The Responsibility to Protect

Also by Aidan Hehir

INTERNATIONAL LAW, SECURITY AND ETHICS: Policy Challenges in the Post-9/11 World (*co-edited with Andrew Mumford and Natasha Kuhrt*)

HUMANITARIAN INTERVENTION: An Introduction

KOSOVO, INTERVENTION AND STATEBUILDING: The International Community and the Transition to Independence (*editor*)

HUMANITARIAN INTERVENTION AFTER KOSOVO: Iraq, Darfur and the Record of Global Civil Society

STATE-BUILDING: Theory and Practice (*co-edited with Neil Robinson*)

The Responsibility to Protect

Rhetoric, Reality and the Future of Humanitarian Intervention

Aidan Hehir

palgrave
macmillan

First published 2012 by
PALGRAVE MACMILLAN

Palgrave Macmillan in the UK is an imprint of Macmillan Publishers Limited, registered in England, company number 785998, of Houndmills, Basingstoke, Hampshire RG21 6XS.

Palgrave Macmillan in the US is a division of St Martin's Press LLC, 175 Fifth Avenue, New York, NY 10010.

Palgrave Macmillan is the global academic imprint of the above companies and has companies and representatives throughout the world.

Palgrave® and Macmillan® are registered trademarks in the United States, the United Kingdom, Europe and other countries

ISBN 978–0–230–28917–8 hardback
ISBN 978–0–230–28918–5 paperback

This book is printed on paper suitable for recycling and made from fully managed and sustained forest sources. Logging, pulping and manufacturing processes are expected to conform to the environmental regulations of the country of origin.

A catalogue record for this book is available from the British Library.

A catalog record for this book is available from the Library of Congress.

10 9 8 7 6 5 4 3 2 1
21 20 19 18 17 16 15 14 13 12

Printed in China

For Sarah, Esmé, Elsie and Iris

Contents

Acknowledgements

Thanks to Steven Kennedy at Palgrave Macmillan who encouraged me to write this and provided excellent advice throughout. Thanks also to everyone at the Department of Politics and International Relations at the University of Westminster.

I would also like to thank Helen Caunce, James Pattison, Robert W. Murray, Jennifer Welsh, Theresa Reinold, Ysis Lorenna Souza, Bolarinwa Adediran, Elisa Randazzo, Pol Pedreny, Robert Pollard, Tobin Sprout, Lou Barlow, Ryan Nelson, Melissa Quinley, Readers' Wives, Richard Ford, Janice Erlbaum and John G.

As ever thanks to my family, George, Mainie, Niamh, Paul, Hazel, Jay, Nial, Rita, Aishling, Aran, Katie, Hannah, Emily, Chris, Lola Bee, Barney, Sue, and Lucy.

Biggest thanks and love go to my wife Sarah and my daughters, Esmé, Elsie and Iris ... *'you're never fully dressed without a smile'*.

AIDAN HEHIR

Chapter 1

Introduction: Rhetoric and Reality

On 17 December 2010 Mohamed Bouazizi, a 26-year-old-street vendor, set himself alight outside the governor's office in Sidi Bouzid, Tunisia. Bouazizi, who later died from his injuries, sought to draw attention to his government's corruption and mismanagement. Within weeks, a wave of protests swept across North Africa and the Middle East leading to the removal of the regimes in Tunisia and Egypt. While many leaders sought to pre-empt the protestors by initiating democratic reforms, others were less conciliatory. The subsequent violence which erupted in Libya, Bahrain, Syria and Yemen, pitted unelected governments and their powerful military against pro-democracy protestors. These images of violence reinvigorated the debate on humanitarian intervention. While this debate continues to rage, two things are clear: first, that humanitarian intervention remains a pertinent and emotive issue. Second, that there is still much that needs to be done to improve the international community's response to intra-state crises.

Discussions of whether, how and when to intervene, have in recent years been dominated by the term 'responsibility to protect'. The concept, usually abbreviated to R2P, emerged from the debates on humanitarian intervention in the mid to late 1990s. Following the controversy surrounding NATO's intervention in Kosovo in 1999, the International Commission on Intervention and State Sovereignty (ICISS) was established by the Canadian Government. The ICISS published its report, *The Responsibility to Protect*, in December 2001. The report argued that sovereign states had certain responsibilities towards their own citizens which, if not honoured, should become a matter of international concern, and possibly grounds for external intervention. Though largely overshadowed by the events of September 11th, the report became a key focus for the debate on humanitarian intervention and, thanks to the advocacy of many NGOs, academics and policymakers, soon made its way on to the international political agenda. At the 2005 World Summit the concept was formally recognized by all UN member states and it has been referred to since in both Security Council and General Assembly resolutions. In short the term has, undoubtedly, made a swift ascension from the periphery to the centre of international political discourse.

In the process of this ascension, R2P has dethroned the ostensibly old-fashioned and/or pejorative term 'humanitarian intervention'. Supporters of what would have previously been termed humanitarian intervention now invariably champion R2P. By default, to oppose R2P is to be perceived as a critic of humanitarian intervention. I believe, however, in the necessity of humanitarian intervention and while I share a number of the same core beliefs as R2P's many supporters, it is my contention that R2P cannot, in its present form and trajectory, significantly alter the cycle of inconsistency that has been the 'international community's' response to intra-state humanitarian crises. This book is a modest attempt to redirect this trajectory so that the momentum in favour of intervention and proscriptions against internal repression does not dissipate in the face of failure.

In his 2009 book, *What's Wrong With the United Nations and How to Fix It*, Thomas Weiss wrote, 'By not imagining a fundamentally different system, we make the continuation of the current lacklustre one all the more inevitable' (2009b, p. 225). Earlier in the book he declared, 'To halt at least some conscience-shocking future cases of mass suffering or to stabilize other kinds of international conflicts, there simply will be no viable alternative to international military forces' (ibid, p. 132). I agree wholeheartedly with both statements and this book is an explicit attempt to contribute to the imagining of a 'fundamentally different system', including the establishment of a standing UN military force, without lapsing into indulgent idealism. Weiss is, however, one of the most vocal supporters of R2P whereas I am not. This is illustrative of the fact that supporters of humanitarian intervention and UN reform need not be advocates of R2P. This book will hopefully go some way towards disproving the widely held perception that critics of R2P are recalcitrant purveyors of *realpolitik* and sovereign inviolability (Evans, 2008, p. 3). Some are, but not all.

There is clearly a broad constituency of activists, academics and policymakers who believe that there are circumstances when external intervention in the affairs of a sovereign state is necessary. This book seeks to constructively engage with this constituency by initially identifying the limitations of R2P, which is currently the pre-eminent pro-intervention framework. The critique of R2P, contained in Part I of this book, argues that while the concept has undeniably raised international consciousness regarding humanitarian intervention and the limits of sovereign inviolability, it has reached the limits of its utility and, in fact, come to obscure the structural barriers to effective humanitarian action. Part II advances an alternative strategy that seeks to re-orientate the focus of the pro-intervention constituency in the hope that a new, more effective movement for reform can be mobilized. This introductory chapter initially provides a succinct overview of the basis for my argument, which is developed in greater detail in subsequent chapters, and latterly an overview of each chapter.

The illusion of progress?

A major inspiration for writing this book was the obscure phrase, 'eirenic munificence' which appears on the final page of Simon Chesterman's *Just War or Just Peace* (2002, p. 236). In the context of humanitarian intervention, Chesterman warned of the dangers of moving away from international law towards a more subjective regulatory framework, which would necessarily be influenced by the prevailing distribution of power and the temporal whims of those who wield it, both regionally and internationally. The broader implications of Chesterman's warning impelled me to look at the issue of humanitarian intervention with a view to determining whether it was possible to move towards a system more responsive to intra-state humanitarian crises while avoiding the fate of a world without international law, or rather a world where, 'international law is deprivileged to become just one policy justification among others' (ibid, p. 236). Simply put, I believe that humanitarian intervention is too important an issue to be dependent on the exigencies of the Great Powers; the only viable solution to the near perennial problem of how we should respond to man-made intra-state humanitarian crises is a strengthening of international law involving significant reform of the UN. This book's primary aim is to defend this contention and outline the parameters of reform.

Another inspiration was my growing concern at the trajectory of the debate on humanitarian intervention precipitated in recent years by the rise of R2P, particularly since the 2005 World Summit. Effusive appraisals of R2P abound; Alex Bellamy cites R2P as 'the single most important development' on the question of intra-state humanitarian crises (2009, p. 2); Anne-Marie Slaughter describes the recognition of R2P in the 2005 World Summit Outcome Document as 'an enormous normative step forward, akin to an international Magna Carta' (2011); while Gareth Evans claimed R2P has made 'major contributions that seem likely to have a lasting impact' (2008, p. 39) and more effusively characterized R2P as 'a brand new international norm of really quite fundamental importance and novelty ... that is unquestionably a major breakthrough' (2009, p. 16). The number of books and articles published on the subject in recent years is remarkable: as UN Special Adviser on R2P, Ed Luck, exclaimed, 'The ever-expanding literature on the responsibility to protect could now fill a small library. The number of graduate theses alone devoted to the topic has been nothing less than staggering' (2010). Whether this popularity, if not ubiquity, is evidence of R2P's efficacy, real and/or potential, is less clear.

It would be disingenuous, and perhaps gratuitously cynical, to deem the popularity of the concept as being indicative of its weakness. Nonetheless, this popularity is, in many respects, a function of at least one characteristic of R2P which I contend *does* undermine its utility, namely its ambiguity. As Carsten Stahn noted, R2P is, 'a multifaceted concept with various elements'. This diversity has certainly broadened the constituency of 'R2P advocates' and generated a more inclusive, pluralist debate about related issues but this broadening has (arguably) come at a cost. Accordingly, Stahn wrote: 'The notion became popular because it could be used by different bodies to promote different goals' (2007, p. 118). The various tangents increasingly emanating from the concept is reflected in the diverse applications of the term and the extent to which 'R2P' has become an obligatory reference point in academic discourse on the issue of humanitarian intervention. The burgeoning literature on R2P could be said to have diluted the focus of an idea which really stemmed from a debate on how to *respond* to mass atrocities within states. This dilution has been made possible, I contend, because R2P has failed to consolidate its identity since its initial formulation. With the exception of the agreement at the World Summit in 2005 on the four crimes that constitute grounds for intervention, R2P has added surprisingly little clarity or innovative proposals to the pre-existing debate on humanitarian intervention. Its malleability has enabled a plethora of authors and advocacy groups to declare that their work on, for example, climate change, education reform and mental health, constitute R2P-type initiatives. This is certainly testimony to the goodwill which is associated with the term but this would seem to constitute the instrumental usage of R2P as a slogan, a means by which pre-existing theories and concerns garner increased publicity. This is not unique to R2P of course; many initiatives have, quite understandably, sheltered under the umbrella of the prevailing catch-phrase, be it, 'Never Again!' or 'Make Poverty History'. The history of temporarily popular rallying cries suggests popular usage and tangible influence cannot be readily conflated. As I discuss in Chapter 2, R2P does have certain referent points and key moments in its evolution, but the contested issues and difficult questions which inspired the debate on humanitarian intervention in the 1990s remain, sadly, largely unanswered.

While the rise of the R2P industry – which today comprises many advocacy groups and centres across the world – is an interesting phenomenon in itself, a more pressing reason for my seeking to expose the concept's limitations is the fact that R2P has deflected attention away from potentially useful avenues of research and indeed advocacy, most particularly UN reform. Frustration with the ostensibly vacuous nature of R2P has led certain observers, not opposed to the idea of humanitarian intervention, to become disillusioned by what they see as the hype surrounding R2P (Reinold, 2010; Strauss, 2010). The time, money and effort expended on R2P would be better focused elsewhere; those who genuinely seek to resolve the problem posed by intra-state humanitarian crises, as the majority of R2P advocates surely do, would be more fruitfully employed in exploring truly innovative approaches to this issue and this book seeks to contribute to building an alternative pro-intervention constituency.

The limits of moral advocacy

That intra-state crises occasionally demand military intervention is, I argue in Chapter 6, axiomatic. That R2P has come to dominate the debate on intervention is equally irrefutable. The confluence of these truisms has, perhaps naturally, led many to champion R2P and to articulate their views through R2P's rhetorical framework. There is an increasing sense that R2P is the only viable solution to the problem posed by humanitarian intervention, and that, while it has its flaws, we must 'try to make it work'.

It is the contention of this book, however, that this is a misplaced strategy. Those eager to see an end to the spectre of inertia that has too often characterized the international 'response' to intra-state crises need not, and I believe they should not, seek to achieve these aims by adhering to the prevailing strategy currently employed by R2P's most vocal champions. R2P has changed international political discourse, perhaps irrevocably, but it has not changed the practice of international politics, nor will it do so as long as the focus is on generating moral pressure to act. The term may have achieved an enviable ubiquity in international political discourse but close examination of R2P reveals a discursiveness that comprises a medley of less important abstractions from 'pillars' to 'thresholds' which obscure the real problem. At its core R2P is a reassertion of the status quo and an eloquent appeal to behave in accordance with moral norms. Of course, moral advocacy is not new and its influence, though not negligible, has always been limited.

Gary Bass's *Freedom's Battle* does much to explode the myth that humanitarian advocacy, including for military intervention, is a post-Cold War phenomenon. Bass points to a number of cases during the nineteenth century when egregious oppression and violence compelled both individuals and states to advance arguments in favour of what we now call humanitarian intervention. He writes:

> emotional pleas were a regular feature of international politics throughout much of the nineteenth century, resulting in several important military missions. The basic ideas go all the way back to Thucydides, who, horrified at bloody ancient civil wars, hoped for the endurance of 'the general laws of

> humanity which are there to give a hope of salvation to all who are in distress'. (Bass, 2008, p. 4)

The nineteenth century, as Bass notes, is today synonymous with imperialism and hardly a particularly rich source of evidence for humanitarian concern. Bass's analysis, however, identifies a tension between the proponents of *realpolitik* and the agitation of what he calls 'the atrocitarians' which has obvious parallels with contemporary debates (ibid, p. 6). Bass argues that as a consequence of the emergence of the free press and the lobbying of groups like the London Greek Committee established in 1823, 'Humanitarian intervention was once a relatively familiar European practice, and was understood as such' (ibid, pp. 4–5). Again the parallels with today's 'CNN effect' and 'global civil society' are clear.

Nonetheless, while many people in the nineteenth century did eloquently espouse cosmopolitan ethics, their existence and vocal advocacy does not constitute proof that they compelled states to look beyond their narrowly defined national interests. The most one can deduce from Bass's analysis is that in the nineteenth century, as today, there were those who argued that states *should* do something about suffering overseas, and occasionally statesmen did advance humanitarian justifications for their military interventions. Yet, in the context of Britain and France's wilful imperial excesses, the periodic expression of humanitarian concern appears glaringly hypocritical. Indeed, Bass notes that many of the more powerful and vocal exponents of enlightened rhetoric who aligned themselves with 'the atrocitarians' in the nineteenth and early twentieth centuries, such as William Gladstone, Theodore Roosevelt, David Lloyd George and Woodrow Wilson, 'held loathsome racial attitudes that played out in the subjugation of countless people' (ibid, p. 343). Evidence for the influence of humanitarian activists on European and US foreign policy during this era of rampant colonialism and the subjugation of human rights under the banners of the 'white man's burden' and the '*mission civilisatrice*' is, however, modest. This contrast between the policies of the colonial powers and their benign rhetoric should constitute a salutary lesson for those who equate the increased usage of R2P in international discourse with its increased influence.

Yet, this appears to have been overlooked in the rush to

proclaim that a new era is within our reach. In his book *The Responsibility to Protect*, Gareth Evans outlines a litany of atrocities, genocide, mass rape and human cruelty which he attributes to the principle of sovereignty. States, jealously possessive of their sovereign rights, are portrayed as morally bankrupt, introverted and implacably disposed to singularly pursue the national interest. And perhaps Evans is right; human history from 1648 to 1992 can make for depressing reading with acts of altruism exceedingly rare. It is difficult to understand, however, why this disposition, embedded in statecraft for the previous 350 years, should suddenly dissipate in the early 1990s. The contemporary foreign policy change required to achieve Evans' goal – as per his book's sub-title – of *Ending Mass Atrocity Crimes Once and for All* would be of such a magnitude that it would constitute a veritable revolution. Yet, this putative revolution, quite uniquely, involves no constitutional or institutional change. The revolution, it seems, will, to borrow Gil Scott-Heron's line, 'not be televised' as it will be one which takes place not in a tangible, observable way, but rather in the hearts and minds of statesmen across the world leading to the proliferation of 'good people, good governments, and good governance' (Evans, 2008, p. 7). This belief in the capacity of 'good' to triumph over 'evil' is on one level somewhat inspiring but it is also laden with normative assumptions that undermine its utility. Instances of intra-state crises are the result, we must assume, of 'bad' people perpetrating 'bad' deeds while others look on, thereby behaving 'badly'. There is little, if indeed any, engagement with other possible factors such as the potentially deleterious influence of the structure of the international system in its various forms, namely economic, political and legal. The 'bad' people commit these acts, it seems, because of their nature while the observers who do not intervene are by definition behaving badly; countervailing circumstances, context and the possible existence of a hierarchy of responsibilities are essentially discounted in this near Manichean world view. The solution – namely the allegedly normative power of R2P – is, ultimately and essentially, the global dispersal of individual benevolence and what Robert Drinan calls 'the mobilization of shame' which he defines as, 'the moral power which, more than laws or economic sanctions, will induce nations to follow the less followed road that leads to democracy and equality' (2001, p. 32).

This faith in the power of words and ideas to effect momentous change is illustrative of what Reinhold Niebuhr criticized as 'bourgeois individualism'. This view, based on an unshakeable faith in progress, overlooked, and still overlooks, the fact that within any society personal and group interests differ; the inevitable plurality of interests always necessitates structures – economic, political and judicial – to regulate interactions because promises are unreliable and unity of purpose and interests, though not impossible, is only ever temporal. Niebuhr decried those who exhibited, 'a touching faith in the possibility of achieving a simple harmony between self-interest and the general welfare on every level' (1986, p. 164). This melding of self-interest and general welfare – which if realized would obviously remove the need for legal codes – is precisely what R2P advocates seek to achieve, and indeed, appear to expect to realize.

Of course, most progressive political, legal and social changes have been catalysed by the insights of certain figures and groups who have converted masses to their cause; there is nothing unusual about calling for a new way of thinking and behaving. Where these ideas have succeeded, however, they have been accompanied by institutional change so as to codify the new system/paradigm. For example, exposing Eastern European 'communism' as morally and economically bankrupt and generating mass societal opposition to the ruling elite was obviously not enough; the system, including the constitution and the institutions, had to be changed to consolidate the revolution. R2P, on the other hand, aspires to achieve hugely expansive aims but calls for little tangible change: instructional, legal or structural.

The first point on the list of aims advanced by the ICISS in *The Responsibility to Protect* was, 'to establish clearer rules, procedures and criteria for determining whether, when and how to intervene' (2001a, p. 11). This explicit focus on clearer rules is a worthy, and surely reasonable, aim. It is striking, however, how this has been largely abandoned by contemporary advocates of R2P. As discussed in Chapters 3 and 8, R2P has not changed international law or suggested the codification of new binding guidelines on intervention and this reform strategy is in fact no longer even seen as necessary. Immense faith has been placed in the capacity of 'good' people to convince states to behave in certain ways by publicizing atrocities and 'shining a light' on unacceptable inaction through the media. The willingness of the international media, however, to highlight crises and publicize the advocacy of the 'good' people calling for action is not assured. In the context of the conflict in Darfur, Steve Crawshaw of Human Rights Watch highlighted the hypocrisy of the media's position:

> There was much editorial soul-searching in April [2004] over the failures to chronicle the Rwandan genocide that had taken place 10 years earlier. That soul-searching was, however, accompanied by an almost complete disregard for the crimes against humanity that were being committed in Darfur at the very same time ... Even when the UN Secretary-General, Kofi Annan, used his Rwanda anniversary speech on April 7 to address the subject, few newspapers took much notice. A colleague noted: 'The international media don't seem to send reporters to cover genocides. They cover genocide anniversaries.' (Crawshaw, 2004)

Eventually, of course, the international media did take up the issue of Darfur but even then the effect on the Security Council was hardly appreciable (Bassiouni, 2009). The lesson is surely that the mobilization of moral pressure to intervene is not readily achievable and even if realized, such pressure can be resisted by the permanent five members of the Security Council (P5).

The critique offered above and throughout this book will no doubt be challenged by many. One oft-repeated rebuttal to the above charges is the claim that it is too early to write off R2P: that we must wait for it to take root and to gradually increase its influence. There is merit to the argument that changes in international politics take time, though periodically sudden shifts also do occur. Nonetheless the 'let's give it time' refrain is neither convincing nor applicable in this context because, paradoxical though it may seem, R2P existed before R2P was formally created. At its core, R2P constitutes an appeal for states to treat their citizens better and to be ready to take action to protect citizens of other states. This principle, as Bass noted, can be traced back at least two millennia to Thucydides (2008, p. 4). Such moral advocacy has also been a constant feature of the post-Charter era. The utility of R2P is further undermined by the fact that the existing agreement as to its meaning is shallow and thus its ostensible power as a 'norm' is inherently weak. As Theresa

Reinold notes, beyond the general, and relatively modest, consensus that states should not commit certain acts against their citizens and that the international community may get involved if they do, the concept is underdeveloped. She argues that R2P lacks both conceptual clarity and consistent application in state practice and therefore, 'norm internalisation cannot occur ... the responsibility to protect clearly has not evolved into a norm, that is, an intersubjectively shared standard of appropriate behaviour' (Reinold, 2010, p. 74).

The paradox is, however, that the R2P industry has reached a point where it has become seemingly impossible for some to admit that the strategy has not worked, and cannot work within the confines of the current systemic structure. Inconvenient instances when R2P demonstrably failed to effect change – such as the international community's response to both the conflict in Darfur and the massacres in Sri Lanka – are downplayed in favour of those cases where R2P ostensibly played a role (see Chapter 4).

What is to be done?

I do not reject R2P on the basis of a theoretical (or personal) rejection of the very idea of humanitarian intervention, nor do I suggest that power politics is so pervasive that it is inconceivable that norms governing the use of force can evolve and ultimately effect change both in positive law and normative ideals. Rather, I argue that the issue of humanitarian intervention has highlighted the profound need for fundamental structural reform of the UN. Lofty declarations proscribing certain acts are insufficient; if they were not then how do we explain the many instances of unabated genocide since the signing of the 1948 Genocide Convention? Somewhat ironically, Evans criticizes the Genocide Convention on the basis that it constituted little more than empty rhetoric: 'It was almost as if, with the signing of the Genocide Convention', he wrote, 'the task of addressing man-made atrocities was seen as complete: it was rarely invoked and never applied' (2009, p. 17). Why R2P, which has significantly less legal character and is more nebulous and contested than the Genocide Convention, should avoid this faith is unclear.

To simply criticize R2P, however, would be to add little of any constructive value to the debate. To this end, Part II of this book outlines a justification both for humanitarian intervention and my preference for international law – including a new legal institutional arrangement – as the only viable regulator of such action. In Chapter 8, I outline a (clearly ambitious) proposal for reforming the international system which comprises two key features:

- The creation of a judicial body with the power to judge how to respond to a particular intra-state humanitarian crisis.
- The establishment of a standing, independent UN military force deployable by the judicial body.

These reforms would, if ever implemented, constitute a quite obviously profound reform of the UN system. Additionally, while I have endeavoured to cover the potential pitfalls, it is quite possible that the proposals advanced in Chapter 8 require further refinement and alteration. If these proposals only help trigger a debate on how such reforms might be introduced and operationalized, however, then that is a good start.

Libya 2011 and R2P

During the course of writing this book, the Security Council passed resolution 1973 sanctioning the imposition of a no-fly zone over Libya. On 19 March, military action against Libya began and by October Colonel Gaddafi was dead and his regime destroyed. Many lauded this intervention as evidence of R2P's influence (Thakur, 2011). Indeed, in response to Security Council Resolution 1973, UN Secretary-General Ban Ki-Moon stated:

> The Security Council today has taken an historic decision. Resolution 1973 affirms, clearly and unequivocally, the international community's determination to fulfil its responsibility to protect civilians from violence perpetrated upon them by their own government. (2011)

The actions of the Security Council were undeniably significant and for many, myself included, surprisingly swift and robust. If we are to believe some of the rhetoric that accompanied the intervention, especially the statements issued by Susan Rice, the US Ambassador to the UN, this intervention was inspired by R2P and motivated by a desire to protect the rebels from the violence executed and ominously promised by Colonel Gaddafi.

The intervention predictably reinvigorated old debates about humanitarian intervention, with opponents decrying US imperialism, the West's thirst for oil and the clash of civilizations, and supporters stressing the humanitarian imperative and the normative power of global civil society and specifically R2P. Personally, I supported the military intervention on the basis that the Gaddafi regime was intent on slaughtering the pro-democracy movement and had demonstrated a capacity to do so; his public threat to the people of Benghazi, 'We are coming tonight ... We will find you in your closets ... We will show no mercy' was unequivocal (Heneghan, 2011). Such overt declarations of murderous intent are highly unusual (Bellamy, 2011, p. 3; Chesterman, 2011a, p. 4). Additionally, the calls by the rebels themselves for intervention, after their initial reluctance, was of huge significance as was the vocal support of the Arab League, the Organization of Islamic Conference and the Gulf Cooperation Council. I do not believe, however, that the existence of R2P was a significant factor in the decision by the Security Council to sanction action.

In sanctioning action against Libya, the Security Council utilized the powers available to it under Chapter VII of the Charter. As explored in greater detail in Chapter 3, these competencies pre-date R2P and were used a number of times in the 1990s. 'Security Council Resolution 1973', Chesterman notes, 'was consistent with resolutions passed in the heady days of the immediate post-cold war era' and thus 'hardly groundbreaking' (2011a, pp. 1–2). Interestingly, while Resolution 1973 includes the sentence 'Reiterating the responsibility of the Libyan authorities to protect the Libyan population', which can plausibly be said to relate to R2P, there is no mention in either of the resolutions of the international community's 'responsibility to protect' or the action being a function of this responsibility. This omission, Jennifer Welsh argues, is significant and suggests that the notion of an international responsibility to protect, 'was still contested by some members of the Security Council' (2011, p. 1). As Chesterman notes, formulations of the phrase 'responsibility to protect' have been used previously, even prior to the 2005

World Summit; he notes that in the context of the situation in Georgia, the Abkhazi were said by the Security Council in 2002 resolution to have 'a particular responsibility to protect' returnees (2011a, p. 2). The Security Council has, therefore, always had the power to undertake such action and R2P did not provide the Security Council with a previously unavailable means by which to sanction military action against Libya. It has been asserted that Resolution 1973 was 'especially important' for the fact that 'it is the first time that the Security Council has authorized the use of military force for human protection purposes against the wishes of a functioning state' (Bellamy, 2011, p. 1). Chesterman argues, however, that the issue of consent is actually 'not legally significant' in the context of a Chapter VII mandated operation (2011a, p. 2). Additionally, in 1994, the Security Council passed Resolution 940 authorizing the establishment of 'a multinational force' with the power 'to use all necessary means' to remove the military junta in Haiti that had deposed the democratically elected President Aristide. Technically the Security Council had the consent of the Haitian government (in exile) but given that Aristide had fled the country in 1991 the de facto government – the junta – were opposed to the intervention. The ostensible novelty of Resolution 1973 is, therefore, dubious and predicated on a punctilious interpretation of 'government'.

This aside, the Security Council's use of its Chapter VII powers has been erratic, and dependent on the assent of each member of the P5. The intervention in Libya again illustrated the centrality of the P5 and the pervasive influence of the whims of these states; had either Russia or China vetoed the resolution, military action would not have been sanctioned by the Security Council. That neither did was certainly a welcome development but one predicated on a coincidence of factors rather than collective adherence to a principle. Bellamy accepts that without the support of the Gulf Cooperation Council, the Organization of Islamic Conference and the Arab League, 'China and Russia would have certainly vetoed Resolution 1973' (2011, p. 4). The Russian and Chinese position was, therefore, very obviously a function of regional politics in the Middle East rather than a principled adherence to R2P. Indeed, Bellamy acknowledges, 'This confluence of factors is unlikely to be often repeated' (ibid, p. 4). Likewise Weiss suggests that the lesson of the intervention in Libya is 'we can say no more Holocausts, Cambodias, and Rwandas – and occasionally mean it' (2011, p. 5). The 'occasionally' here clearly doesn't constitute a particularly firm basis for hope; the international community has always 'occasionally' done the right thing, but these occasions have been far outnumbered by instances of inertia and apathy.

If, for argument's sake, we assume that the three states that pushed for the resolution – the US, France and the UK – were genuinely motivated by humanitarian concerns and a desire to adhere to R2P, though this is itself not assured, can we plausibly make the same claims about Russia and China? Is it likely that during the deliberations in Moscow and Beijing, which led both countries to decide to acquiesce, decision makers were ultimately swayed by a collective concern to abide by their prior commitments to R2P? That Gaddafi's representatives travelled to China to buy, '$200 million worth of rocket launchers, anti-tank missiles, portable surface-to-air missiles designed to bring down aircraft, and other weapons and munitions' from state-controlled arms companies during NATO's intervention surely calls into question China's humanitarian credentials (Barnard, 2011; Branigan, 2011). Michael Walzer argued, in fact, that 'Russia and China, who opposed the intervention, abstained on the final Security Council vote, perhaps because they can't imagine an outcome that better suits their interests in the Middle East and Africa' (2011).

The fact that R2P exists and the Security Council sanctioned action are not necessarily related. It is noteworthy that President Obama's landmark speech justifying the intervention on 28 March made no mention at all of R2P (White House, 2011) nor did the joint article written by Barak Obama, David Cameron, Nicolas Sarkozy (Obama, Cameron and Sarkozy, 2011). The US sought Security Council authorization for its invasion of Iraq in 2003 not because it believed it was imperative but rather because it would have added to the arsenal of justifications (Malone, 2006, pp. 265–6; Thakur and Sidhu, 2006, p. 5).

Would similar action be sanctioned in response to comparable violence in Israel or Saudi Arabia or Pakistan? It is highly unlikely, if not inconceivable due to the national interests of the P5 in each case and indeed regional opinion. To suggest that national interest influenced the decision to intervene in Libya does not mean one adheres to a conspiratorial view whereby the

'West' hatched a nefarious plan to plunder Libya's oil fields. It seems quite reasonable to suggest that Western states would have preferred the situation in Libya to not have deteriorated: military action against Libya was not a plan waiting for an excuse. Rather, a combination of factors including events on the ground, the favourable regional disposition, Libya's geostrategic importance and Gaddafi's pariah status, reputation for violence and exceptionally public declaration of intent – plus doubtless myriad domestic considerations – combined to induce the leaders to push for action. Indeed, President Obama acknowledged that the intervention was undertaken 'because our *interests* and values are at stake'. More explicitly, later in the same speech he stated, 'America has an important strategic interest in preventing Qaddafi from overrunning those who oppose him' (White House, 2011). In other words the action taken derived from Obama's world view which comprises, 'a pragmatic assessment of individual cases' rather than his adherence to a law or principle (Chesterman, 2011a, p. 5). This union of interests and values is far from unique or shocking. What would be truly shocking is if the P5 had acted purely on the basis of values.

If David Cameron, Barack Obama, Nicolas Sarkozy – the chief proponents of the intervention – pushed for action because of their desire to honour the commitments their predecessors made to R2P, such a collective unity of purpose would of course be an interesting phenomenon in itself, but would it actually constitute evidence that R2P was likely to *continue* to make a difference? Action taken on the basis of a commitment to a principle derived from altruistic *individual impulses* cannot be reasonably cited as constituting a precedent or new norm. Rather, it is more accurately described as aberrant, albeit welcome, behaviour impelled by a unique constellation of necessarily temporal factors. This, indeed, is the explanation proffered by Bernard-Henri Lévy, who worked with President Sarkozy in generating support for the intervention. He wrote:

> [Libya] is the absolute exception ... the question should be worded inversely. Not 'it's strange, suspect even, that what we did in Libya has not been done elsewhere', but 'how is it that what we have done nowhere, absolutely nowhere else, we have done in Libya?' ... here is the answer. A blend of factors is involved, a mixture of chance and necessity with ... this

> unforeseen element that is, by definition, impossible to generalize: the political will of one man, the President of the French Republic, Nicolas Sarkozy. (Lévy, 2011)

The fact that the intervention in Libya was the function of a coincidence between humanitarian suffering and national interests – 'a mixture of chance and necessity' – should not, however, lead us to conclude that this intervention was unjustifiable or that it does not qualify as a 'humanitarian intervention': purity of motives is surely an unreasonably onerous requirement. The refrain commonly uttered to condemn the intervention – 'what about Syria/Yemen/Bahrain/Israel, etc?' – may speak to a broader issue but it does not necessarily influence the humanitarian credentials of the Libya case. Indeed, the selectivity argument, James Pattison notes, 'shows not that the intervention in Libya is itself morally problematic, but that the failure to act in response to similar cases ... is morally wrong' (2011, p. 6). The people saved by the use of force in Libya can surely not be ignored in favour of those who have died at the hands of similarly repressive governments elsewhere. The unique nature of this intervention must, however, give pause for thought and scepticism as to the broader meaning and implications of the Libyan case.

Even accepting the Libya case – which as I say I consider a welcome aberration – non-intervention has continued to be the normal response of the 'international community' since the emergence of R2P. There have been a number of cases where large-scale human suffering perpetrated by states against their own people has been, effectively, ignored by the Security Council. This is because, as discussed at length in Chapter 3, the P5 are under no obligation to act and continue to decide how to react to intra-state crises on a case-by-case basis with their national interests as the guiding determinant. R2P has not altered the decision making process at the Security Council: indeed Nicola Reindorp of the Global Centre for R2P accepted that this is an unresolved issue noting, 'The thing that we're leaving on the table that we haven't come back to is how the Security Council is going to act' (Reindorp, 2009). She argued, however, that while R2P had not brought about 'a fundamental change in what the Security Council can and can't do' it had led to, 'a shift in clearer expectations of what the Security Council *ought* to do' (ibid). R2P has, it is thus argued, created a new environment or culture which, albeit not reflected in positive law, has influenced the decision making of the P5. Reindorp argued: 'It is much, much tougher now than it was in 1994, for the Russians to stand there and say "no, no, this is just a matter of internal concern"' (ibid). While the intervention in Libya has, understandably, been cited as proving the veracity of this claim, there is, however, much evidence to suggest that this is not in fact the case.

First, quite logically no member of the P5 will ever openly declare that their refusal to sanction intervention in a particular case is due to their lack of concern for the suffering people within the state or a principled rejection of R2P; since the inception of the UN system, the P5 have creatively explained their non-intervention many times and doubtless will continue to do so. The idea that R2P has created some form of moral trap is, therefore, unconvincing. Additionally, on an evidential basis the claim that the Russian government, and the P5 more generally, today find it more difficult to look the other way as atrocities occur overlooks the Security Council's response to the recent situations in both Darfur and Sri Lanka. The crisis in Darfur is dealt with later in this book and the lamentable international reaction surely must give us reasons to doubt the influence of R2P. The war crimes allegedly perpetrated by the government of Sri Lanka occurred mostly from January to May 2009 in the Eastern Provence as the government's forces closed in on the retreating Tamil Tigers. The alleged atrocities clearly fall within the post-R2P timeframe and the concept's purview. A US Department of State report detailed various war crimes committed by the Sri Lankan government in the course of the military campaign including the targeting of civilians, the destruction of hospitals, and the killing of captives or combatants seeking to surrender (2009). The Security Council's response, however, was patently ineffective and essentially mute; in fact, throughout 2009 the Security Council failed to pass a single resolution on the situation in Sri Lanka. Crawshaw reflected on the implications of this inaction for R2P:

> That [situation in Sri Lanka] was something that the responsibility to protect absolutely fitted. It should have been used to put greater pressure on the Sri Lankan government ... it was interesting to see there was a failure to address the Sri Lankan

> issue and that, I think, can be said to be where the gap between the words and the reality is ... So R2P was there and yet basically nothing happened on Sri Lanka. (2009)

Only the very naive would be surprised that the P5 have a record of ignoring mass atrocities; the interests of these states naturally leads them to respond to situations in states in different ways (Bosco, 2009). Post-R2P, this remains the case; indicatively Allen Buchanan and Robert Keohane criticize the Security Council's historical failure, 'to authorize justified humanitarian interventions against genocide, war crimes, crimes against humanity, and ethnic cleansing' and also note, 'there is no evidence that this disposition toward inaction has been rectified' (2011, p. 51). The 2005 World Summit *Outcome Document*, which arguably has the strongest claim to carry legal weight of all documents and declarations related to R2P, reiterates the centrality of the Security Council and advances no obligations or duties to act; the discretionary power of the P5 is explicitly recognized by virtue of the wording of Paragraph 139 which recognizes that signatories are 'prepared to take collective action ... on a case-by-case basis'. Reflecting on this 'preparedness' and 'case-by-case approach', Stahn argued, 'This dual condition ... appears to reflect the view of those states that questioned the proposition that the Charter creates a legal obligation for Security Council members to support enforcement action in the case of mass atrocities' (2007, p. 109). The wording, therefore, is explicitly designed to enable the kind of selectivity that permitted inaction in Rwanda in 1994, Darfur from 2003 onwards and Sri Lanka in 2009, but, when convenient, the use of Chapter VII powers in response to certain situations such as in Haiti in 1994 and Libya in 2011.

The intervention in Libya, therefore, is perfectly consistent with the Security Council's record of inconsistency and an instance when the cessation of slaughter was dependent on the 'eirenic munificence' of the P5 (Chesterman, 2002, p. 236). A unique coincidence of variables led to the decision to sanction action and there is nothing in Resolution 1973 which can reasonably be deemed evidence that R2P has catalysed a permanent change in the disposition of the P5. The optimistic appraisals of the intervention are reminiscent of the 'euphoria' which greeted the Security Council's sanctioning of force to repel Iraqi forces from Kuwait in 1991 and the subsequent imposition of no-fly zones over Northern and Southern Iraq to protect civilians from Saddam's aggression (Malone, 2006, p. 11). The temporal unity regarding Iraq was, however, 'short lived' (Berdal, 2003, p. 15). Subsequent inertia at the Security Council in the 1990s further shattered this optimism as the P5 demonstrated a predisposition to respond to cases on the basis of expediency rather than humanitarian need. The international response to intra-state crises, lampooned so accurately by David Brooks (2004), has a tragic inevitability which persists today, even post-Libya.

Structure and overview

Chapter 2, 'The Evolution of the Responsibility to Protect', provides a brief overview of the original ICISS report including the catalysts for its inception and its central tenets. The chapter then analyses the international reaction to the report and the nature of the contention surrounding its publication. The inclusion of two paragraphs in the 2005 World Summit *Outcome Document* referring directly to an international 'responsibility to protect' was heralded by many as a triumph; this chapter argues, however, that the variant of R2P included in the 2005 *Outcome Document* constituted a significant diminution of the tenets of the ICISS report and in effect constituted no more than a restatement of existing international law and a nebulous commitment to 'help to protect populations from genocide, war crimes, ethnic cleansing and crimes against humanity'.

In July 2009 the General Assembly held a three-day debate on R2P. Representatives of over 180 states took part in this debate thus providing a unique insight into the international community's views on R2P. Chapter 2 demonstrates that though there was a general endorsement of the idea of a 'Responsibility to Protect', there were significant differences in the interpretation regarding both what this responsibility entails domestically and also the nature of the international community's responsibility to protect those suffering within states. Thus the 'consensus' reached on R2P in 2009 was not an innovative development but rather the triumph of the lowest common denominator.

In Chapter 3, 'Responsibility to Protect, Authority and International Law', I argue that neither the 2005 World Summit *Outcome Document* nor the 2009 General Assembly debate constitute a reform of existing international law. R2P is a restatement of existing law both in terms of the responsibility of states to their citizens and the international mechanisms for responding to egregious intra-state humanitarian crises. The primary question the ICISS sought to address related to the existing laws governing the right of external actors to intervene in the affairs of a sovereign state for humanitarian purposes. Security Council practice during the 1990s had demonstrated that the provisions of Chapter VII of the Charter enabled the Security Council to sanction such an intervention but the question of unilateral humanitarian intervention remained controversial. R2P does not constitute, or even advance, a new legal principle regarding unilateral intervention but rather restates the primacy of the Security Council. Additionally, there is no provision compelling the Security Council to act and thus we are left with what has been described as a discretionary entitlement: precisely the same unsatisfactory situation that pertained prior to the 2001 ICISS report. I argue, therefore, that contemporary intra-state crises are dealt with in accordance with the same legal, and indeed political, processes that have existed since 1945.

The evolution of R2P since the ICISS report evidences a pronounced shift in emphasis towards preventing humanitarian crises rather than halting them. While the original ICISS did emphasize the importance of prevention, the key issue, which catalysed the report and constitutes its primary focus, was halting rather than preventing egregious humanitarian crises. In Chapter 4, 'The Responsibility to Prevent: The Last Refuge of the Unimaginative?', I argue that it is folly to focus on prevention without also ensuring that there are robust and effective means by which the four crimes included in R2P's remit are halted. While prevention conceptually precedes reaction, I have structured Part I in the order in which issues have been posed, hence the treatment of prevention in Chapter 4.

R2P is now being championed as primarily an initiative aimed at *preventing* intra-state mass atrocities and this constitutes a significant alteration of its original *raison d'être* and an answer to a question that wasn't the original impetus behind R2P. The shift to prevention, I argue, is a function of the inability of proponents of R2P to affect change in the area of responding to humanitarian crises and thus many have retreated to the more abstract and less immediate issue of promoting dialogue, pluralism and political and social reform within states. To add empirical evidence to bolster this chapter's claims, I analyse the role of the Special Adviser on the Prevention of Genocide established in 2004 which constitutes the only tangible innovation linked both to prevention and R2P. I demonstrate that this new office has very limited powers, manpower and budget, and that this is indicative of the lack of real interest in prevention and hence illustrative of the need to contrive effective means to respond to the inevitable outbreak of intra-state crises.

The 'humanitarian impulses' of world leaders has become a key focus of R2P advocates keen to address the manifest gap between humanitarian rhetoric and humanitarian action. Indeed, to a striking extent advocates of R2P have come to predicate its entire utility on changing the disposition of statesmen. In Chapter 5, 'Political Will and Non-intervention', I argue that we must have reservations about R2P if it is this heavily dependent on something as transitory as political will and the disposition of statesmen. The depressing litany of 'inhumanitarian non-intervention' is a function of a *lack* of political will and this, rather than any political or legal restrictions, was the cause of the collective inertia in the face of the Rwandan genocide. Why this reluctance to accept a responsibility for the welfare of citizens suffering egregious human rights violations in other states should now dissipate in the face of the emergence of R2P is unclear. It is argued that while it is comforting to think that eloquent appeals to governments to 'do something' will be effective there is little empirical basis to suggest this will be the case given that since 1945 many grandiose declarations – most obviously 'Never Again!' in relation to the Holocaust and genocide – have been of little demonstrable utility in practice. The focus on 'generating political will' has led to the emergence of a plethora of NGO's specifically committed to promoting R2P and while these organizations have succeeded in raising the profile of R2P, I maintain that the capacity of such groups to affect real change is limited and that there are a number of problems associated with the enactment of international policy being contingent on NGO activism, particularly the mixed record of success.

Additionally I argue that the fact that states consider their own interests when deciding whether or not to intervene is neither necessarily immoral nor amoral. Indeed, the primary duty of all governments is to their own citizens and it is not indefensible to determine that as a particular intervention would imperil the state it should not be undertaken. Thus, when advocates of R2P focus on moral arguments to pressurize states into taking action they are not engaging in a one-way moral discourse; states can advance strong and indeed morally sound arguments in defence of non-intervention. The idea that states which refuse to 'send in the troops' are morally bereft is not, therefore, axiomatic.

Chapter 6, 'In Defence of Humanitarian Intervention and the Potential of International Law', begins with a defence of humanitarian intervention. In contrast to the majority of critics of R2P, and humanitarian intervention generally, I believe that it is necessary to enable external intervention for humanitarian purposes under certain circumstances. I base my argument not on a particular ideological, theoretical or religious conviction but rather on a broadly humanist argument that egregious humanitarian crises retard both our claims to, and our actual, ethical and societal progress. While history is replete with evidence of man's capacity and propensity to both commit and ignore extreme violence, evidence also suggests that it is within our capabilities to arrest mass human suffering.

The second part of this chapter draws on the work of Hans Kelsen and Martti Koskenniemi to justify why I believe international law rather than religion, ethics or political ideology is best suited to regulating humanitarian intervention and inter-state relations more generally. I argue, however, that international law can only fulfil its potential if there is a clear separation between politics and law enforcement analogous to the separation between the executive and the judiciary within democracies. So long as the subjects of international law – that is, states – continue to constitute the architects of law's design, interpretation and implementation it will continue to be compromised by politicization. In addition to this normative approach, I highlight the capacity of international law to evolve to reflect changes in prevailing moral norms and thus I argue that change is not just possible but inevitable. Drawing on the major advances in international law since 1945, I argue that the trajectory of international law evidences two key trends: the expansion of human rights covered by international law, and the preference for the objective judgement of the violation of these rights. These points will serve as a basis for the prescriptions advanced in Chapter 8.

Many proponents of R2P have advanced a caricature of sovereignty which overlooks a number of sovereignty's real and normative positives. I argue in Chapter 7, 'Understanding the Tension between Sovereignty and Intervention', that finding a means of responding to intra-state humanitarian crises must begin with an endorsement of the basic tenets of sovereignty but that this does not equate with absolute sovereign inviolability. In contrast to the claims routinely made by many of R2P's chief proponents, sovereignty and humanitarian intervention *can* be reconciled and the focus on undermining both sovereign inviolability and sovereign equality is counter-productive. Additionally, I argue that the image of the developing world as implacable champions of an anachronistic conception of sovereign inviolability is empirically unsound. The chapter concludes by arguing that evidence suggests that provided certain guarantees are met the developing world are likely to support reform which facilitates a consistent and effective international response to intra-state crises.

Having outlined a defence of humanitarian intervention in Chapter 6, in Chapter 8, 'Grasping the Nettle: The Parameters of Viable Reform', I identify the key issue which must be addressed if there is to be a solution to the perennial problem posed by humanitarian intervention, namely the power of the Security Council. Attempts to contrive a means of responding consistently, quickly and effectively to intra-state crises which recognize the Security Council as the final arbiter of when and how to respond are destined to fail. Significant reform of the Security Council – in terms of its powers rather than its composition – is therefore required and is here suggested. The key components of the reform advocated are the establishment of a new body (elected by, and accountable to, the General Assembly) with powers to determine what the international response to a particular crisis should be in the event of Security Council paralysis, and the establishment of an independent UN military force capable of being deployed in the event that states are unwilling to volunteer troops. In addition to ensuring a non-partisan decision making process such reform would liberate states from the burden of supplying their own troops for military operations not in the national interest, as argued in Chapter 5.

This chapter does not aim to advance a precise structure for such a force but rather to achieve two things: first to demonstrate why such reform is the only means by which consistent and effective responses to egregious intra-state crises can be realized; second, to highlight the evidence that such reform, far from constituting a utopian fantasy, coheres with existing preferences amongst the majority of the world's states. This latter point is defended with reference to the concerns expressed by the developing world through various G-77 declarations and General Assembly debates and declarations. While few states, or coalitions of states, have openly and explicitly called for such reform, the nature of the concerns routinely raised by the developing world suggests a willingness to endorse the parameters of the prescriptions I advance.

Part I

The Responsibility to Protect: Sound and Fury …?

Chapter 2

The Evolution of the Responsibility to Protect

Though it is obviously necessary to provide some historical background on the evolution of R2P, this is not the primary intention of this chapter. There are myriad books and articles which provide a detailed historical narrative of this evolution (see for example, Bellamy, 2009; Weiss, 2007a). Rather, this chapter traces the evolution of R2P as a concept in international politics – that is, as a concept with an agreed meaning amongst states – highlighting a number of key junctures and their effect on the meaning of the term. As Alex Bellamy notes, R2P has 'changed in important respects from the way it was originally conceived by the ICISS' (2009, p. 195) and it is necessary, therefore, to identify the key moments when changes occurred, and to evaluate these changes. The aim here is to identify the original impetus for the emergence of the concept and, more importantly, the nature of R2P as it exists today and how the concept has failed to evolve into a significant influence on the behaviour of states. This chapter serves, therefore, as the foundation for Chapters 3, 4 and 5 which explore in depth the key characteristics of the contemporary manifestation of R2P.

Tracing the historical evolution of R2P is not especially contentious: there are five key events which have exercised the greatest influence on the evolutionary trajectory of R2P namely, the Rwandan genocide in 1994, NATO's intervention in Kosovo in 1999, the publication in 2001 of the seminal report by the International Commission on Intervention and State Sovereignty (ICISS), the 2005 World Summit, and the 2009 General Assembly debate on R2P. Significant disagreement exists, of course, as to whether R2P has increasingly become an embedded norm with positive legal form and normative power (Evans, 2009; Schulz, 2009), or been gradually diluted to the point that it is nebulous and ineffectual (Hehir, 2010b; Reinold, 2010). As discussed in Chapter 1, my perspective falls within the latter category but before justifying this diagnosis (the focus of Chapters 3, 4 and 5), I wish to contrast the aims and expectations of the proposal originally advanced by the ICISS with the contemporary manifestation of R2P and identify what has been jettisoned from the original report, what has been ignored, and what new agendas have been artificially added to try to reinvigorate the concept.

'Acts of Genocide': Rwanda 1994

NATO's intervention in Kosovo in March 1999 is regularly cited as the primary catalyst for the establishment of the ICISS and the birth of R2P. While there is an undeniable link between the controversy generated by Operation Allied Force, too much emphasis on this event – this 'intervention' – obscures the extent to which non-events – 'non-interventions' – played as significant a role in the emergence of R2P. Operation Allied Force was primarily controversial because NATO intervened without a Security Council mandate and this provoked great fear about an imminent increase in unilateral interventionism by the West and, more broadly, the subversion of the entire UN system for regulating the use of force and preserving sovereign equality (Chandler, 2002). This was, however, but one aspect of the broader debate on humanitarian intervention. The 'problem' posed by humanitarian intervention was not only how to restrain states from taking precipitate military action, but also how to overcome the unedifying spectacle of non-intervention that so often characterized the international 'response' to intra-state crises. As Simon Chesterman noted, historically the problem has been the regularity of 'inhumanitarian non-intervention' rather than a surfeit of purportedly 'humanitarian' interventions (2003, p. 54). It is for this reason, therefore, that the emergence of R2P must been seen as inspired by the non-intervention in response to the Rwandan genocide as much as it was to the intervention in Kosovo in 1999. The significance of this point will become clearer in Chapter 5.

The failure to act in the face of the dreadful events which occurred in Rwanda in 1994 is described by Paul Kennedy as 'the single worst decision the United Nations ever made' (2006,

p. 103). Whether 'the United Nations' made a decision not to intervene is a contentious point, however; the capacity of the UN to independently, that is, without the Security Council's assent, order an intervention and to deploy troops was (and remains) non-existent and thus a 'UN intervention' to stop the egregious violence could only have been sanctioned by the permanent five members of the Security Council (P5). A more accurate appraisal of the response to the genocide, therefore, is that the P5, rather than the UN, consciously chose not to intervene. Nonetheless, the UN cannot be fully exonerated; on 11 January 1994, Romeo Dallaire, Force Commander of the UN Assistance Mission for Rwanda (UNAMIR), cabled the UN Department of Peacekeeping Operations (DPKO) in New York with intelligence suggesting Hutu militias were planning to kill UN troops and murder 1,000 Tutsis every twenty minutes. Dallaire stated that he had been given information regarding the location of caches of weapons and he requested permission to seize these arms (Dallaire, 2003, p. 145). The DPKO refused his request as they felt this would exceed UNAMIR's mandate and potentially endanger UN peacekeeping troops. The DPKO did not inform the members of the Security Council of Dallaire's warning prior to the Security Council's meeting on 5 April, the day before the genocide began. According to Michael Barnett, UN officials with the capacity to influence events failed to meet their responsibilities; the DPKO failed to inform the Security Council about Dallaire's cable, UN Secretary-General Boutros Boutros-Ghali was 'positively anaemic', and within the UN Secretariat civil servants were, Barnett claims, 'timid, indecisive, and deceitful'. The UN, he concludes, 'responded to the genocide with wilful ignorance and indifference' (Barnett, 2002, pp. 3–4). The UN's own enquiry was also critical of the performance of many of its organs and especially its early warning system citing Rwanda as compelling evidence for the need to radically alter the structure of the UN (Security Council, 1999, pp. 3, 54–5).

Nonetheless, while there are certainly grounds for criticizing the UN's performance before, during and even after the genocide in 1994, the majority of the blame has been, and arguably should continue to be, levelled against the P5. On 20 April 1994, two weeks after the slaughter began, UN Secretary-General Boutros Boutros-Ghali put three options to the Security Council: the first was the deployment of thousands of additional troops under a

Chapter VII mandate to force a ceasefire. The second involved reducing UNAMIR's contingent to some 270 troops, while the third option was the complete withdrawal of UNAMIR. On 21 April, in what now appears an incredible act of callousness, the Security Council voted for the second option. Nicholas Wheeler noted that while there was clearly no way UNAMIR could have acted effectively under its original mandate once the genocide began this did not mean the contingent of UN troops had to be withdrawn. The alternative option, and that which was most likely to stem the slaughter, was 'a change of mandate and the deployment of an effective fighting force' (Wheeler, 2002, p. 222). With respect to this option, Barnett recalled there was 'a brief discussion' about the possibility of strengthening UNAMIR to halt the escalating violence, but added, 'I was (and still am) unaware of a single member state who offered their troops for such an operation' (1997, p. 559). Nearly a month later, as the slaughter continued and the international response was becoming increasingly obviously inadequate, the Security Council acted, though again, in a decidedly half-hearted fashion. On the 17 May, the Security Council passed Resolution 918 which neglected to use the word 'genocide' but more obliquely referred to, 'the killings of members of an ethnic group with the intention of destroying such a group in whole or in part'. This resolution modestly altered UNAMIR's mandate and increased its number to 5,500 troops. According to Chesterman, however, 'intense lobbying by the United States' ensured that the deployment would take place in two phases with phase one comprising the deployment of merely 150 unarmed observers and 800 Ghanaian soldiers with the sole task of securing Kigali airport (2002, p. 145).

Throughout the near three-month period, during which some 800,000 Rwandans were massacred, states, and the US in particular, shied away from using the obviously appropriate word 'genocide' to describe the killings, evidently fearing that to do so would compel them to take more robust action as per the 1948 Genocide Convention (Schabas, 2000, p. 496). In this vein, Security Council Resolution 925 on 8 June noted, 'acts of genocide have occurred in Rwanda' and issued a call for member-states to 'respond promptly to the Secretary-General's request for resources, including logistical support capability for rapid deployment of additional UNAMIR forces'. Logistically this deployment could have taken up to three months to organize. On the 18 June, however, France announced that it was willing to launch an intervention to establish a safe area in South-West Rwanda and four days later the Security Council, somewhat reluctantly, given suspicions about France's motives (see Jones, 1995), passed Resolution 929 sanctioning Operation Turquoise.

In the aftermath of the genocide, outrage at the international response was loud and routine; Dallaire in particular decried the obfuscation and railed against, 'the inexcusable apathy by the sovereign states that made up the UN that is completely beyond comprehension and moral acceptability' (Shawcross, 2001, p. 115). When US President Clinton subsequently travelled to Rwanda in 1998 to apologize for the inaction, he told his audience his administration, 'did not fully appreciate the depth and the speed with which you were being engulfed by this unimaginable terror' (New York Times, 1998). This 'if only we'd known then what we know now' defence has been rejected by many who have since uncovered evidence that Clinton, and indeed others, did in fact know that genocidal violence was underway (see, Carroll, 2004; Power, 2001). Indeed, Dallaire later described Clinton's speech as 'outright lies' (2009, p. 357).

Rwanda's legacy

The genocide was the catalyst for two themes which would come to dominate debate on humanitarian intervention during the latter half of the 1990s: first, the term 'Never Again!' once again gained currency and thereafter UN officials frequently referred to the events of 1994 whenever their earnest speeches on the need for UN reform required unconditional head-nodding: second, the rights afforded to sovereign states were increasingly challenged with an equation drawn between sovereignty and the occurrence of human rights' abuses (Jones, 1995, p. 226; Chatterjee and Scheid, 2003, p. 4).

It is curious that the primary 'lessons' propounded after the Rwandan genocide appear to have had little to do with the actual cause of the desultory international response. The origins of 'Never Again!' date back to the collective guilt felt in the aftermath of the Holocaust and the rhetorical commitment made to banish such organized slaughter. The refrain 'Never Again!', though often solemnly articulated, often appeared as little more than an empty slogan when contrasted with the glacial pace of reform and the international community's erratic response to instances of alleged and clear genocide in the modern era. The decision, therefore, to repeat a slogan that had wide currency prior to the genocide – and manifestly negligible influence – does not make a lot of sense. Additionally, while Rwanda sparked great outrage at the immorality of sovereign inviolability, the lack of intervention in 1994 had very little, if indeed anything, to do with sovereignty; Wheeler for example noted that during UN deliberations on how to respond, 'the principle of sovereignty was never raised ... no state tried to defend the UN's stance of non-intervention on the grounds that genocide fell within Rwanda's domestic jurisdiction' (2006, p. 36). The primary cause of the much criticized 'response' to the genocide was predominantly the unwillingness of the P5, and indeed all the other major powers, to take action, a point noted by the UN's own enquiry into the international response to the genocide (United Nations, 1999, p. 3). This catastrophe, therefore, exposed in graphic detail both the absolute centrality of the P5 in determining the UN's response to intra-state humanitarian crises and mass atrocities, and the primacy of political will – and its narrow scope – in determining how states, in particular the P5, respond to unfolding genocide and grave crimes against humanity more generally. Thus, while the Rwandan genocide was one of the 'immediate stimuli' for the ICISS's report (Weiss, 2007a, p. 88), and *The Responsibility to Protect* opens with the declaration, 'We want no more Rwandas' (ICISS, 2001a, p. XIII), the key cause of the manifestly lamentable international response in 1994 was arguably ignored, or certainly overlooked: this point will be explored in greater detail in Chapters 3 and 8.

'How should we respond?' Kosovo 1999

The end of the Cold War convinced many observers, and indeed statesmen, that humanitarian intervention was poised to become a more established and consistent practice in international relations. Now that the East–West rivalry that had stifled collective action at the Security Council was no more, many, not unreasonably, assumed that a new era had dawned. The UN-sanctioned action to repel Iraqi forces from Kuwait in 1991, and the subsequent intervention to protect the Kurds and Shiites in Northern and Southern Iraq through the imposition of no-fly zones, suggested that this optimism was well founded. Apart from earlier resolutions condemning the racist regimes in Rhodesia and South Africa in 1977, the passing of Resolution 688 on the 5 April 1991 was the first time the Security Council had described a humanitarian crisis as a threat to international peace and security (Malone, 2006, p. 88). Resolution 688 did not explicitly sanction military intervention or even the imposition of no-fly zones, though the subsequent military operation was justified as 'consistent with United Nations Security Council Resolution 688' (Wheeler, 2002, p. 512). The actions of the Security Council in this instance, and indeed the subsequent willingness of certain members of the P5 to creatively and expansively interpret Security Council resolutions to facilitate robust humanitarian action, coupled with the deployment of UN-mandated troops to Somalia in 1992, led to great optimism about the future of humanitarian intervention (Smith, 1998, p. 66). The Security Council mandated an unprecedented number of interventions under Chapter VII in the 1990s, further suggesting that a new humanitarian dispensation had achieved ascendancy.

These Security Council-mandated actions in the 1990s, however, evidenced a strong correlation between the action taken and the national interests of the P5 (Cassese, 2005, p. 347; Chesterman, 2002, p. 5). For example, the sanctioning of coercive military action – which was ultimately unnecessary – to restore the democratic government in Haiti in 1994 appeared to herald a new intolerance of military coups against democratically elected governments. In fact, the US had a significant interest in stemming the flow of refugees from Haiti and protecting its economic ties to the country (Chesterman, 2002, p. 153), while China, more cynically, acquiesced with the operation because the US promised it support for a World Bank loan if it did so (Voeten, 2008, p. 51). NATO's intervention in Kosovo in 1999, however, reinvigorated the optimists. Here, it seemed was a case where states had transcended both their narrow national interests and the restrictive provisions of international law to halt suffering.

Following the breakdown of negotiations with Slobodan Milošević's Federal Republic of Yugoslavia over the situation in Serbia's southern province of Kosovo, NATO began air strikes on 24 March 1999. The campaign lasted far longer than NATO's key political leaders anticipated and led to a dramatic increase in forced displacement of the Kosovar Albanian population; indeed, Misha Glenny described the displacement organized by Milošević and precipitated by NATO's campaign as of 'biblical proportions' (1999, p. 658). At the end of the 78-day campaign, however, Milošević agreed to extricate all his troops and police from Kosovo and permit the deployment of K-FOR, a NATO-led force which also comprised Russian troops.

In terms of the international reaction to Operation Allied Force, both China and Russia strongly opposed NATO's actions, as did India (Bellamy, 2002, p. 166). Additionally the West's traditional allies, such as Japan, Indonesia and South Korea, far from being supportive of NATO, were 'mute in their response' (ibid, p. 167). Indeed, General Assembly Resolution 377 passed in 1950 – the so-called *Uniting for Peace* resolution which enables the General Assembly to act when the Security Council is unable to unanimously sanction action – was, according to Nigel White, 'conveniently forgotten' prior to NATO's intervention (2000, p. 41). NATO governments declined to put the intervention to a vote in the General Assembly because officials felt it was highly unlikely that the requisite two thirds of the Assembly members would support it (Chesterman, 2003, p. 57).

The international response among states to NATO's action was thus mixed. Critics of this assertion point to Russia's failed attempt to have Operation Allied Force condemned by the Security Council and the support afforded to the operation by the Organisation for Islamic Conference (OIC) (Caplan, 2000, p. 24). While the fact that on the 26 March the Security Council voted 12–3 against Russia's draft resolution condemning 'NATO aggression' may appear conclusive, Wheeler pointed to the fact that five of the twelve who voted against the resolution were members of NATO and only three of the remaining seven spoke in support of the intervention (2002, p. 291). The OIC's support for the intervention was largely the consequence of an expression of solidarity with Kosovo's predominantly Muslim population rather than support for the principle of unilateral intervention *per se*. Indeed, 50 of the 57 members of the OIC were among the 133 states in the G-77 that later voted twice to condemn NATO for using force without Security Council authorization.

The intervention, supporters argued, highlighted the changed attitudes of Western states and the power of global civil society to influence foreign policy. Constituting 'the first war of humanitarian intervention ever carried out by the Western military powers' (Coll, 2001, p. 128), the extensive humanitarian rationale espoused by the leaders of the intervening states – such as Tony Blair's statement that this was a war fought for 'values' (Chatterjee and Scheid, 2003, p. 7) – suggested that the pressure exerted by proponents of intervention for the promotion and preservation of human security had significantly influenced NATO states. Bellamy claimed that the intervention evidenced, 'a heightened degree of liberal institutionalism in global politics' and illustrated, 'the extent to which international values and interests have begun to come together during the 1990s' (2002, pp. 211 and 214). Operation Allied Force was thus held to illustrate the capacity of the human rights movement and global civil society to compel Western states to alter their priorities from narrow national interests towards a universal concern with human security (Thomas and Tow, 2002, p. 178).

Critics argued, however, that NATO's action was inspired by more traditional national interests, specifically the general desire to proliferate capitalism and also to project power into Eastern Europe to fill the vacuum left by the collapse of the Soviet Union (Wood, 2000; Johnstone, 2000). The argument that NATO was compelled by moral concerns for the plight of the ethnic Albanian population in Kosovo was deemed implausible by some given the West's history of oppression and general disregard for human rights (Chomsky, 1999, p. 74). NATO's intervention was thus seen by many as the precursor to greater Western expansionism and an attempt to subvert the existing norms governing sovereignty and the use of force in international relations which restricted the West's power (Chandler, 2002, p. 17). Realist critiques asserted that the intervention – and the new norm it heralded – would destabilize the international system and set a dangerous precedent. They argued that the pursuit of humanitarian objectives is firstly hypocritical but also, even if genuine, against national interests as it distracts from strategic and economic interests and angers rival powers (Kober, 2000; Bandow, 2000; Mandelbaum, 1999). In contrast to the controversy which surrounded the Rwandan genocide, therefore, NATO's intervention in Kosovo led to fears that the international system was posed for a proliferation of interventions which would lead to instability and the erosion of the laws and norms regulating the use of force.

Kosovo: a missed opportunity

In the wake of this furore, UN Secretary-General Kofi Annan sought to use this debate to highlight the fact that the time had come to finally address the apparent conflict between sovereignty and humanitarian intervention. After becoming Secretary-General in 1997, Annan had periodically raised concerns about the contested status of humanitarian intervention and specifically the tension in the UN Charter, and international law more generally, between the rights of states and the rights of individuals. In a speech in 1998 he argued that the UN Charter, 'was never meant as a license for governments to trample on human rights and human dignity' (Roberts, 2006, p. 86). In a widely cited article in *The Economist* published after NATO's intervention Annan further argued, 'State sovereignty, in its most basic sense, is being refined', noting: 'individual sovereignty – by which I mean the fundamental freedom of each individual, enshrined in the Charter … has been enhanced by a renewed and spreading consciousness of individual rights' (1999, p. 49). In a landmark speech to the General Assembly in 2000 Annan asked

> if humanitarian intervention is, indeed, an unacceptable assault on sovereignty, how should we respond to a Rwanda, to a Srebrenica – to gross and systematic violations of human rights that affect every precept of our common humanity? (ICISS, 2001a, p. vii)

It was this very question which led to the convening of the ICISS and ultimately the publication of *The Responsibility to Protect* in 2001.

NATO's intervention, therefore, generated heated debate about the laws and norms governing the use of force and the very efficacy of international law. Operation Allied Force had, in the words of the ICISS, 'brought the controversy [surrounding humanitarian intervention] to its most intense head' (2001a, p. vii) and seemingly illustrated the limitations of the *status quo* and the need for significant reform (Guicherd, 1999, p. 20;

Simma 1999, p. 6). The unwillingness of China and Russia to support what many claimed was an obviously morally necessary intervention called into the question the legitimacy of the P5's veto which, many argued, was an anachronism that saddled legitimate action with the stigma of illegality (Reisman, 2000; Bellamy, 2002, p. 212).

Interestingly, however, despite the obvious opposition of many states to NATO's actions it is possible to discern, even at this juncture, agreement around two key points: that states had a responsibility to protect their populations from mass atrocities and that the international community could legitimately become involved if this responsibility was not fulfilled. As Bellamy notes, states (with the exception of China) opposed NATO's action not on the grounds that external intervention for the purpose of halting egregious oppression was inherently wrong, but rather on the basis that the intervention lacked a Security Council mandate and could constitute a precedent which would degrade international law and increase incidents of war. The intervention, therefore, Bellamy argues, 'helped lay the foundations for the grand consensus on sovereignty as responsibility' (2010, p. 45). NATO's intervention was famously described by the Independent International Commission on Kosovo (IICK) as 'illegal but legitimate' (2000, p. 10) and it was precisely this disconnect between legality and legitimacy that troubled the UN Secretary-General. The question he posed in 2000 – 'how should we respond to a Rwanda, to a Srebrenica – to gross and systematic violations of human rights that affect every precept of our common humanity?' – was the direct catalyst for the establishment in 2000 of the ICISS which described its report as a 'response to this challenge' (ICISS, 2001a, p. vii).

This was, therefore, a defining moment in the history of humanitarian intervention, one which, perhaps uniquely brought together all the key elements of the debate and forced the issue to the top of the international agenda. While the international response to NATO's actions was clearly marked by division, as Bellamy notes there were grounds for some optimism. The main source of contention was not so much the idea that states should refrain from oppressing their own people or that external intervention was occasionally permissible, but rather the means by which such intervention was regulated. The debate, therefore, focused attention on the Security Council and the veto power of the P5. It was, in short, an ideal opportunity to think creatively about this structural configuration and to exploit the international disquiet to push for reform. As previously discussed in Chapter 1, the fact that this window of opportunity did not lead to a focused proposal for reforming the international institutions constituted, I believe, a missed opportunity. Part II of this book, particularly Chapters 7 and 8, calls for a change in direction back to a focus on the institutions and laws governing the use of force rather than moral advocacy as was in fact promoted after Kosovo by R2P.

The International Commission on Intervention and State Sovereignty

In response to the perceived need for clarity on the issue of humanitarian intervention, and specifically the call for new thinking issued by the UN Secretary General in 2000, the Canadian Government established the International Commission on Intervention and State Sovereignty (ICISS) in 2000. The ICISS began its work in August 2000, convening a series of roundtables across the world to feed into work simultaneously undertaken by a core group of scholars and practitioners. Owing to the terrorist attacks against the US in September 2001, the publication of the final report was delayed until December 2001.

The ICISS was determined that its report would have real impact and influence declaring, 'We want no more Rwanda's and we believe that the adoption of the proposals in our report is the best way of ensuring that' (ibid, p. xiii). Rather than pose the issue in terms of the rights of intervening states, the ICISS placed the onus on states to meet their responsibilities to their own citizens. The primary responsibility for individuals, the ICISS argued, lay with their host state. In the event that a state failed to meet this responsibility the international community had a responsibility to protect citizens within this state. The ICISS outlined three aspects of this responsibility: the responsibility to prevent, the responsibility to react and the responsibility to rebuild. The idea of a 'responsibility to prevent' was that states have a responsibility to ensure that domestic tensions are addressed before they escalate (ibid, pp. 19–27). The 'responsibility to rebuild' placed a responsibility on an intervening state, or states, to contribute to a lasting settlement to the original conflict (ibid, pp. 39–45). The 'responsibility to react' is most closely related to the central dilemma posed by humanitarian intervention and the aspect of the ICISS's report which attracted greatest attention, though, as Chapter 4 attests, this emphasis has altered quite significantly since the publication of the report. The ICISS noted that 'above all else' R2P constitutes, 'a responsibility to react to situations of compelling need for human protection' (ibid, p. 29). If a state is either unable or unwilling to meet its responsibility to protect its citizens then the responsibility transfers from the state to the international community.

The ICISS employed the concept of 'human security' as the basic framework for its approach (ibid, p. 15). Building on the 'emerging principle' inherent in this idea the Commission argued that military intervention could only be legitimate when 'major harm to civilians is occurring or imminently apprehended, and the state in question is unable or unwilling to end the harm, or is itself the perpetrator' (ibid, p. 16). International intervention to stop human rights abuses, the report also emphasized, need not only take the form of military intervention (ibid, p. 29). The ICISS offered six 'Principles for Military Intervention' – criteria which must be met for an intervention to be legitimate – namely, right authority, just cause, right intention, last resort, proportional means and reasonable prospects (ibid, p. 32). In terms of 'just cause' the ICISS advanced two thresholds: 'large scale loss of life, actual or apprehended ... or large scale "ethnic cleansing", actual or apprehended'. With respect to 'right intention' the ICISS suggested that the intervening party must be motivated primarily, though not exclusively, by humanitarian aims. Regarding 'last resort' the ICISS advised that every diplomatic and non-military avenue must have been explored, though not actually tried provided there were good grounds for discounting alternative options. On 'proportional means' the ICISS advised that all interventions must be executed in strict adherence with international humanitarian law and aim to use the minimum degree of force possible. The final criterion – 'reasonable prospects' – advised that interventions should only be undertaken if the action is likely to be successful (ibid, pp. 32–7). These criteria were in themselves neither especially new nor controversial; indeed, the ICISS's supplementary research publication noted these amounted to a re-expression of an existing consensus which constituted a 'modified just war doctrine' (2001b, p. 140).

Regarding 'right authority', the subject of an entire chapter of the report, the ICISS clearly privileged the UN as the entity with the legitimacy to order an intervention; all those seeking to launch an intervention, the ICISS advised, must seek the Security Council's approval. The ICISS warned that acting without explicit Security Council approval ran the risk of undermining the UN and international law more generally. Membership of the UN, the ICISS claimed, carries an obligation not to unilaterally use force but also an obligation to use force on behalf of the UN if so sanctioned (ICISS, 2001a, pp. 48–9). While the ICISS was clear as to the importance of the Security Council it did criticize the unrepresentative nature of the P5 and its lack of accountability to the General Assembly. In terms of addressing the biggest issue influencing the Security Council's record on humanitarian intervention – the veto power of the P5 – the ICISS suggested a 'code of conduct' whereby, 'a permanent member, in matters where its vital national interests were not claimed to be involved, would not use its veto to obstruct the passage of what would otherwise be a majority resolution' (ibid, p. 51). If, however, the Security Council did not act when a crisis passed the just-cause threshold the ICISS suggested the matter should be taken to the General Assembly which could employ the powers vested in it through the *Uniting for Peace* resolution. Additionally, the ICISS suggested that regional organizations could undertake an intervention and seek to have retrospective legitimacy bestowed on their actions by the Security Council.

The issue which generated the controversy about NATO's intervention in Kosovo was the permissibility of unilateral intervention, namely action taken by a state or group of states without explicit approval from the Security Council or the General Assembly. The ICISS outlined 'two lessons' which should guide thinking in respect to this issue. First, they warned that in the face of Security Council inaction, 'it is unrealistic to expect that concerned states will rule out other means and forms of action to meet the gravity and urgency of these situations'. Such interventions 'may not be conducted for the right reasons or with the right commitment to the necessary precautionary principles'. Second, if action is taken without the Security Council's approval and this action proves successful 'then this may have enduring serious consequences for the stature and credibility of the UN itself' (ibid, p. 55). This was, in effect, a tacit acknowledgment that unilateral humanitarian intervention could be legitimate but there was little here which developed a means by which this legitimacy could be objectively judged or, more importantly, how such action could be regulated.

After ICISS

In response to the publication of *The Responsibility to Protect* many critics argued that it created a framework that could be an easily manipulated by powerful Western states, and indeed powerful states generally, to intervene at will under the pretext of humanitarianism. Mohammed Ayoob, for example, argued that the report 'raises the spectre of a return to colonial habits and practices on the part of the major Western powers' (2002, p. 85). David Chandler argued that the post-Cold War systemic configuration, though favourable to the West and particularly the US, provided no 'framework which can legitimize and give moral authority to new, more direct forms of Western regulation'. This 'crisis' led to the assertion of the liberal peace thesis which constitutes, 'the convergence of morality and *realpolitik*' (Chandler, 2004, p. 85). R2P, ostensibly part of this liberal peace thesis, was thus a means by which the tenets of international law could be manipulated and subverted to facilitate the national interests and expansionist ambitions of Western states.

Undoubtedly, for many the 2003 invasion of Iraq confirmed these fears. Like Operation Allied Force in 1999, this intervention was undertaken without the Security Council's authorization and championed most vociferously by the US and the UK. While the invasion of Iraq was initially primarily justified on what we now know to have been spurious security concerns, Operation Iraqi Freedom was also justified as an act of liberation, particularly in retrospect when the fabled weapons of mass destruction failed to materialize (Hehir, 2008a, pp. 59–65). It was not difficult, therefore, to claim continuity between the two interventions and to cite R2P as facilitating unilateralism.

Nonetheless, a causal link between the publication of *The Responsibility to Protect* and the invasion of Iraq can only be sustained if we can determine that, without the framework advanced by the ICISS report, the US-led coalition would not have been able to justify their invasion on humanitarian grounds. This is patently not the case. Prior to the publication of the ICISS report, myriad interventions were spuriously justified on humanitarian grounds; in the ten cases between 1945 and 1990 when humanitarian justifications for intervention were offered the ICISS's research directorate found, 'the rhetoric of humanitarianism had been used most stridently in cases where the humanitarian motive was weakest' (Weiss, 2007a, p. 37). The abuse of humanitarian rhetoric was prevalent prior to the emergence of R2P which cannot, therefore, be charged with creating a previously unavailable justificatory framework. The fear that *The Responsibility to Protect* would precipitate a flood of interventions has not materialized – though the invasion of Iraq cannot be ignored in this context – and as Weiss notes, 'Overzealous military action for insufficient humanitarian reasons ... certainly is no danger' (ibid, p. 52).

In assessing the ICISS's report, certain achievements are noteworthy. First, conceptually the new terminology did have some terminological attraction offering, as it did, a means by which to navigate around the divisive and, according to some, value-laden debate on 'humanitarian intervention'. Few could, and indeed did, oppose the idea that states have a 'responsibility to protect' their own citizens and the external dimension of R2P regarding the international responsibility was not solely focused on military intervention thereby allaying certain fears that invasions and military interventions were now to become routine (Roberts, 2006, p. 72). Additionally, the report advanced the debate by offering specific details on long-debated issues: in particular by drafting a set of criteria for military intervention and, within the 'just cause' criterion, thresholds for intervention. While these criteria and thresholds were certainly not now law, they did at least provide a framework around which debate could focus.

There were, however, significant weaknesses: the ICISS report's threshold criteria both use the ambiguous term 'large scale'. Despite the lack of clarity inherent in this term, the ICISS stated it wished to 'make no attempt to quantify "large scale" [as this] will not in practice generate major disagreement' (ICISS, 2001a, p. 33). In fact, as Bellamy rightly argued, this indeterminacy potentially enabled the P5 to block interventions by claiming that the thresholds have not been breached meaning that the determination of when to intervene would continue to be based on political rather than legal or factual grounds (2006a, pp. 148–9). Additionally, though a significant section of the report was devoted to the question of right authority, the final recommendation – the 'code of conduct' – was a highly idealistic, if not in practice unworkable, solution. A non-binding agreement in itself is a problematic legal, and even moral, mechanism to implement, while the very idea that the P5 would collectively have no interests in the outcome of a particular intra-state conflict was arguably quite naive. Additionally, even if, hypothetically, a particular intra-state conflict was of no strategic interest to the P5 then the likelihood that one of the P5 would oppose an intervention is slim precisely because they would have no objection to such an act given their lack of national interests and thus the code is somewhat tautological. Even in such cases, however, the horse trading that too often characterizes the P5's response to events means that events in relatively insignificant corners of the world are nonetheless used as pawns in a larger strategic game of power politics (Berdal, 2003, pp. 9–10). A final, and hugely significant issue, was the fact that the ICISS essentially fudged the issue of unilateral humanitarian intervention. While the report intimates that such action could conceivably be legitimate, it refrains from offering either an endorsement of such action in the event of Security Council paralysis or from proposing an alternative means by which humanitarian interventions could be legitimized in the absence of formal Security Council authorization.

The 2005 World Summit

The ICISS's report was published three months after the 11 September attacks and unsurprisingly conceded much of the limelight to the global 'war on terror' and the ensuing preoccupation with a different type of military action, namely self-defence (Gow, 2011; Hehir, 2008b). The ICISS's report was initially favourably received by Canada, the UK and Germany while Argentina, Australia, Colombia, Croatia, New Zealand, Norway, Peru, the Republic of Ireland, Rwanda, South Korea, Sweden and Tanzania all expressed broad support (Bellamy, 2006a, p. 151). East Asian countries were 'more cautious' in their response while, perhaps most importantly, the P5 were quite negative (Macfarlane, Thielking and Weiss, 2004, p. 982). In May 2002 the Security Council discussed the ICISS report: the US 'was noticeably unenthusiastic about the debate' while additionally 'there was widespread opinion in the meeting that if new situations emerged … the five permanent members and broader Council would lack the political will to deliver troops and would limit themselves to condemnatory resolution' (Welsh, 2006, pp. 185 and 210). The US rejected the idea of being bound to commit troops should the ICISS's thresholds be breeched while China and Russia opposed any diminution of the Security Council's monopoly on the legitimization of the use of force. Though the G-77 did not offer a specific unified response, it did suggest amending the ICISS report's provisions to strengthen the principles of territorial integrity and sovereignty (Bellamy, 2006a, p. 152). At the July 2003 'Progressive Governments Summit' the prime ministers of Canada and the UK attempted to include references to R2P in the final communiqué but this was rejected with Argentina, Chile and Germany particularly opposed. This marked 'a surprising new kind of hostility among countries that earlier might have been counted among the supporters of the concept' (Macfarlane, Thielking and Weiss, 2004, p. 984). The fallout from the divisive invasion of Iraq and the general rhetoric of the Bush administration since 11 September 2001 had created a 'poisonous' atmosphere in the General Assembly and a new unwillingness on the part of many states to support interventionism or countenance any expansion of the permissible grounds for the use of force (Weiss, 2007a, p. 125).

In September 2003, Kofi Annan commissioned the High Level Panel on Threats, Challenges and Change to examine the UN's role in addressing international security concerns. The report argued that membership of the UN and recognition of a state's sovereignty carried certain responsibilities. There was also an explicit acknowledgment that the international community had a 'responsibility to protect' citizens in other states when the host state failed in its domestic responsibility to do so (High Level Panel on Threats, Challenges and Change, 2004, p. 66). The report adopted the just-cause thresholds and precautionary principles contained in the ICISS's report with some minor amendments and, though it advanced a cautious perspective on revising the rules governing the use of force, suggested that the Security Council needed to 'enhance its capacity and willingness to act in the face of threats' (ibid, p. 80). Kofi Annan welcomed the findings and included the recommendations in his report *In Larger Freedom* which he presented to the General Assembly in March 2005.

At the 2005 World Summit, held on the 14–16 September in New York, two paragraphs – 138 and 139 – were included in the final *Outcome Document* explicitly endorsing the notion of a responsibility to protect (see extract overleaf). The fact that this endorsement of R2P was included in the *Outcome Document* was heralded by advocates of R2P as a significant success, especially as the World Summit itself had achieved relatively modest, if not disappointing, progress in other areas. The compromises which secured the inclusion of these paragraphs, however, arguably undermined the essence of the original proposal and the result was an ambiguous conception of R2P (Chesterman, 2011a, p. 2; Reinold, 2010, p. 64).

Bellamy suggests three major concessions were made to ensure the inclusion of the references to a 'responsibility to protect' in the two paragraphs. First, regarding the question of authority, the idea of the P5 agreeing not to use their veto powers – the ICISS's 'code of conduct' – was abandoned early in the negotiations at the behest of the P5 thereby ensuring there was no concession by the P5 on decision making. Additionally, the notion of legitimate intervention without explicit Security Council approval was 'sidestepped' (Bellamy, 2006a, p. 155). Second, the just-cause threshold included in the *Outcome Document* in fact technically restricted the instances when the Security Council could legitimately intervene. Security Council practice in the 1990s had substantially broadened the Security Council's remit to act, with the term 'threats to international peace and security' in Chapter VII of the Charter being used in a number of cases where the actual threat to international peace and stability was quite obviously minimal. This was arguably most evident with respect to Haiti, first with resolution 842 in June 1993 and later in July 1994 when resolution 940 authorized military force (ICISS, 2001b, pp. 102–4). With the *Outcome Document* once again explicitly vesting exclusive authority with the Security Council, and the criteria for intervention limited to 'genocide, war crimes, ethnic cleansing and crimes against humanity', the scope for intervention was actually somewhat restricted (Byers, 2005b; Wheeler, 2005). Third, while the ICISS stated that the responsibility to protect transferred from the state

Box 2.1 Paragraphs 138 and 139 of the 2005 World Summit *Outcome Document*

138 Each individual State has the responsibility to protect its populations from genocide, war crimes, ethnic cleansing and crimes against humanity. This responsibility entails the prevention of such crimes, including their incitement, through appropriate and necessary means. We accept that responsibility and will act in accordance with it. The international community should, as appropriate, encourage and help States to exercise this responsibility and support the United Nations in establishing an early warning capability.

139 The international community, through the United Nations, also has the responsibility to use appropriate diplomatic, humanitarian and other peaceful means, in accordance with Chapters VI and VIII of the Charter, to help protect populations from genocide, war crimes, ethnic cleansing and crimes against humanity. In this context, we are prepared to take collective action, in a timely and decisive manner, through the Security Council, in accordance with the Charter, including Chapter VII, on a case-by-case basis and in cooperation with relevant regional organizations as appropriate, should peaceful means be inadequate and national authorities manifestly fail to protect their populations from genocide, war crimes, ethnic cleansing and crimes against humanity. We stress the need for the General Assembly to continue consideration of the responsibility to protect populations from genocide, war crimes, ethnic cleansing and crimes against humanity and its implications, bearing in mind the principles of the Charter and international law. We also intend to commit ourselves, as necessary and appropriate, to helping States build capacity to protect their populations from genocide, war crimes, ethnic cleansing and crimes against humanity and to assisting those which are under stress before crises and conflicts break out.

(General Assembly, 2005)

to the international community when the host state was deemed 'unable or unwilling' to exercise its responsibilities, in the *Outcome Document* this was amended to cases where the host state was guilty of a 'manifest failure' – a semantic change but one which raised the threshold for international action.

Assessing the World Summit

Supporters of R2P sought to achieve a number of goals at the World Summit: they wanted the General Assembly to make a commitment to the tenets of the original ICISS document and they sought to persuade the Security Council to do three things: first to adopt a resolution committing it to act whenever the just-cause thresholds were crossed, second to submit its decisions to public deliberation about the use of force based on the precautionary principles, and third to agree not to use the veto in cases of humanitarian emergencies where they did not have some clear national interests at stake (Bellamy, 2006a, p. 153). The two major initiatives proffered by adherents to R2P – that of securing the P5 endorsement of an obligation to act, and the agreement to remove the veto – were not incorporated into the *Outcome Document*. Additionally, the goal of further strengthening the capacity of states to legitimately act outside of the Security Council was unsuccessful as the endorsement of the basic tenets of the ICISS report was made conditional on the re-statement of the Security Council's absolute primacy. The consensus reached on R2P and included in the *Outcome Document* was, therefore, arguably achieved only by conceding key aspects of R2P and restricting the evolution of the permissibility of intervention (Reinold, 2010, p. 62; Wheeler, 2005, p. 105). Thus the *Outcome Document* constituted for some, 'a step-backward ... R2P lite' (Weiss, 2007a, p. 177).

The 2005 World Summit *Outcome Document*, more so than the ICISS's report, today constitutes the agreed meaning of R2P. It is, as is clear, quite a modest achievement which leaves many of the main questions which catalysed the emergence of R2P unanswered. The preceding section outlines the extent to which the P5 shaped the variant of R2P which ultimately emerged from the World Summit negotiations. While accepting the real influence of the P5, and the US in particular, during the negotiations, I maintain that the absence of significant improvements to the means by which intra-state crises are addressed cannot reasonably be attributed solely to mendacity on the part of the P5. The P5 were, quite naturally, always likely to oppose any diminution in their power, and their tactics, therefore, could hardly have occasioned any surprise. The real problem was that the ICISS, and R2P advocates more generally, had failed to propose any coherent alternative to the Security Council for the regulation of intervention which other states could rally behind and promote. As Bellamy argued with respect to the developing world's response to NATO's intervention in Kosovo, and discussed in greater detail in Chapter 7, the key source of concern for the developing world was, and remains, ensuring consistency, not preserving absolute inviolability. There was scope, therefore, for proposing an alternative system which, while allaying the developing world's fears of neo-colonialism, was orientated towards objectively regulating humanitarian intervention. In the absence of a coherent proposal for an alternative, objective means by which to regulate humanitarian intervention, the developing world was, in effect, forced to adopt a 'better the devil you know' approach and support the restatement of the status quo in 2005. The P5 is obviously an imperfect institution but, it is quite obviously preferable to a system where the use of force for humanitarian intervention is deregulated. Had the ICISS articulated a proposal for institutional reform which would ensure consistency this may have been opposed by the P5 but, crucially it could have become a unifying rallying cry for the developing world. Powerful as the P5 are, they have not always been able to block major institutional innovations, as the creation of the International Criminal Court proves. This point is developed further in Chapters 7 and 8.

The 2009 General Assembly debate

In the aftermath of the 2005 World Summit, it was agreed that the General Assembly would at a later date formally discuss how to implement paragraphs 138 and 139 of the *Outcome Document*. After some delay, during which time certain states that had signed up to the *Outcome Document* somewhat curiously suggested that they hadn't in fact agreed to the idea of a 'responsibility to protect' (Evans, 2009, p. 52), a date was set and the General Assembly debate on R2P began on 21 July 2009.

The debate was framed by the report, 'Implementing the Responsibility to Protect', drafted by UN Secretary-General Ban Ki-Moon and presented to members states at the General Assembly six months prior to the debate. In his report Ban Ki-Moon warned against attempting to broaden the scope of R2P, reiterating that its parameters were limited to 'genocide, war crimes, ethnic cleansing and crimes against humanity' (2009a, p. 8). The Secretary-General offered a conception of R2P based on three pillars: Pillar 1: the protection responsibilities of states; Pillar 2: international assistance and capacity building, and Pillar 3: timely and decisive response. The Secretary-General stressed that R2P had been accepted by states in 2005 and constituted a commitment that could not now be retracted. He urged the General Assembly to implement R2P and to, 'make their words come to life and to make the aspirations of people everywhere for a safer, more secure world for "We the peoples" a reality' (ibid, p. 30).

Over the course of three days – 23, 24 and 28 July – General Assembly member states gave their views on the Secretary-General's report, and R2P more generally. In total over 90 governments made presentations and more were represented by regional organizations such as the Non-Aligned Movement and the Caribbean Community. Following the debate, a number of very positive appraisals lauded the event as a significant achievement. The International Coalition for R2P described the debate as, 'a success for both advocates and victims working to prevent and halt genocide, war crimes, crimes against humanity and ethnic cleansing' (2009, p. 1). Similarly, a report by the Global Centre for R2P noted that UN member states 'were overwhelmingly positive about the doctrine' and declared, 'What emerged was a clear commitment from the vast majority of member states to be part of efforts to prevent and halt atrocity crimes and to make a reality of "Rwanda, never again"' (2009b, p. 1). UN Secretary-General Ban Ki-Moon described the debate as 'heartening' and 'forward-looking' (2009b). In the course of the debate, a number of themes reoccurred and it is possible to identify five principles around which there was effectively unanimity: each are discussed in the subsequent paragraphs.

Many states highlighted the African Union's 2000 Constitutive Act as a significant development in the evolution of R2P. The Act was cited as indicative of the move from 'non-interference' to 'non-indifference' and of the willingness of states in the developing world to adhere to, and advance, principles on human rights protection often characterized as culturally specific or 'Western'. The critique suggesting that R2P was designed to legitimize Western imposition of particularist humanitarian standards and facilitate a return to pre-Charter colonial interference under the rubric of human rights was countered by many states who referred to Article 4(h) of the Constitutive Act which recognizes, 'The right of the Union to intervene in a Member State pursuant to a decision of the Assembly in respect of grave circumstances, namely war crimes, genocide and crimes against humanity'. R2P was, therefore, generally endorsed as a universal principle of non-indifference in keeping with the cultural norms extant in the developing world and not a 'Western' norm.

Additionally, it was consistently stressed that prevention was a key component of R2P. While R2P clearly stems from the 1990s debates on humanitarian intervention, many states argued that R2P involved much more than military intervention and further, that its greatest potential efficacy lay in its capacity to prevent, rather than halt, humanitarian crises. This will be dealt with in greater detail in Chapter 4.

There was also widespread agreement that R2P was not a new legal principle, as Ban Ki-Moon had emphasized in his pre-debate report (2009a, p. 5). The impetus for this line of argument appears to have been the perceived need to counter the suggestion that R2P was not in conformity with existing international law and thus that it could be rejected on the grounds either that it has no legal basis, or that it is in conflict with existing international law. While certain states disagreed with the view that R2P was based on established legal doctrine this was very much the minority position; even states such as North Korea, Sudan, Myanmar and Iran acknowledged that the basic principles underpinning R2P could be found in existing international law. As will be argued in Chapter 3, however, the fact that R2P does not constitute a new legal principle may well negate the argument that it is somehow contrary to existing international law, but this also means that it necessarily constitutes a reassertion of the discredited *status quo*.

A fourth area of agreement was that R2P could only be applied to the four crimes listed in paragraph 138 of the World Summit *Outcome Document*, namely genocide, war crimes, ethnic cleansing and crimes against humanity. In May 2008 certain international observers, such as then French Foreign Minister Bernard Kouchner, claimed that the humanitarian crisis caused by the hurricane in Myanmar was being exacerbated by the ruling military junta's inability, if not unwillingness, to provide aid to the needy and thus the situation demanded external intervention (Reuters, 2008). This was unfavourably received in many parts of the world, by both critics and supporters of R2P, and criticized as an unjustifiable expansion of R2P's remit (Evans, 2008, p. 65): this was reflected in the general consensus during the 2009 debate on the limitations of R2P's applicability. During the debate the French ambassador did, however, argue that by endorsing R2P states could not thereafter 'watch helplessly' if a government refused to help its own people in the wake of crisis precipitated by a natural disaster (France, 2009, p. 6). Singapore, however, indicative of the broader opposing view described this expansive interpretation of R2P as 'patently unhelpful' (Singapore, 2009, p. 2).

The fifth point on which there was general agreement related to the need for the mobilization of political will. This call for a new will to act echoed paragraph 138 of the 2005 World Summit *Outcome Document* and Ban Ki-Moon's pre-debate report (2009a, pp. 8–9). Obviously, the absence of political will in any situation will undermine effective action and it is certainly true, therefore, that R2P's efficacy is influenced by the disposition of states. The problem, however, as discussed in detail in Chapter 5, is that political will is a variable upon which the entire utility of R2P is now predicated. With respect to Pillar 2, there is neither a compulsion to act or punishment for inaction and thus R2P is, in Frank Berman's succinct description, a 'discretionary entitlement' which can be operationalized only if states are inclined to do so (2007, p. 161).

R2P after the 2009 debate

Thus, the 2009 debate certainly evidenced welcome agreement around a number of issues and was not marred by the rancour and division that all too often characterizes General Assembly debates. Nonetheless, while this air of cordiality served as the basis for the many positive analyses published in the wake of the debate, closer analysis both of what states actually agreed to and also what they neglected to discuss, gives cause for concern (Hehir, 2011). Indeed, it is debatable whether disagreement on any of the five issues previously discussed was ever likely; what state could, or at least publicly would, object to any of these principles? Chapters 3, 4 and 5 argue that the key contentious issues which catalysed the emergence of R2P in the wake of the non-intervention in Rwanda in 1994 and NATO's 1999 intervention in Kosovo were essentially sidelined in 2009 (and previously at the 2005 World Summit) and that the agreed variant of R2P we have today constitutes the triumph of the lowest common denominator. A conspicuous omission during the debate was a discussion of the process by which the international community can, and more importantly will, become involved in a particular situation without the host state's consent. There was no clarification in 2009 of the criteria for intervention; while the original ICISS report included six criteria for military intervention, these were not included in the 2005 World Summit *Outcome Document* nor were they clarified in 2009. Additionally, and perhaps most significantly, there is as yet no answer to the key question, 'In the event that an intra-state crisis reaches a particular nadir and the host state is evidently unable or unwilling to address the situation, what happens if the Security Council fails to respond?' There remains no consensus on the permissibility of unilateral intervention – action taken without the Security Council's support – yet this was a key catalyst for this debate. In light of these omissions, therefore, the R2P which we have today as a result of the 2009 debate does not appear to constitute a viable solution to the problem the ICISS was established to solve. This is the focus of the following three chapters.

Conclusion: 'what is R2P?'

It *is* possible to identify what R2P is, at least in terms of what states agree it is. While individuals and organizations have imbued the concept with both positive and negative connotations, and at times exaggerated its tenets and remit, when we speak of R2P we must adhere to that manifestation which has been agreed to by states. As Bellamy argues, it does not make sense today to discuss R2P in terms of the original ICISS variant or even less so in terms of subjective interpretations as to its 'true' character (2009, p. 195).

In summation, R2P has the following characteristics:

1 States agree that they have an internal responsibility to protect their citizens (Pillar 1 in Ban Ki-Moon's 2009 formulation).
2 States agree that R2P applies only to four crimes: genocide, war crimes, ethnic cleansing and crimes against humanity.
3 R2P comprises a commitment by all states to prevent the occurrence of the four crimes within their own state and to work with other states in preventing the outbreak of such crimes.
4 As per the wording of the 2005 *Outcome Document*, states agree that when a state, 'manifestly fail[s] to protect their populations from genocide, war crimes, ethnic cleansing and crimes against humanity' the international community 'are prepared to take collective action, in a timely and decisive manner, through the Security Council, in accordance with the Charter', using force only as a last resort.
5 States agree that R2P does not alter existing law governing the use of force and in particular that it recognizes the Security Council as the sole authority with the power to sanction intervention.
6 With the exception of the establishment of the Office of the Special Adviser on the Prevention of Genocide and the Special Adviser on the Responsibility to Protect, R2P does not involve the creation of any new UN organs or institutions or any alteration in the mandate or powers of existing UN organs or institutions.
7 R2P's provisions on coercive intervention constitute a political commitment by member states which is not based on set thresholds for intervention and does not include automatic triggers for intervention.

The following three chapters argue that the agreement that today exists among states as to the meaning of R2P, evidenced during the 2009 debate and summarized above, is shallow and that its practical influence can only ever be minimal. Those seeking the achievement of a consistent, impartial and effective means by which large-scale intra-state humanitarian crises can be addressed will be disappointed if they expect R2P in its present form to effect such change. This is because R2P restates existing commitments, fails to address the key sources of contestation and offers no proposals on institutional and/or legal reform. Chapter 3, 4 and 5 argue that the variant of R2P endorsed in

2005 and reaffirmed in 2009 constitutes the articulation of a series of political promises devoid of any concrete duties or meaningful responsibilities.

Not only is R2P unlikely to contribute anything of value to the means by which the international community responds to intra-state crises, it may actually retard progress in this area. Despite the positive analyses emanating from some quarters in the wake of both the 2005 World Summit and the 2009 General Assembly debate, the future efficacy of R2P has in fact been limited, rather than increased, by both the nature of the recent consensus achieved as to its meaning and the difficulty in reinterpreting, or significantly altering, the now set status of R2P. Today, R2P has a fixed referent point and established constituent principles; while its meaning cannot be described as immutable, definite parameters now exist which restrict (re)interpretation. While in certain respects this may be a positive development – in particular with respect to those who seek to either expand its applicability or exaggerate its provisions – in other respects the emergence of this fixed identity diminishes the possibility that R2P can spearhead meaningful reform given the nature of the anodyne principles which today constitute its agreed meaning.

Chapter 3

The Responsibility to Protect, Authority and International Law

Chapter 2 charted the evolution of R2P, stressing and analysing the impact of five key junctures – the 1994 Rwandan genocide, the 1999 intervention in Kosovo, the 2001 ICISS report, the 2005 World Summit and the 2009 General Assembly debate – thereby establishing the contemporary tenets of the concept. This chapter focuses on one particular aspect of R2P, namely its legal status.

As will be explored in greater detail in Chapter 6, the efficacy of international law is a matter of some debate. While the traditionally dominant view within International Relations was that international law was somewhat irrelevant, and definitely secondary to power politics, in the post-Cold War era this has changed. Many have argued that international law, though certainly weak and undeniably prone to politicization, potentially holds the key to the resolution of some of the primary controversies in international relations. Clearly, as presently structured, the international legal system formally recognizes and reflects the existing power hierarchy and in addition to this structural constraint on the efficacy of international law, there also exists a manifest tension between the rights of individuals and the rights of sovereign states accentuated by the obviously imperfect, if not fundamentally flawed, enforcement mechanisms.

The debates on humanitarian intervention in the 1990s, perhaps uniquely, necessitated a discussion about both international law and international relations which generated considerable inter-disciplinary debate. The specific catalysts for this debate were two-fold: the question of the internal responsibilities of states, and the corollary regarding the international community's right to intervene (not only in the military sense) in the domestic affairs of states when national responsibilities had not been fulfilled. The refrain 'something must be done' periodically rang out in the face of humanitarian crises and the Rwandan genocide precipitated an outraged chorus of 'Never Again!' Yet, precisely *who* should do *something* quickly emerged as a contested issue. In light of the non-intervention in Rwanda and the 'illegal but legitimate' intervention in Kosovo, the existing regulations appeared unsuitable, if not anachronistic.

The ICISS acknowledged that there were a number of problems with the existing legal system and cited as its first objective, '[to] establish clearer rules, procedures and criteria for determining whether, when and how to intervene' (2001a, p. 11). This chapter argues that R2P does not in fact achieve these aims. The evolution of R2P from the ICISS report to the present day evidences no legal innovation and constitutes an endorsement of the very international legal system – including the legal architecture and the laws themselves – which was so discredited by the end of the 1990s. The fact that R2P amounts to an endorsement of the *status quo* can only be regarded as a significant failing unless one dismisses the importance, and deleterious influence, of the UN system for regulating the use of force. To understand how little has changed it is necessary to detail the legal system, and its record, prior to the emergence of R2P. The chapter thus begins by assessing the legal status of humanitarian intervention prior to the establishment of the ICISS and then proceeds to assess the legality of R2P on the basis of its two main components, namely, the internal responsibilities of states and the international responsibility of states.

The legal status of humanitarian intervention pre-R2P

The legal status of humanitarian intervention has long been a divisive issue in international law (Farer, 2003, p. 143). The end of the Cold War and the growing clamour to 'do something' in response to the intra-state humanitarian crises which erupted in the early 1990s, particularly in the Balkans and East Africa, generated an increased focus on this contested legal status. In terms of what 'humanitarian intervention' constitutes, there are, predictably, differing views. For the purposes of this chapter, I use the following definition: 'Military action taken by a state, group of states or non-state actor, in the territory of another state, without that state's consent, which is justified, to some significant extent, by a humanitarian concern for the citizens of the host state' (Hehir, 2010a, p. 20).

Humanitarian intervention and the UN Charter

A particularly important aspect of the debate surrounding the legality of humanitarian intervention has been the question of the necessity of UN authorization, often advanced in the context of the question 'who decides?' The UN Charter does not refer to a right of humanitarian intervention for either individual states or the UN Security Council. Article 2.4 prohibits the threat or use of force against the territorial integrity or political independence of any state while Article 2.7 explicitly prohibits the UN from unsolicited involvement in the domestic affairs of its member states. Many subsequent treaties, resolutions and statements reaffirmed these principles. Articles 53 and 64 of the 1969 Vienna Convention on the Law of Treaties state that these provisions are *jus cogens* and accepted by the international community as principles from which no derogation is permitted. General Assembly Resolution 2131 in 1965 affirmed member's opposition to all forms of intervention, 'for any reason whatsoever' and declares that 'armed intervention is synonymous with aggression'. In 1970, the General Assembly passed Resolution 2625 which reaffirmed the prohibition on 'the threat or use of force against the territorial integrity or political independence of any State'. Clause IV of the Helsinki Accords Final Act of 1975 notes, 'The participating states will respect the territorial integrity of each of the participating states. Accordingly they will refrain from any action ... against the territorial integrity, political independence, or the unity of any participating state.' Both the Charter and supplementary international law, therefore, explicitly recognize the inviolability of the state and outlaw the use of force, even if with purportedly humanitarian intent (Gray, 2000; Murphy, 1996; O'Connell, 2000).

In the 1990s, however, the Security Council expanded its interpretation of its Chapter VII powers to include intra-state humanitarian crises. Chapter VII outlines the circumstances under which the Security Council may sanction the use of force. Under Article 39 the Security Council can determine, 'the existence of any threat to the peace, breach of the peace, or act of aggression' and decide what measures need to be taken. If peaceful measures fail then the Security Council, acting under Article 42, can sanction more robust measures, 'as may be necessary to maintain or restore international peace and security.' During the Cold War this provision was understood restrictively; indicatively the UK and France argued that while the 1960 Sharpeville massacre perpetrated by the South African police was regrettable, it was not an issue which fell under the Security Council's purview as detailed in Chapter VII. In the landmark Resolution 688 in 1991, however, the Security Council declared: '[The Security Council] Condemns the repression of the Iraqi civilian population in many parts of Iraq, including most recently in Kurdish populated areas, the consequences of which threaten international peace and security in the region'. This signalled a new willingness on the part of the Security Council to broaden its interpretation of Chapter VII. Stretching this provision of the Charter to include humanitarian crises provoked some controversy; indicatively, the Independent International Commission on Kosovo (IICK) noted, 'At present the Charter does not explicitly give the Security Council the power to take measures in cases of violations of human rights' (2000, p. 196; see also Danish Institute of International Affairs, 1999, p. 62; White, 2004; Armstrong, Farrell and Lambert, 2007, pp. 132–3). Whether the application of Chapter VII powers to intra-state humanitarian crises was consistent with the Charter was, therefore, of some doubt, and a number of states, particularly in the developing world, were concerned that the UN was becoming more interventionist (Roberts, 2006, p. 73).

Despite these valid concerns, an intervention authorized by the Security Council has a very strong legal case and authorized interventions have not, historically, been sources of great legal contestation. As Anne Peters notes, 'Since the 1990s it has been uncontroversial that the Security Council may authorize humanitarian military action as a matter of international law' (2009, p. 538). Of greater concern, however, was the inconsistent use of Chapter VII in the post-Cold War era; while the permanent five members of the Security Council (P5) had reinterpreted their powers, they had not advanced any coherent framework outlining how their new understanding of Chapter VII would be consistently and impartially applied in practice. In his assessment of the 'remarkable transformation' in the Security Council's use of Chapter VII, Simon Chesterman observed that the application of this provision was haphazard, leading to 'ambiguous resolutions and conflicting interpretations' (2002, p. 5). According to Chesterman, action taken by the Security Council under Chapter VII was driven by the national interests of the P5 at the expense of issues of procedural legality (ibid, p. 165; see also Cassese, 2005, p. 165). The Security Council's authorization of the use of force in Haiti in 1994 is illustrative of this selectivity.

In 1991, the democratically elected President of Haiti, Jean-Bertrand Aristide, was ousted in a military coup and in response the UN imposed economic sanctions. By 1994 the sanctions were deemed to have been ineffective and in July 1994 the Security Council passed Resolution 940, which determined that the situation in Haiti constituted a threat to international peace and security and ordered an intervention to restore the democratically elected President Aristide. In practice, however, non-democratic regimes and benefactors of military coups were not considered to constitute this grave threat in every instance. In addition, in keeping with other uses of Chapter VII during the 1990s, this Security Council resolution was officially deemed an exception. Resolution 940 recognized 'the unique character' of the situation and stated: '[Haiti's] extraordinary nature ... [requires] an exceptional response'. Similarly the sanctioning of action in Somalia in 1992 under Chapter VII was premised on it being, 'an exceptional response' and the sanctioning of the deployment of troops in Rwanda in 1994, through Resolution 929, was described as, 'a unique case'. The purportedly 'exceptional' nature of these actions was a means to avoid any compulsion to act or create precedents which would demand consistency and automaticity in the future (Danish Institute of International Affairs, 1999, p. 74). While the inconsistent use of Chapter VII angered many states who accused the Security Council of hypocrisy (Cassese, 2005, p. 347), the 'exception' justification facilitated selective responses and enabled the influence of political exigencies in the decision making process of the P5. This selectivity, and subjectivity with respect to thresholds, will be explored in greater detail later in this chapter.

By the end of the 1990s, therefore, it was clear that the P5 understood Chapter VII as enabling it to authorize a military intervention against a state without that state's consent for humanitarian purposes – a 'humanitarian intervention' to all intents and purposes (Chesterman, 2011a). Action taken without

Security Council authorization proved a far more controversial issue, however, as evidenced by the debate generated by NATO's intervention in Kosovo in 1999 (see Chapter 2).

There are two exceptions to the prohibition on the use of force without Security Council authorization. First, there is the right of self-defence: Article 51 of the Charter reads, 'Nothing in the present Charter shall impair the inherent right of individual or collective self defence if an armed attack occurs against a member of the United Nations'. This is premised, however, by the declaration that the use of force in self-defence is only permissible, 'until the Security Council has taken measures necessary to maintain international peace and security' and that this right of self-defence'shall not in any way affect the authority and responsibility of the Security Council'. The International Court of Justice (ICJ) ruled in the 1986 *Nicaragua v The United States* case that the notion of self-defence should be understood restrictively and thus Article 51 does not apply with respect to preventing or halting egregious intra-state humanitarian crises (Guicherd, 1999, p. 21).

The second permissible derogation from the prohibition is the 1950 General Assembly Resolution 377, *Uniting for Peace*. This resolution empowers the General Assembly to act when the Security Council is unable to unanimously sanction action or demand a cessation to ongoing military action when there is a threat to international peace and security. The General Assembly may take up an issue under two conditions: first, when nine members of the Security Council vote to move the issue to the General Assembly. This vote is immune from the P5 veto. Second, when a majority of UN members states vote to bring the issue to the General Assembly (Krasno and Das, 2008, p. 175). The General Assembly can only take the lead on an issue if it is not already under consideration at the Security Council but, provided this condition is met, then technically the General Assembly can sanction a military intervention if two-thirds of its members so agree. The procedures outlined in Resolution 377 were drafted at the behest of the US in response to the conflict in Korea when the Soviet veto paralysed the Security Council, though the first actual reference to 'Uniting for Peace' occurred during the Suez Canal crises in 1956 (Bosco, 2009, p. 60). The Danish Institute of International Affairs (DIIA) found that the *Uniting for Peace* resolution 'Has lost much of its importance [and] is no legal basis for the authorization of humanitarian intervention' (1999, p. 61). Additionally, moving divisive issues such as those posed by humanitarian intervention to the General Assembly is no guarantee that they will be swiftly dealt with and thus the utility of the provision is dubious; at times use of the *Uniting for Peace* resolution simply created another forum for unproductive rhetoric and division (Krasno and Das, 2008, p. 189). Nonetheless, an increased role for the General Assembly, specifically through the utilization of the *Uniting for Peace* resolution, has been mooted as a possible solution to paralysis at the Security Council and the representativeness of the General Assembly is obviously additionally attractive (Evans, 2008, p. 136; ICISS, 2001a, p. 53).

Under existing codified international law, therefore, there is no law explicitly sanctioning unilateral humanitarian intervention. In its key ruling in the 1949 *Corfu Channel* Case the ICJ declared that it could

> only regard the alleged right of intervention as the manifestation of a policy of force, such as has, in the past, given rise to most serious abuses and as such cannot, whatever be the present defect in international organization, find a place in international law. Intervention ... would be reserved for the most powerful states and might easily lead to perverting the administration of international justice itself. (DIIA, 1999, p. 86)

In its ruling in the 1986 *Nicaragua* v. *the United States* case, the ICJ further declared, 'While the US might form its own appraisal of the situation as to respect for human rights in Nicaragua, the use of force could not be the appropriate method to monitor or ensure such respect' (ibid, p. 83). In 1986 the UK Foreign Office found against the legality of humanitarian intervention noting 'the scope of abusing such a right argues strongly against its creation (Holbrook, 2002, pp. 140–1). Similarly, the US 1987 *Restatement of Foreign Relations Law* noted, 'Whether a state may intervene with military force in the territory of another state without its consent not to rescue the victims but to prevent or terminate human rights violations, is not agreed or authoritatively determined' (Burton, 1996, p. 428). This apparent consensus on the illegality of humanitarian intervention, however, was increasingly challenged in the post-Cold War era.

Rethinking the proscription

Article 2.4 of the Charter has been cited as one potential legal basis for unilateral humanitarian intervention. The article reads, 'All Members shall refrain in their international relations from the threat or use of force against the territorial integrity or political independence of any state, or in any other manner inconsistent with the Purposes of the United Nations'. It has been claimed that a true humanitarian intervention would not be directed against 'the territorial integrity or political independence' of the targeted state and would thus not be 'inconsistent with the purposes of the United Nations' (Tesón, 1998, p. 150; Weiss, 2007a, p. 17). The IICK rejected this argument, however, noting:

> Charter provisions relating to human rights were left deliberately vague, and were clearly not intended when written to provide a legal rationale for any kind of enforcement, much less a free-standing mandate for military intervention without UN Security Council approval. (2000, p. 168)

Additionally, Chesterman's analysis of the preliminary meetings held to discuss the UN Charter determines that the 'dominant' legal opinion as to the meaning of Article 2.4 holds that it does not provide any scope for humanitarian intervention (2002, p. 53).

A second potential source of legality is the 1948 Genocide Convention which includes obligations for states to act when genocide occurs. The Convention defined genocide as a crime against humanity and a matter of concern for the international community as a whole. In this sense genocide cannot be deemed an exclusively domestic matter as per Article 2.7 of the UN Charter, and if committed constitutes legitimate grounds for external involvement. The ICJ considers the prohibition of genocide to be a peremptory norm of international law (*jus cogens*) from which no derogation is permitted (Akhavan, 1995, pp. 229–30).

The Genocide Convention addresses both prevention and punishment, but is directed more to the latter (Schabas, 2000, p. 447). The punitive provisions of the Convention have rarely been invoked due to the fact that the mechanisms through which this is achieved rely on the active cooperation of states and the

Security Council. While states not involved in the genocide have certain obligations under the convention they cannot be held to be in contempt of the Convention for not acting to prevent or halt genocide, though they may be culpable if they indirectly support the commission of the atrocity (Milanović, 2006, p. 571). States have, however, historically proven unwilling to invoke the Genocide Convention for reasons of national interest (Akhavan, 1995, p. 231). This problem has also adversely affected the preventative aspect of the Convention as, again, there has been an evident unwillingness on the part of states to initiate action against states committing genocide. The Genocide Convention makes no mention of unilateral action and, therefore, the legality of unilateral intervention to prevent genocide is not established by the Convention (Dinstein, 2005, p. 72; Schabas, 2000, p. 491). Indeed, in 2004 in his testimony before the United States Senate Foreign Relations Committee, Secretary of State Colin Powell declared, 'genocide has been committed in Darfur'. Powell blamed the government of Sudan but stated that this did not mean that any coercive action had to be taken (US Department of State, 2004). Morally questionable as this may seem, Powell was correct according to a strict reading of the Genocide Convention; his assertion that genocide was occurring only compelled the US to refer the matter to the Security Council – which they did – rather than to take unilateral action (Dinstein, 2005, pp. 72–3; Schabas, 2000, p. 495). The duty incumbent upon states as per the Genocide Convention is, therefore, quite obviously 'flimsy' (Milanović, 2006, p. 571).

There is, additionally, the so-called 'link theory' justification as initially proffered in particular by Richard Lillich (1967) who argued that, while under Article 24.1 the Security Council has 'primary responsibility for the maintenance of international peace and security', under Article 1.1 UN member states have a responsibility to maintain international peace and security when the Security Council is unable to carry out its duties in this respect. Under certain circumstances, therefore, it is claimed that the onus is on member states to act and the prohibition on the use of force as outlined in Article 2.4 is suspended. Geoffrey Robertson similarly argues that Article 2.4 'really means to prohibit any armed attacks which are inconsistent with Charter purposes, and does not necessarily exclude those which are directed to uphold those purposes' (2002, p. 434).

In its assessment of the merits of the link theory, the DIIA identified three flaws. First, there is no explicit basis for this rationale outlined in the UN Charter. Although Article 24.1 states that the Security Council has *primary* rather than *exclusive* responsibility for the maintenance of international peace and security, according to the DIIA, '[This] refers to a subsidiary responsibility of other organs of the UN, notably the General Assembly, but not of the Members states'. Second, it is not legally sound to assert that the Charter must be suspended when the Security Council fails to act as there is no legal basis for this assertion. Third, the prohibition on the use of force is a tenet of customary international law and has evolved independently of the UN Charter and, therefore, 'can hardly be conditioned upon the effectiveness of collective security under Chapter VII' (DIIA, 1999, p. 82). This view is supported by Thomas Franck and Nigel Rodley; those who drafted the human rights legislation, they note, never intended it to be used as a justification for unilateral action. Such action would, in fact, 'bring to a standstill' the very process of defining and codifying human rights (Franck and Rodley, 1973, p. 300).

Given the lack of evidence within positive international law for a legal basis for unilateral humanitarian intervention, the remaining potential source is customary law. The landmark judgment of the US Supreme Court in the *Paquete Habana Case* of 1900 established that in addition to codified doctrines, treaties and court judgments, international law is based on the customary behaviour of states and this is codified in Article 38 of the Statute of the ICJ. By definition, customary law begins with a breach of existing positive law followed by what Antonio Cassese describes as 'the fundamental elements constituting custom' namely, 'state practice (*usus* or *diuturnitas*) and the corresponding views of states (*opinio juris* or *opinio necessitates*)' (2005, p. 157). In this sense, there may be a legal basis to a principle, such as humanitarian intervention, that has not been formally codified and states may be considered to be bound by a customary law even if they have not signed a treaty to that effect. For example, in 1986 the ICJ ruled that the Geneva Convention applied to all states, even those who had not signed it, as it had become part of customary international law.

An analysis of customary international law prior to the inception of the UN Charter, however, suggests that no customary law of humanitarian intervention existed at this time (Chesterman, 2002, p. 24). Thus, the only possible means by which unilateral humanitarian intervention could be considered customary international law is state practice since 1945. Anthony Arend and Robert Beck's analysis of the Cold War period, however, concludes, 'between 1945 and 1990 there were no examples of a genuinely humanitarian intervention' and in addition, during this period finds '[there was] no unambiguous case of state reliance on the right of humanitarian intervention' (1993, p. 137). In those cases during this period where the greatest case for a 'humanitarian' justification could have been made, such as Vietnam's intervention in Cambodia in 1978 and Tanzania's intervention in Uganda in 1979, neither intervening state articulated a humanitarian justification and certainly neither asserted that a legal right of humanitarian intervention existed. 'Thus', according to Philip Hilpold:

> it can be inferred from these events and reactions that the necessary elements for the formation of a customary rule allowing measures of humanitarian intervention were not only not present but relevant state practice was a thorough confirmation of the rule which excludes the permissibility of such interventions. (2001, p. 445)

Humanitarian intervention thus clearly did not constitute an international 'norm' at this juncture and these interventions were framed as acts of self-defence so as to appear to coincide with the prevailing norms regarding the use of force. The ICISS confirmed that 'the many examples of intervention in actual state practice throughout the 20th century did not lead to an abandonment of the norm of non-intervention' (2001a, p. 12).

NATO's intervention in Kosovo in 1999 dramatically highlighted the contestation surrounding unilateral humanitarian intervention and reinvigorated these debates. Conscious of the willingness of Russia and China to veto any proposal for military intervention, NATO circumvented the Security Council and intervened unilaterally. While some legal justification was indeed formally offered, the lack of Security Council authorization was primarily justified on the grounds that to have done nothing was unconscionable. In terms of objective assessment, the dominant (though by no means unanimous) legal view was that NATO acted unlawfully. Indicatively, the UK House of Commons Foreign Affairs Select Committee concluded that NATO's intervention was 'of dubious legality in the current state of international law' (2000, para. 1138). The finding of the IICK that NATO's intervention was 'illegal but legitimate' has since become an oft-quoted and widely accepted appraisal of the intervention (2000, p. 4).

Nigel Rodley and Basak Cali note that, at the time, three perspectives on the legality of NATO's actions emerged: first, the minority view that Operation Allied Force was legal, second, the majority view that it was illegal and a third view, which held that it was 'a potential harbinger of future legality' (2007, p. 278). Therefore, while the dominant view was that NATO acted contrary to international law, many who acknowledged this illegality argued, and indeed hoped, that as Operation Allied Force had so emphatically illustrated the deficiencies with the existing legal regime, legal reform would subsequently follow. The need for fundamental legal reform was stressed by certain observers conscious of the politicized nature of P5 decision making and uncomfortable with the permissibility of 'illegal but legitimate' action (Guicherd, 1999; Simma, 1999). Many preferred to find some means to reconcile the two: indicatively Michael Burton asked, 'Why saddle legitimate intervention with the stigma of illegality?' (1996, p. 430). Additionally, others feared that without clearer guidelines unilateral intervention would become a more common practice and one which would destabilize the international system (High Level Panel on Threats Challenges and Change, 2004, p. 63; Whitman, 2005): a fear which according to some manifested in 2003 with the US invasion of Iraq (Newman, 2009, p 81). The ICISS, a self described response to the legal deficiencies exposed by NATO's intervention, noted, 'the issue of international intervention for human protection is a clear and compelling example of concerted action urgently being needed to bring international norms and institutions in line with international needs and expectations' (2001a, p. 3).

In the original ICISS proposal there were three aspects to R2P, namely, the responsibility to prevent, the responsibility to react, and the responsibility to rebuild. As noted in Chapter 1, the responsibility to react is the aspect of R2P that has generated most debate. The responsibility to react has two components: the internal responsibility of states to protect their own citizens from the four crimes, and the external responsibility of the international community of states to act when a state is unable or unwilling to protect its own people from the four crimes. The following sections analyse the ICISS report, the 2005 *Outcome Document* and the 2009 General Assembly debate, and assesses the legal implications of each on both the internal and external responsibilities of states.

The internal responsibility to protect

The starting point for the ICISS's report was the principle that states have a duty to protect their own populations from certain harms, hence the idea of 'sovereignty as responsibility'. The origin of the term derives from a report published in 1996 by Francis Deng in his capacity as Special Representative on Internally Displaced People. Deng argued, 'sovereignty carries with it certain responsibilities for which governments must be held accountable'. The right of sovereign inviolability, he argued, was conditional on a state, 'effectively discharging its responsibilities for good governance' (Deng *et al.*, 1996, p. 1). Sovereign inviolability was not, therefore, an immutable attribute enjoyed by states without qualification, but rather a quality dependent on internal behaviour. The logic behind the ICISS's inclusion of this initial principle was the Commission's desire to alter the prevailing focus and terminology used in the debate on 'humanitarian intervention': previously, discussions primarily focused on the rights of states to intervene. Presenting the issue in terms of states having the primary responsibility to protect their own population, the ICISS argued, charted a way out of the 'outdated and unhelpful' debate on the right to intervene (ICISS, 2001a, p. 11).

This internal responsibility, the ICISS suggested, had a threefold manifestation: first, 'state authorities are responsible for the functions of protecting the safety and lives of citizens and promotion of their welfare', second, 'national political authorities are responsible to the citizens internally and to the international community through the UN' and third, 'the agents of the state are responsible for their actions' (ibid, p. 13). The report at times advanced quite ambitious benchmarks for responsible governance arguing that states should 'protect their citizens from chronic insecurities of hunger, disease, inadequate shelter, crime, unemployment, social conflict and environmental hazard' (ibid, p. 15). While these crimes were discussed under the broad umbrella of 'human security' they were not presented as grounds for either automatically condemning a state for violating its sovereign responsibility, or external intervention. The report did, however, place particular importance on certain crimes cited as inexcusable violations of the state's responsibility. Thus, '[protecting] communities from mass killing, women from systematic rape and children from starvation' was one formulation (ibid, p. 17) but the more explicitly titled 'threshold criteria' were the crimes, 'large scale loss of life actual or apprehended, with genocidal intent or not ... large scale ethnic cleansing actual or apprehended, whether carried out by killing, forced expulsion, acts of terror or rape' (ibid, p. 32). The ICISS was clear that while certain acts and crimes were reprehensible – such as lower level human rights violations and the denial of democratic rights – they were not justifiable grounds for military intervention, but quite possibly justifications for economic sanctions (ibid, p. 34). It is additionally important to note that the ICISS report was not singularly focused on military intervention; this was but one aspect of its remit and thus the 'threshold criteria' applied only to the extreme case where intervention was deemed legitimate and hence lower level offences were not ignored but considered to be best remedied in a less dramatic fashion.

This conception of sovereignty as responsibility was reiterated in the 2004 report of the High Level Panel on Threats, Challenges and Change which asserted:

> In signing the Charter ... States not only benefit from the privileges of sovereignty but also accept its responsibilities. Whatever perceptions may have prevailed when the Westphalian system first gave rise to the notion of State sovereignty, today it clearly carries with it the obligation of a State to protect the welfare of its own people. (2004, p. 17)

The 2005 World Summit *Outcome Document* echoed both the ICISS and the High Level Panel's approach to the internal aspect of R2P, noting in paragraph 138, 'Each individual State has the responsibility to protect its populations from genocide, war crimes, ethnic cleansing and crimes against humanity. This responsibility entails the prevention of such crimes, including their incitement, through appropriate and necessary means'.

At the 2009 General Assembly debate on R2P, there was widespread and emphatic support for the idea that states had a responsibility to protect their own citizens from the four crimes, termed 'Pillar 1' by the UN Secretary-General in his pre-debate report. Indeed, some of the more eloquent and forceful endorsements came from states not usually associated with responsible governance; Myanmar and North Korea endorsed the idea while the Iranian ambassador stated, 'it goes without saying that it is the obligation and prerogative of any State to defend its own people against aggression and protect them from genocide, war crimes, ethnic cleansing and crimes against humanity' (Iran, 2009, p. 2). The Sudanese representative articulated a fulsome endorsement of the principle:

> These duties are conferred on the sovereign State by what is known in political philosophy jurisprudence as the social contract between the governed and the governor or between the crown and its subjects. (Sudan, 2009, p. 1)

At no point in the debate did any state argue that sovereignty entitles a state to treat its population *anyway it pleases*: a point that has significance for the argument presented later in Chapter 7.

A restatement of existing law

Clearly the consensus at the General Assembly in 2009, and the evolution of thinking which preceded it, is to be welcomed; the refusal by a state to accept responsibility for the welfare of its citizens would clearly give cause for concern. Yet, whether this constitutes a significant evolution or a meaningful commitment likely to have real impact is debatable. First, since at least the inception of the UN, states have accepted that they have certain responsibilities to their citizens and that, though they may enjoy sovereign inviolability as per Article 2.7 of the UN Charter, there were certain acts they were prohibited from committing against their own people (Thakur and Weiss, 2009, pp. 26–8). As Carsten Stahn notes in his critique of the novelty of R2P, 'It is well understood that sovereignty entails duties on the international plane'

(2007, p. 112). Since 1945 there have been a number of international treaties proscribing certain violations of human rights such as the Convention for the Prevention and Punishment of the Crime of Genocide (1948), the Convention on the Elimination of All Forms of Racial Discrimination (1965), the International Covenant on Civil and Political Rights (1966), the Convention on the Elimination of all Forms of Discrimination against Women (1979), the Convention against Torture (1984) and the 1993 Vienna Declaration and Programme of Action. Todd Landman's statistical analysis of human rights law in the post-Charter era concluded that there has been 'an expansion in both the breadth and depth' of the international human rights legal regime and that, 'an increasingly larger set of human rights has found positive legal expression, while on the other hand a larger number of states have ratified these main instruments' (2005, p. 14). It is clear, therefore, that states, since at least 1945, have been willing (and able) to agree on certain universal human rights laws, and to have, by definition, accepted that as sovereign states they had certain responsibilities to their own population. The principle of internal responsibility has not, therefore, been a source of contestation; Alex Bellamy notes that, during the writing of his influential report on IDPs, Deng met with over thirty countries to discuss the idea of sovereignty as responsibility and during these discussions 'not a single leader challenged the assertion that sovereigns had a responsibility towards their own citizens' (2010, p. 42).

At the conclusion of the 2005 World Summit, Tony Blair declared: 'For the first time at this summit we are agreed that states do not have the right to do what they will within their own borders' (Fisher, 2007, p. 109). This is simply untrue. Since the 1945 Nuremberg trials it has been clear that states accept that they cannot not do 'what they will' to their own citizens. Many legal developments during the Cold War, such as the Genocide Convention, the Universal Declaration of Human Rights, and the International Covenant on Civil and Political Rights, outlined the responsibilities states had towards their citizens. Thus, even prior to the post-Cold War era, states could not reasonably claim a legal entitlement to do *whatever* they wanted to their own citizens. It is not the case, therefore, that thirty years ago states charged with orchestrating and/or committing egregious internal crimes against humanity could have legitimately claimed the right to do whatever they wanted. Such states may have claimed that the issue was 'an internal matter' but this is not the same as saying 'we admit we are committing these acts and we claim the right to do them'. The idea that today's discourse is qualitatively different because R2P alone has forced states to accept that there are limits to what they can do to their own people is simply not true.

Of course, compliance with international laws, treaties and commitments on human rights, and internal state responsibility more generally, has been erratic (Armstrong, Farrell and Lambert, 2007, p. 157). Every year since 1945 there have been man-made humanitarian crises, oppression and violations of international human rights law committed by states against their own people; indeed, over the course of the twentieth century, far more people were killed by their own governments than were killed in all inter-state wars put together (Lu, 2006, p. 54). Rhetorical commitments to accept a responsibility to protect ones citizens are, therefore, of dubious utility. The proliferation of these expressions of concern for, and commitment to, human rights have not been accompanied by an attendant alteration in the Charter's provisions for dealing with violations of human rights. The result is a large body of both treaty and customary law related to human rights, which lacks a clear means by which these laws can be enforced in the event that a state wilfully violates the law. States are subject to scrutiny by UN bodies such as the Human Rights Council (formerly the UN Commission on Human Rights), the Human Rights Committee and the Office of the UN High Commissioner for Human Rights. Compliance with even just the supervisory role of these organizations, however, is poor and the enforcement capacity and effectiveness of these organizations is minimal.

The nature of human rights differentiates this sub-set of international law from the laws governing inter-state relations. As Malgozia Fitzmaurice states, 'Human rights treaties are not contractual in nature and do not create rights and obligations between States on the traditional basis of reciprocity; they establish relationships between States and individuals' (2006, pp. 205–6). States, therefore, may well agree amongst themselves the standards they *should* uphold domestically but ultimately under the current system the necessarily domestic nature of compliance with these agreements limits the effect the inter-state context of the original treaty can have. With the exception of the possibility that the Security Council will designate a situation to warrant a Chapter VII intervention, a major ask given that technically the situation must constitute a 'threat to international peace and security', non-compliance with human rights treaties results in negative consequences only for the domestic citizenry and not other signatories to the treaty. In this respect, as Louise Henkin notes, 'compliance with human rights law … is wholly internal' (1990, p. 250). As R2P has not changed either the legal architecture or the laws themselves, this unsatisfactory situation remains.

One must wonder, therefore, at the significance, and more importantly the efficacy, of the commitments made in 2005 and 2009 if states such as Myanmar, North Korea, Iran and Sudan can feel comfortable endorsing them. The fact that states gathered in the General Assembly in 2009 to commit to protecting their citizens certainly did not constitute a unique, and hence praiseworthy or significant, occasion in the post-Charter era. No state accused of genocide, war crimes, ethnic cleansing or crimes against humanity has ever admitted they were perpetrating such acts but argued that they were legally entitled to do so. The problem has not been the *principle* of internal state responsibility but rather putting this into practice and enforcing compliance. Additionally, it is not the case that R2P's proscription against the four crimes is novel; these acts have long been prohibited under international law and thus the consensus manifest in 2005 and 2009 related to the prohibition of certain acts that had already been proscribed. According to Chesterman, 'by the time RtoP was endorsed by the World Summit in 2005, its normative content had been emasculated to the point where it essentially provided that the Security Council could authorize, on a case-by-case basis, things that it had been authorizing for more than a decade' (2011a, p. 2). Likewise, in his 2009 report 'Implementing the Responsibility to Protect' the UN Secretary-General acknowledged that Pillar 1 'rests on long-standing obligations under international law' (Ki-Moon, 2009a, p. 10). In short, therefore, the idea that states have a responsibility, under international law, to protect their own citizens predates the emergence of R2P; clarifying that states have an internal responsibility was not, and is not, part of the problem R2P sought to solve.

The international responsibility to protect

The aspect of the ICISS's report which attracted most attention was the recommendation that if states fail to meet their responsibility to protect their own citizens this responsibility transfers to the international community. This proposal, of course, raised profoundly important questions: in the event that a state did manifestly fail to meet its internal responsibility who would/should/could intervene? Membership of the UN, the ICISS claimed, carries an obligation not to unilaterally use force but, the report noted: 'the corollary, not always as readily accepted, is that states should be willing to use force on behalf of, as directed by, and for the goals of the UN' (2001a, p. 49). States, therefore, should accept that in addition to their internal responsibility, they have a wider responsibility to act to help the UN maintain international peace and security and uphold international humanitarian standards.

As noted in Chapter 2, the ICISS warned about the potentially deleterious consequences of permitting unilateral intervention but did suggest that such action could be potentially legitimate. Yet, rather than suggest a means by which unilateral action could be legalized, the better option, according to the ICISS, was to continue to respect the authority of the Security Council; the report noted: 'the commission is in absolutely no doubt that there is no better or more appropriate body than the Security Council to deal with military intervention issues for human protection purposes' (ibid, p. 49). 'The task', the ICISS emphasized, 'is not to find alternatives to the Security Council as a source of authority but to make the Security Council work much better than it has' (ibid, p. 49). Recognizing the obstacle presented by the veto power of the P5 – evident during NATO's intervention in Kosovo in 1999 – the ICISS put forward the 'code of conduct' proposal (ibid, p. 51). With respect to the possibility that the P5 failed to abide by this code of conduct the Commission argued: 'it would be impossible to find consensus ... around any set of proposals for military intervention which acknowledged the validity of any intervention not authorized by the Security Council' (ibid, p. 54). Instead, the ICISS relayed, 'two important messages' to the Security Council namely that it was, 'unrealistic to expect that other states will rule out other means and forms of action to meet the gravity and urgency of these situations', and additionally that if an action taken without the P5's assent were to occur and if this action was widely lauded as legitimate, 'this may have enduring serious consequences for the status and credibility of the UN itself' (ibid, p. 55).

Paragraph 139 of the World Summit *Outcome Document* referred to the external aspect of R2P and the relevant wording in the paragraph stated:

> we are prepared to take collective action, in a timely and decisive manner, through the Security Council, in accordance with the Charter, including Chapter VII, on a case-by-case basis and in cooperation with relevant regional organizations as appropriate, should peaceful means be inadequate and national authorities manifestly fail to protect their populations from genocide, war crimes, ethnic cleansing and crimes against humanity.

The principle that the international community had the right to become involved, via the Security Council, in the domestic affairs of states if the four crimes were occurring was, therefore, clearly affirmed by all states in 2005.

At the 2009 General Assembly debate, very few states voiced a principled objection to the principle that the international community had a right to become involved in the internal affairs of states in the event that a crisis spiralled out of control. Even North Korea accepted that the international community had the right to 'encourage and assist sovereign States in their efforts to fulfil their responsibility to protect their own people' (Democratic People's Republic of Korea, 2009, p. 17). While Iran, Pakistan and Sudan did argue that endorsing R2P in 2005 did not, and should not, denote support for coercive military intervention, these were very much minority perspectives and, in truth, legally accurate analyses. There was, therefore, widespread consensus at the 2009 General Assembly debate that the international community had the legitimate right to become involved, to some degree, in the internal affairs of states.

Authority and consistency: unanswered questions

While the preceding evolution regarding the external dimension of R2P from the ICISS to the 2009 General Assembly debate clearly supports the idea that states agree that they are not absolutely inviolable under international law, many questions remain unanswered and the nature of the consensus is very thin. There is nothing new in the fact that states have agreed that the international community has the right to become involved in the domestic affairs of states (Hakimi, 2010, pp. 343–4; Peters, 2009, p. 525). In the first decade of the post-Cold War era, the legality of external involvement was not an especially contentious issue – in principle – and not one of the key sources of controversy which compelled the ICISS to issue its report. Indeed, the ICISS found in its consultations, 'even in states where there was the strongest opposition to infringements on sovereignty, there was a general acceptance that there must be limited exceptions to the non-intervention rule for certain kinds of emergencies' (2001a, p. 31). This acceptance of *a* role for the international community was reiterated time and time again during the General Assembly debate in 2009 (Hehir, 2011). Yet, this is not significant in itself; the Security Council's use of Chapter VII in the 1990s had amply demonstrated that internal events, including humanitarian catastrophes, could be deemed of international concern and importance and, potentially, grounds for external intervention. The permissibility of Security Council mandated intervention for the purpose of human protection was already proven.

There are, in particular, two fundamental and related issues which have manifestly *not* been resolved; the permissibility of action taken without Security Council authorization, and what to do to ensure greater consistency in Security Council decision making. With respect to the first issue, NATO's intervention in Kosovo led to questions being raised about the authority of the Security Council and whether intervention without the Security Council's assent could be, and should be, legalized within certain narrow parameters. Second, with respect to the Rwandan genocide, many asked how the international response to egregious intra-state crises could be made more consistent and automatic. Indeed, the ICISS noted that one of its aims was 'crafting responses that are consistent' (2001a, p. 5). R2P has failed to answer either of these questions and is, at most, a re-statement of the very international legislation and systemic regulation which suffered such disrepute in the 1990s that the ICISS was established in the first place.

Action without Security Council approval – unilateral intervention – has not been endorsed and is clearly not part of R2P today. The ICISS failed to make a concrete recommendation on this point, offering instead, the 'two important messages' referred to previously. These messages, however, appear to overlook a number of salient points: first, that states may act without Security Council authorization is simply stating the obvious given the historical record. It is precisely one such instance – NATO's intervention in Kosovo – that led to the establishment of the ICISS, so warning about the possibility of this happening somewhat undermines the idea that the ICISS was a means of resolving exactly this controversy and the tension between legality and legitimacy it exposed. Second, the second 'important message' suggests that the P5 have an interest in upholding the credibility of the UN; perhaps they *should*, but even a cursory glance at the historical record amply demonstrates that when the P5 take action the 'status and credibility' of the UN is not high on their list of priorities. The principle, as stipulated in Article 24.1, that the P5 are mandated to protect the UN's primacy and act on behalf of all member states is, in fact, an inverse of the reality of this relationship (Berdal, 2008). In essence, this is not a warning likely to carry any weight. As discussed in Chapter 2, during the negotiations that led to the 2005 *Outcome Document* the idea of alternative sources of authority other than the Security Council and the permissibility of unilateral humanitarian intervention were not entertained and the final wording of paragraph 139 clearly restates that the Security Council has sole authority (Bellamy, 2006a, p. 155). The 2009 debate additionally evidenced a commitment to the primacy of the Security Council; no alternative sources of authority, or criteria for legitimate unilateral intervention were advanced and Ban Ki-Moon's report on the matter reiterated the absolute need for Security Council authorization (2009a, p. 25).

The second fundamental issue not as yet addressed by R2P goes back to the non-intervention in Rwanda in 1994, as discussed in Chapter 2, and relates to the question of ensuring that the Security Council does act when a situation breaches a certain threshold. As yet there has been no alteration to the legal process governing the response to intra-state crises that ensures ensures consistency and automaticity. As discussed in Chapter 2, following the publication of the ICISS report, the P5 emphatically distanced themselves from accepting any obligation to take action (Welsh, 2006). During the course of the 2005 negotiations at the World Summit the reluctance of P5 states to accept an *obligation* to intervene was very evident. In a letter to the President of the General Assembly prior to the summit John Bolton, then US Ambassador to the UN, suggested amending the section in the draft document regarding the responsibility to protect, arguing: 'the Charter has never been interpreted as creating a legal obligation for Security Council members to support enforcement action in various cases involving serious breaches of international peace' (Bolton, 2005). The draft *Outcome Document* originally read:

> The international community, through the United Nations, also has the *obligation* to use diplomatic, humanitarian and other peaceful means, including under Chapter VI and VIII of the Charter to help protect populations from genocide, war crimes, ethnic cleansing and crimes against humanity. [Emphasis added]

Bolton demanded that this be changed to read:

> The international community, through the United Nations, also has *moral responsibility* to use appropriate diplomatic, economic, humanitarian and other peaceful means, including under Chapter VI and VIII of the Charter to help protect populations from such atrocities. [Emphasis added]

The final wording for paragraph 139 actually chosen reads: 'The international community, through the United Nations, also has the responsibility.' 'Responsibility' and 'obligation' are clearly very different, as will be explored in Chapters 5 and 7. Additionally, instead of the sentence, 'In this context, we recognize our shared responsibility to take collective action', Bolton suggested, 'In this context, we stand ready to take collective action.' The final wording of paragraph 139 – 'In this context, we are prepared to take collective action' – corresponds more closely to Bolton's preference.

Paragraph 139, therefore, states that the international community, acting through the UN, has a 'responsibility' rather than an obligation to act and that the Security Council is 'prepared' to act. These changes, in conjunction with the reaffirmation of primacy of the Security Council enable the P5, therefore, to determine what, if indeed any, action to take in response to a humanitarian crisis thereby removing any obligation to act in all situations where the threshold is breached. In a letter to UN member states prior to the World Summit Bolton made the US's position clear: 'We do not accept that either the UN as a whole, of the Security Council, or individual states, have an obligation to intervene under international law' (Reinold, 2010, p. 67). Clearly Paragraphs 138 and 139 of the *Outcome Document* signify *some* degree of consensus regarding a 'responsibility to protect' and a rejection of complete sovereign inviolability. Yet, it is debatable whether any substantive change that would ensure the 'Never Again!' refrain commonly articulated after Rwanda in 1994 has really occurred. As Nicholas Wheeler noted, the *Outcome Document:*

> fails to address the fundamental question of what should happen if the Security Council is unable or unwilling to authorize the use of force to prevent or end a humanitarian tragedy, and secondly, it fails to address the question of how this norm could be better implemented to save strangers in the future. (2005, p. 97)

As a 2008 research paper commissioned by the UK House of Commons on R2P succinctly noted, 'It remains unclear whether in the event of Security Council paralysis, a unilateral intervention would prove legitimate or legal' (Brown, 2008, p. 3). The wording regarding the responsibility to protect in the *Outcome Document* creates significant scope for politically determined *ad hoc* interventionism. Paragraph 139 does nothing to address the question of political will which has been the primary barrier to the sanctioning of humanitarian intervention.

As discussed in Chapter 2, during the 2009 debate there was very discussion about how to ensure consistency and automaticity. Certain states did, however, raise concerns about this very issue: the Sri Lankan ambassador asked:

> Who will define a particular situation and determine that it is a candidate for preventative or reactive intervention? How do we define its scope? … What are the means of ensuring that

> institutional, ideological or even personal prejudices do not creep into early warning analysis, conclusions and recommendations? (Sri Lanka, 2009, p. 1)

Similarly the Nicaraguan ambassador stated, 'For my country, the general principles of the responsibility to protect agreed in 2005 are not controversial. What concerns us is how to interpret those principles and their potentially selective implementation' (Nicaragua, 2009, p. 1). The 2009 debate did little to clarify this issue; during the debate the P5 distanced themselves from any automaticity; the UK ambassador cautioned against thresholds or 'checklists' for action warning, 'Every situation is different' (UK, 2009, p. 2), and hence a political decision has to be agreed. The Chinese ambassador stated unambiguously:

> the Security Council has a role to play but it must make judgments and decisions tailored to specific circumstances and must act prudently. Here it must be pointed out that the responsibility entrusted to the Council by the Charter is the maintenance of international peace and security. (China, 2009, p. 2)

This reference to maintaining 'international peace and security' is an obvious, and indeed legally accurate, reference to the limits of the Security Council's *raison d'être*; while increased pressure has been put on the P5 to 'do something' in response to a number of intra-state crises since the end of the Cold War, humanitarian action was not, and is not, an explicit aspect of its mandate as detailed in Chapter V of the UN Charter. There has been no development, therefore, which can be cited as insurance that there will be a consistent, impartial response in future; decisions will continue to be made in an *ad hoc* fashion dependent on political whims and exigencies. The implications of this are detailed in Chapter 5.

During the 2009 General Assembly debate many states, such as Algeria, Bangladesh, Benin, Brazil, Ecuador and Guatemala, noted that the key variable which has led to the record of what Chesterman describes as 'inhumanitarian nonintervention' (2003, p. 54) was not legal proscriptions but the lack of will amongst the P5 to sanction the requisite action. As with internal compliance with R2P, the external aspect of the concept – Pillar

III in Ban Ki-Moon's formulation – remains entirely dependent on political will and finds no coherent legal expression. R2P's utility, therefore, is ostensibly that it can be employed to put pressure on the Security Council to sanction action: a means by which the political will to intervene can be generated through the advocacy of those groups and individuals with the capacity, and financial resources, to influence the behaviour of states. It is certainly true that during the 2009 General Assembly debate a number of states called for greater consistency from the Security Council, with some, such as Gambia, Italy, Singapore, South Korea and New Zealand (see Hehir, 2011), in fact, urging a more pro-active stance. The capacity of these small powers to influence the decision making dynamic amongst the P5 is, however, quite naturally minimal given the enormous disparities in wealth and military might (Charlesworth and Kennedy, 2009, p. 407). Whether the P5 will be susceptible to the blandishments of concerned NGOs, individuals and states is additionally questionable given the historical litany of inaction in the face of international pressure to 'do something'.

Conclusion: 'in short, it is nothing new'

The impetus for the establishment of the ICISS was the controversy surrounding NATO's intervention in Kosovo and also, it is important to stress, the reprehensible international response to the genocide in Rwanda in 1994. The questions raised by these two events largely focused on three issues: Who has the legitimate authority to intervene? What constitutes the threshold for outside intervention? How can the international response to egregious intra-state crises be made more consistent and effective? The evolution of R2P has certainly answered the second of these questions; it is today clear that R2P applies only to four crimes – genocide, war crimes, ethnic cleansing and crimes against humanity – as detailed in paragraphs 138 and 139 of the 2005 World Summit *Outcome Document*. Yet, with respect to the questions regarding authority and consistency, there has been no resolution of the original dilemmas which actually led to the establishment of the ICISS in the first place.

Many, conscious that Kosovo-type disagreements amongst the P5 were likely to re-occur, were concerned that without clear legal rules on who could legitimately intervene in the absence of Security Council authorization the very basis of international law would be eroded. Additionally, while the 1990s had proved that the Security Council *could* intervene by creatively interpreting their Chapter VII powers, there was no guarantee that it would, as was so graphically illustrated during the 1994 Rwandan genocide. Given that these two issues catalysed the heated debate on humanitarian intervention which led to the establishment of the ICISS, it is striking that R2P, as it is today, fails to articulate any meaningful prescriptions for legal, procedural or institutional reform which could be said to address either. The focus on 'sovereignty as responsibility' is thus arguably both unhelpful and unoriginal: unhelpful insofar as the barrier to humanitarian intervention was not sovereignty but rather political will, and unoriginal in that states have accepted, since at least 1945, that they have certain responsibilities towards their own population. The doctrine of 'sovereignty as responsibility', Bellamy concedes, is 'neither new ... nor radical' (2009, p. 20).

The ICISS acknowledged that the question of authority is a particularly divisive issue but claimed, 'it would be impossible to find consensus' on a proposal for regulating humanitarian intervention absent the explicit consent of the Security Council or General Assembly (2001a, pp. 54–5). Bellamy concurs noting that the issue of authority is too 'thorny' (2009, p. 54). This means, however, that one of the central dilemmas R2P aims to solve remains unresolved, namely, what to do in the event that the Security Council is unwilling to take action in response to an egregious intra-state humanitarian crisis. The ICISS equivocated on the issue of intervention without a Security Council mandate, warning both that such action could fundamentally undermine the UN but also that it was 'unreasonable' to expect states not to intervene if the Security Council failed to act: a tacit acknowledgement that action without Security Council authorization *could* be legitimate. Rather than tackle this issue by advancing a proposal for substantive UN reform, the ICISS, Bellamy admits, 'sidestepped the question of Security Council reform almost entirely' (ibid, p. 63). The only proposal advanced by the ICISS was the 'code of conduct' which amounts to a non-binding 'gentleman's agreement'. This appears to overlook the fact that the national interests of the P5 are invariably involved and, if a case arises where they are not, there is unlikely to be a major problem anyway. Aside from the fact that the ICISS's 'code of conduct' was highly idealistic, it was dropped from the 2005 World Summit, as was any tentative suggestion that action outside of a Security Council could be potentially legitimate; indeed Bellamy argues this concession to the Security Council's primacy was a *sine qua non* during the 2005 World Summit discussions (2009, p. 73). The General Assembly debate on R2P in 2009 was notable for the absence both of support for unilateral intervention and specific proposals for reform in this area.

During the 2009 debate it was widely acknowledged that R2P did not constitute a legal innovation; indicatively, Chile's spokesman asserted, '[R2P is] based on long-standing obligations arising from international law. In short, it is nothing new' (Chile, 2009, p. 2), while Brazil argued, '[R2P] it is not a principle proper, much less a novel legal prescription' (Brazil, 2009, p. 2). Under existing international law, the Security Council has a monopoly on the legitimate use of force and, therefore, in the event that a crises reaches a certain point it is the P5 who have the discretion to decide what response, if indeed any, to sanction. The variant of R2P agreed in the General Assembly in 2009 did not amend international law, create any new regulatory body, or change the responsibilities and duties of states; as the Secretary-General noted 'the responsibility to protect does not alter, indeed it reinforces, the legal obligations of Member States' (Ki-Moon, 2009a, p. 5). The fact that the world's states were agreeing to legal principles already contained in the Charter necessarily meant, and means, that as R2P does not comprise any tangible legal or political innovation, it constitutes at most a statement of resolve, a political promise to summon the will to do better in future. It is, Carsten Stahn argues, 'a political catchword, rather than a legal norm' (2007, p. 120).

R2P emerged precisely because events in the 1990s demonstrated that the system was deeply flawed due to this reliance on the P5, and yet R2P has become no more than a re-statement of the very system it was established to change. There is nothing in Chapter VII of the Charter, the ICISS report, the 2005 World Summit *Outcome Document* or the 2009 General Assembly debate which can be construed as *compelling* the Security Council to take action; R2P imposes no positive duty (ibid, p. 117). While many NGOs supportive of R2P heralded the 2009 debate in the General Assembly as a success, an analysis of the content of the debate shows that while there was broad support for the variant of R2P adopted at the 2005 World Summit, this was invariably prefaced by a restatement of commitments to the UN Charter and the primacy of the UN, that is, a renewed commitment to the status quo (Philippines, 2009; Egypt, 2009).

R2P, therefore, very clearly does not constitute a reform of, or addition to, international law: rather it is a political norm. Consequently, in the event that an intra-state crisis is deemed to require external intervention, the only existing legal means by which such action can be authorized is via Chapter VII of the UN Charter which has historically always been applied on the basis of the political calculations of the P5. The significance of R2P's lack of legal status and proposals for legal reform stems from the fact that without legal weight it is difficult to see what R2P actually contributes to the debate on humanitarian intervention given the particular nature of this issue. Re-asserting existing provisions of international law and re-stating previously articulated moral commitments does not constitute a new development likely to address the primary barrier to the timely response to egregious intra-state crises. Thus, without changing existing laws or enforcement mechanisms, the R2P we have today does not significantly reform the discredited system it was originally established to address. Thus, despite the ICISS report, the 2005 World Summit *Outcome Document* and the 2009 General Assembly debate, the manner in which an intra-state humanitarian crisis will be, and legally can be, dealt with today is exactly the same as was the case in 1990. This was evident in the manner in which the Security Council responded to the situation in Libya in 2011; the 'international community's' response was ultimately predicated on the disposition of the P5, and particularly in this case, the view from Moscow and Beijing. There is very little concrete evidence that the existence of R2P in any way influenced the Russians and Chinese who could have vetoed the intervention.

In summation, R2P does not constitute a new international law or, more importantly, constitute legal reform. Therefore, for all the headlines generated by R2P and its near ubiquity in political discourse, it does not carry any innovative legal weight. As UN Secretary-General Ban Ki-Moon noted in his 2009 report on R2P, 'the responsibility to protect does not alter, indeed it reinforces, the legal obligations of Member States to refrain from the use of force except in conformity with the Charter' (2009, p. 5). Likewise Francis Deng – credited by many as the inventor of the term the 'responsibility to protect' – admitted with respect to R2P 'perhaps there's nothing new here' (2010, p. 85–6). The ICISS was determined that its report would have a practical application and ensure there were 'no more Rwandas', claiming their report was 'the best way of ensuring that' (2001a, p. xiii). Yet the fact that R2P does not constitute a legal reform means that its entire utility is predicated on its ostensible *normative* power more than its actual enforceability; this is discussed further in Chapter 5.

Chapter 4

The Responsibility to Prevent: The Last Refuge of the Unimaginative?

Today R2P is increasingly championed as primarily concerned with prevention. Indeed, according to Thomas Weiss, prior to the intervention in Libya, supporters of R2P orientated the debate in such a way that there was a 'virtually exclusive emphasis on prevention' (2011, p. 1). While this does not constitute a totally illogical focus on an unrelated issue, this chapter argues that this new direction for, if not reinvention of, the concept is a dereliction of the concept's original *raison d'être*. As noted in the first sentence of the 2001 ICISS report the origins of R2P stem from the debate surrounding the issue of militarily responding to, rather than holistically preventing, intra-state crises:

> This report is about the so-called right of 'humanitarian intervention': the question of when, if ever, it is appropriate for states to take coercive – and in particular military – action, against another state for the purpose of protecting people at risk in that other state. (ICISS, 2001a, p. vii)

The increased emphasis on prevention is, I argue, indicative of R2P's failure, as detailed in the previous chapter, to affect change in the laws, procedures and institutions regulating the response of the international community.

It is axiomatic that prevention is preferable to humanitarian intervention. Humanitarian intervention, even if successful, constitutes a failure; the initiation of such action is by definition a response to a situation that has degenerated to a particularly catastrophic nadir. Nonetheless, awareness that prevention is preferable to intervention – for both humanitarian and financial reasons – should not constitute grounds for de-prioritizing attempts to reform the manner in which the international community responds to egregious intra-state crises.

That states continue to commit themselves to prevention is obvious; one need only peruse the speeches made during the 2009 General Assembly debate on R2P to read a wide variety of eloquent promises and earnest admonitions. The problem, of course, is that the history of these commitments evidences a dramatic disconnect between rhetoric and reality. The refrain 'Never Again!', so often solemnly articulated since the Holocaust, has often appeared as little more than an empty slogan when contrasted with both the glacial pace of reform and the international community's erratic response to looming crises in the modern era. Reform in the area of early warning mechanisms and streamlined bureaucracy has had limited impact; as Bruce W. Jentleson observes, 'Almost every study of conflict prevention concludes that when all is said and done, the main obstacle is the lack of political will' (2009, p. 293). This problem is exacerbated by the fact that those aspects of R2P related to prevention – in its various forms from the ICISS report to the 2009 General Assembly debate – do very little, if indeed anything, to chart a way out of the cycle of platitudes that has been the history of preventative initiatives. R2P does not advance a coherent or detailed set of prescriptions on prevention and adds very little to the myriad existing theories on why and how we *should* act to prevent crises.

This chapter begins by providing an overview of those elements of R2P focused on prevention with a particular emphasis on the original ICISS report. The next section assesses the remit and record of the Office of the Special Adviser on the Prevention of Genocide (OSAPG) which constitutes the most tangible manifestation of R2P's promotion of prevention. I argue that the OSAPG suffers from a restrictive mandate calculated to accommodate political discretion and that it is designed to operate in a particular way, which limits its efficacy. The subsequent section advances three critiques of the attempt to champion R2P as primarily concerned with prevention, namely that R2P's recommendations regarding prevention are unoriginal and of limited practical utility, that these recommendations are premised on a set of dubious underlying assumptions, and that the shift to prevention constitutes an evasion of R2P's initial remit and a retreat into a less contentious area born of R2P's failure to effect real change on the issue of responding to intra-state crises.

The responsibility to prevent

The responsibility to prevent was one component of the ICISS's tri-partite conception of R2P. The ICISS devoted an entire chapter to prevention and argued that it was 'the single most important dimension of the responsibility to protect' (2001a, p. xi). As with the guidelines contained in the responsibility to react section of the report, the ICISS advanced recommendations on how to prevent intra-state conflict both for states and the international community. The ICISS recommended that states should implement a number of policies including:

> A firm national commitment to ensuring fair treatment and fair opportunities for all citizens ... Efforts to ensure accountability and good governance, protect human rights, promote social and economic development and ensure a fair distribution of resources. (ICISS, 2001a, p. 19)

Conscious that these expansive objectives were routinely flouted, the ICISS placed the greatest emphasis on the role the international community should play in preventing intra-state conflicts in the event that states were unable or unwilling to do so.

A strategy for the effective prevention of conflict, the report noted, requires three interlinked components; effective early warning systems, an understanding of available policy measures, and political will (ibid, p. 20). The ICISS urged the international community to tackle the 'root causes' of internal conflict namely poverty, political repression and uneven distribution of resources (ibid, p. 22). The report additionally asserted that effective prevention may also require addressing 'political needs ... economic deprivation ... strengthening legal protections [and] sectoral reforms to the military and other state security services' (ibid, p. 23) at both national and international level. Both *The Responsibility to Protect* and the supplementary research volume outline a spectrum of policy choices available to the international community to address the causes of conflict before they erupt. These include political, diplomatic, economic and judicial measures incorporating both coercive and non-coercive action (ibid, pp. 23–7). The essay on prevention in the ICISS's supplementary volume stressed the need for better early-warning mechanisms, improved operational capacity, and more coherent institutional capacity (ICISS, 2001b, pp. 35–41). The essay asserted that prevention appealed both to the 'liberal humanitarian ethos' and to '*realpolitik*, national-security logic' by virtue of the fact that prevention was firstly of obvious humanitarian importance but also that it made financial sense given that effective prevention is significantly cheaper than reacting to conflicts in progress (ibid, p. 27). Thus, the essay suggested, 'arguments for conflict prevention should be articulated in the language of interest as much as moral or humanitarian appeals' (ibid, p. 42). The essay did strike a note of caution, however, warning, 'The overwhelming majority of studies cite lack of will as the major cause of failed prevention' (ibid, p. 42).

Paragraphs 138, 139 and 140 of the 2005 World Summit *Outcome Document* affirmed the centrality of prevention; paragraph 138 is primarily concerned with the internal preventative responsibilities of states while paragraph 139 commits states to, 'assisting those [states] which are under stress *before* crises and conflicts break out'. Paragraph 140 reads: 'We fully support the mission of the Special Adviser of the Secretary-General on the Prevention of Genocide'. This new office was established in 2004 and will be explored in greater detail later in this chapter.

During the 2009 General Assembly debate on R2P, states consistently stressed that prevention was the key component of R2P; this was in fact the most commonly articulated sentiment. While R2P clearly stems from the 1990s debates on humanitarian intervention, many states argued that R2P involved much more than military intervention and further, that its greatest potential efficacy lay in its capacity to prevent, rather than halt, humanitarian crises. A number of states, including the UK, Colombia, Indonesia, Nigeria, Peru, South Africa and Sweden (on behalf of the EU), spoke at length about the importance of prevention and in particular urged the re-orientation of the debate on R2P (and by default humanitarian intervention) away from reaction towards prevention. Indicatively the UK ambassador stated:

> what I think we should be trying to achieve here is an R2P-culture, a culture of prevention that is as much about responsible sovereignty as it is international assistance. A culture that in the long-term will help us to prevent mass atrocities and reduce conflict and the cost of conflict. A culture that will help

> us to build an international system which is better equipped and more effective at preventing and responding to conflict. (UK, 2009, p. 3)

A number of R2P's most vocal advocates echo these sentiments; Gareth Evans, co-chair of the original ICISS, argued that prevention is the most important aspect of R2P (2009, p. 79) while Alex Bellamy is more emphatic; 'the overall aim of R2P' he stated, 'has to be to reduce the frequency with which the protection of civilians from genocide and mass atrocities is dependent on the use of non-consensual force by outsiders' (Bellamy, 2009, p. 198). The significance of R2P, he claimed, does not lie in its capacity to guide policy on responses to humanitarian crises; rather the great potential of R2P to make 'a real difference' lies 'in reducing the frequency with which world leaders are confronted with the apparent choice between doing nothing and sending in the Marines' (ibid, p. 3). Contemporary discussions of R2P are, therefore, increasingly characterized by an enhanced focus on prevention.

The ICISS's research volume noted that while states had routinely avowed the importance of conflict prevention, particularly since the 1994 Rwandan genocide, these declarations, 'have not, however, been matched by an equal commitment by member states to build UN preventative capacities' (ICISS, 2001b, p. 29). The establishment of the OSAPG in 2004, however, *did* constitute a definite institutional innovation within the UN architecture specifically focused on conflict prevention and on helping to realize the promise 'Never Again!' The role of the OSAPG was reaffirmed in the 2005 World Summit *Outcome Document* under the section heading 'Responsibility to protect populations from genocide, war crimes, ethnic cleansing and crimes against humanity' and thus this office constitutes the most tangible development linked to R2P specifically related to prevention. The following section analyses the remit and record of the OSAPG with a view to discerning the true level of practical support afforded to prevention by the international community of states and the extent to which this new office has the capacity to match R2P's vision of prevention.

The Office of the Special Adviser on the Prevention of Genocide

The OSAPG has been described as 'pioneering new approaches to genocide prevention that represent an important part of the intellectual history of preventative diplomacy at the UN' (Ramcharan, 2008, p. 180) and 'an authentic basis for hope that the UN may move gradually toward fulfilment of its potential' (Hamburg, 2008, p. 226). The OSAPG is, therefore, of great significance and its powers and record to date are illustrative of the success of R2P's avowal of the need for more focus on prevention and the willingness of the international community of states to prioritize prevention.

The following sections draw on interviews conducted in August 2009 with Dr Francis Deng, the Special Adviser on the Prevention of Genocide; Professor David Hamburg, Chairman of the Office of the Special Adviser on the Prevention of Genocide Advisory Committee; Maria Stavropoulou and Castro Wesamba, both Political Affairs Officers within the OSAPG; Steve Crawshaw, Human Rights Watch's United Nations Advocacy Director; Heather Sonner from the International Secretariat of the Institute for Global Policy; Sapna Chhatpar Considine, Project Manager with the International Coalition for the Responsibility to Protect; Nicola Reindorp, Director of Advocacy at the Global Centre for the Responsibility to Protect; and Professor Thomas Weiss, Director of the Ralph Bunche Institute for International Science, which is affiliated to the Central University of New York.

Establishment and remit

The UN's inquiry into the 1994 Rwandan genocide identified gaps in the early warning capacity of the organization and called for 'an action plan to prevent genocide' aimed at 'improving early warning' (Security Council, 1999, pp. 54–5). This was re-emphasized by Kofi Annan in a 2001 report in which he advocated establishing a new office singularly devoted to prevention (Annan, 2001a, p. 12). In April 2004, on the tenth anniversary of the Rwandan genocide, Annan launched his 'Action Plan to Prevent Genocide' which included the establishment of the OSAPG. While this was not the first time the UN had addressed the issue of preventing genocide, the establishment of this office was unprecedented; as Hamburg reflected: 'It was the first time any prevention professional had been appointed at such a high level ... [and] the first time that a unit focusing specifically on genocide prevention had ever been created at the UN' (2008, p. 224).

The Secretary-General outlined the mandate of the OSAPG in a letter to the Security Council on 12 July 2004:

> The Special Adviser will (a) collect existing information, in particular from within the United Nations system, on massive and serious violations of human rights and international humanitarian law of ethnic and racial origin that, if not prevented or halted, might lead to genocide; (b) act as a mechanism of early warning to the Secretary-General, and through him to the Security Council, by bringing to their attention potential situations that could result in genocide; (c) make recommendations to the Security Council, through the Secretary-General, on actions to prevent or halt genocide; (d) liaise with the United Nations system on activities for the prevention of genocide and work to enhance the United Nations capacity to analyse and manage information relating to genocide or related crimes. (Annan, 2004, p. 2)

Initially, Argentinean human rights lawyer Juan Méndez was appointed Special Adviser in a part-time capacity and, in May 2006, Kofi Annan established an Advisory Committee to support the work of the OSAPG. In May 2007 Francis Deng, former Representative of the United Nations Secretary-General on Internally Displaced Persons, was appointed Special Adviser and in August 2007 the OSAPG was made a full-time position and the status of the Special Adviser was upgraded to Under-Secretary-General.

Humanitarian NGOs generally supported the establishment of the OSAPG; Heather Sonner of the International Secretariat of the Institute for Global Policy argued that while the Secretary-General was tasked with maintaining a generally cordial relationship with UN member states the Special Adviser could, 'speak out on such a sensitive issue as genocide and ... sound the alarm' (Considine and Sonner, 2009). This view was echoed by Steve Crawshaw of Human Rights Watch, who cited 'the wakeup-call potential' of the OSAPG (Crawshaw, 2009). Similarly Nicola Reindorp, Director of Advocacy at the Global Centre for the Responsibility to Protect, argued the existence of the OSAPG meant '[there are] people responsible to ensure that parts of the [UN] bureaucracy are watching for warning signs and driving discussion around policy options' (Reindorp, 2009).

The OSAPG does not have a presence on the ground in potential trouble spots around the world nor has it established a new means of gathering data. Rather it aims to 'filter information' (Stavropoulou, 2009). Yet, many analyses of the genocide in Rwanda in 1994 noted that the most outrageous aspect of the UN's response was the fact that information *was* readily available and alarm bells *were* sounded (see Chapter 2). Establishing an office to manage information about impending genocide can be seen in this context as a solution to a problem that hasn't really been of major import, certainly when compared to the far more profound problem of mobilizing political will amongst the P5 to take timely and effective action. Crawshaw, however, argued, '[In 1994] there wasn't a lack of information but there was a lack of those who had information who were able to cut like a knife through the system' (Crawshaw, 2009). This is not a perspective shared by all, however. According to Michael Barnett, UN officials with the capacity, and indeed the mandate, to highlight looming catastrophe, failed to meet their responsibilities (2002, pp. 3–4). Nonetheless, Crawshaw maintained that the added value of the OSAPG was its potential to expedite information through the UN bureaucracy. On this issue Sonner agreed that while there were certain offices within the UN already mandated to gather information related to the prevention of genocide and mass atrocities – in particular the High Commissioner for Human Rights – there was no single spokesperson mandated to specifically focus on genocide prevention and thus the OSAPG brought a sharper focus to the issue and would be able to, 'prevent the hyper politicisation of that information as it moves up the chain within the Secretariat, which we did see in the case of Rwanda' (Considine and Sonner, 2009). Reindorp claimed it would be 'a real exaggeration to suggest that the appointment of one person ... is going to revolutionise the response to genocide'. Nonetheless, this attempt 'to plug one little piece of the gap in the capacity of the UN secretariat, which itself is one tiny, tiny piece in the whole prevention of genocide architecture' was, she claimed, 'significant', though the OSAPG should not be seen as 'a kind of a panacea' (Reindorp, 2009).

Francis Deng accepted that there was a plethora of sources of information already in existence and that the OSAPG was not going to add significantly to the detection of warning signs. The OSAPG, he thus accepted, did not constitute 'anything dramatically new' and the question of the office's added value was, therefore, 'a valid concern' (Deng, 2009). Nonetheless, he argued that the OSAPG's significance derived from the fact that unlike the many NGOs that issue conflict warnings and collect data, '[The OSAPG is a] UN entity, which was agreed upon as a result of collective thinking about what the UN should be doing to respond to this issue. [It is] a spotlight within the system which is well equipped and capacitated; it can mobilise these resources' (ibid). Deng recalled that prior to the Rwandan genocide Bacre Ndiaye, then UN Special Rapporteur on Extrajudicial, Summary or Arbitrary Executions, submitted a report to the UN warning about the likelihood of massive violence in Rwanda. His report, however, was subsequently lost within the UN bureaucracy. Deng claimed: 'If Ndiaye's report had come to a focal point within the UN system that was charged to make use of such information, to rally forces, to alert the Secretary-General to inform the Security Council, that perhaps would have been more effective' (ibid). The OSAPG was evidently now acting as this 'focal point with the UN system' and thus ostensibly constituted a significant reform of the existing system.

This broad support for the establishment of the OSAPG and endorsement of its utility is not shared by all. According to Thomas Weiss:

> it's not a real job, it's not something you can really do anything about from the inside at this point in time ... I think it would make much more sense to keep this as a focus or a part of the High Commission for Human Rights and keep it live, but not expect it to go anywhere because I don't think it will. (Weiss, 2009a)

Weiss noted that this was a view shared by Evans who expressed similar concerns at a meeting of the OSAPG Advisory Committee. In response to Evan's criticism of the OSAPG, Weiss claims that certain members of the Advisory Committee, such as David Hamburg, and Deng himself, 'went through the ceiling', but added 'they just don't want to hear how few clothes the emperor has' (Weiss, 2009a).

Record to date

The OSAPG has yet to achieve a high profile and it has attracted very little attention within academia, and even within the UN system it has been overlooked at times. Maria Stavropoulou, Political Affairs Officer at the OSAPG, noted that there have been times when the OSAPG was not invited to meetings of the UN inter-agency framework team for conflict prevention. She recalled, 'nobody said, "we don't think you should be part of that meeting", there was never any objection but also there was no automaticity' (Stavropoulou, 2009). It is significant that an office charged with such an important mandate could be overlooked in this way, and is indicative of the OSAPG's low profile.

The fact that the role was initially part-time during Méndez's tenure understandably limited the OSAPG's impact. When Méndez was replaced by Deng the position was quickly made full-time, though according to Hamburg, '[The UN] budget committee gave [Deng] nothing', with the result that Deng had to make do with a skeletal staff for the first year of his tenure (Hamburg, 2009). Indeed, Deng acknowledged that he spent most of his initial twelve months in the post trying to raise money and recruit staff rather than actively working to fulfil his mandate (Deng, 2009). This paucity of financial resources certainly suggests that for all the lofty rhetoric surrounding the establishment of the OSAPG, the actual political commitment was minimal.

Beyond these obvious financial constraints, assessments of the actual work done by the OSAPG vary. Weiss argued that the few press statements issued by the OSAPG had been devoid of significant content and asserted: 'I think Juan Méndez did more in 5 per cent of his time than Francis [Deng] does in 100 per cent of his.' Weiss claimed that this is in part a consequence of the disposition of the current UN Secretary-General Ban Ki-Moon, who, he claimed, 'doesn't want any noise or any waves'. Additionally, Weiss asserted, 'Francis [Deng] doesn't want anybody to be angry at him any of the time' and the combination of these cautious, reticent styles meant '[The OSAPG] is so behind the scenes that it's invisible' (Weiss, 2009a).

Deng himself acknowledged that he is committed to a 'quiet approach' but defended his style by claiming it had proved its effectiveness during his time as Representative of the United Nations Secretary-General on Internally Displaced Persons. He claimed that publicly criticizing states would alienate him and his office; 'doors would be closed and I don't see how I can help people if I cannot even go and see the country and engage the governments in a constructive dialogue' (Deng, 2009). Deng argued further that the results of his efforts were effectively destined to be invisible for two reasons; first, successful preventative action necessarily stops something becoming a major issue and thus it is almost by definition less likely to attract attention than a failure to prevent an atrocity; non-tragedies don't make headlines. Second, behind-the-scenes diplomacy is by definition conducted in private and cannot be publicized if it is effective, so the achievements of the OSAPG are consigned to invisibility.

Nonetheless, the manner in which Deng has chosen to interpret his mandate at the OSAPG is clearly of some concern. This is made all the more significant by virtue of the fact that there was general consensus among NGOs that the potential utility of this office was, almost uniquely, a function of the Special Advisor's capacity to use the OSAPG as a bully pulpit. Crawshaw argued that the OSAPG *must* be outspoken to have any real effect and stated:

> Once you've got that job title on your business card, you have to accept that not everybody's going to like you, so you can stop thinking that you can be everybody's best friend ... yes it's a post which requires diplomacy in many contexts but it also requires very robust speaking. (Crawshaw, 2009)

Sonner noted similarly that her organization initially supported the OSAPG because they believed the office would be 'making the tough calls and really putting pressure on member states to take action in situations that look like they're moving towards genocide' (Considine and Sonner, 2009). They were, therefore, disenchanted with Deng's 'quiet' approach and general unwillingness to openly criticize states. Staff at the OSAPG, perhaps unsurprisingly, rejected this assertion; Stavropoulou argued: 'a public statement can shut many more doors in the short term, and in the long term make the mandate less effective and I don't think NGOs always realise that' (Stavropoulou, 2009). Additionally, the mandate of the OSAPG explicitly commits the Special Adviser to act 'without excessive publicity' and thus while NGOs and others may believe that the OSAPG should act as an alarm bell this is not actually its official remit (Annan, 2004, p. 2). An additional factor in the approach adopted, which is not related to Deng's personal disposition, is the influence of the Secretary-General. Deng highlighted the fact that his capacity to make public statements is dependent on the assent of the Secretary-General:

> Another very important thing that people miss is I am an arm of the Secretary-General and everything I do ... has to be cleared with the office of the Secretary-General and very often ... they advised me against saying anything ... on the Sudan, on Sri Lanka, on Myanmar ... I'm not an independent voice of humanity, I am a tool of the Secretary-General. (Deng, 2009)

While there may be a degree of truth in this, historically a number of UN officials, most notably Mary Robinson in her role as UN High Commissioner for Human Rights, have creatively interpreted their mandate and gone beyond diplomatic conventions to make the best use of their positions. Deng's expressed unwillingness to act without the approval of the Secretary-General, who is widely considered to be overly cautious, appears to support Weiss's view on the impact of Deng's personality and the limited potential of the office as a bully pulpit.

Deng's caution has much to do with the fact that his predecessor was once embarrassingly publicly prevented from addressing the Security Council. This incident occurred on 10 October 2005 when, according to Hamburg, John Bolton, then US Ambassador to the UN, literally marshalled Méndez, then Special Adviser, out of the room before a meeting of the Security Council (Hamburg, 2009; see also Akhavan, 2005, p. 6, and Feinstein, 2006, pp. 15–16). Clearly this public denigration of the OSAPG did little to enhance its status and Deng acknowledges that he was influenced by this incident and determined to avoid any action that would 'create tension between my office and the Security Council' (Deng, 2009). Crawshaw observed that Méndez had been highly critical of the Security Council's ability, and evident willingness, to block the Special Adviser from addressing meetings of the Council (Crawshaw, 2009). In his final report as Special Adviser Méndez recommended that the mandate of the OSAPG be strengthened to ensure that the right to address the Council be clarified. This amendment to the mandate has yet to occur.

The Special Adviser's capacity to address the Security Council has been cited as one of the OSAPG's most significant powers (United Nations Association of the United States of America, 2006, p. 3). The reluctance on the part of members of the P5 to allow the Special Adviser access to Security Council meetings, however, clearly undermines the potential of this aspect of the OSAPG's mandate and in practice, therefore, the OSAPG is not a mechanism that ensures warnings are *always* conveyed to the Security Council, let alone heeded (Janssen, 2008, p. 301). In addition, there is an issue with respect to the novelty of this provision; while it is indeed true that there are few offices within the UN, and fewer outside it, that can address the Security Council directly, it is not the case that without this privilege the perspectives of certain groups can never be heard at Security Council meetings. Article 99 of the Charter empowers the Secretary-General to address the Security Council and, while this provision is rarely used, it is conceivable that the Secretary-General may bring details of a report by a particular UN office or even NGO to the Security Council's attention. In this sense, the capacity of the OSAPG to address the Security Council directly may not be as significant as it first appears. It is also important to reiterate that even if the OSAPG *is* invited or permitted to address the Security Council this in itself is no guarantee that any action will be taken on the basis of his reports and recommendations; the P5 has ultimate discretion and the OSAPG's submissions are no more than advice. Indeed, graphic reports on the deteriorating situation in Darfur were regularly brought to the Security Council's attention from 2003 on, to little effect (Mayroz, 2008, p. 361; Peters, 2009, p. 524).

Paragraph 140 of the 2005 World Summit *Outcome Document* commits all states to 'fully support the mission of the Special Adviser of the Secretary-General on the Prevention of Genocide' though whether this is honoured in practice is open to debate. A lack of cooperation appears to have been evident in late 2008 when a visit to Burundi was cancelled when the government claimed to be unable to provide an official to meet the Special Adviser (Human Rights Council, 2009, p. 13). It is perhaps understandable that states will be somewhat resistant to engaging with 'The Special Adviser on the Prevention of Genocide', given the negative implications suggested by his presence. Indeed, Weiss remarked, 'if you were coming to my country and said "I'm the adviser on the prevention of genocide", the idea that I would welcome you with open arms is clearly not a solid place to start' (Weiss, 2009a). Deng also noted that his work was hampered by a reluctance amongst certain powerful states to engage with the OSAPG claiming 'those who would be called upon to intervene to stop [genocide] tend to be resistant to discussing this issue' (Deng, 2009). Many such states are keen to play down the scale of crises and feel that the OSAPG's presence at a Security Council meeting and public warnings about impending genocide might create a momentum in favour of action.

'A waste of time, and energy and money'?

In his summation of the OSAPG Weiss asserted: 'frankly I think this office is a waste of time, and energy and money'. Evidence that the OSPAG has achieved any significant results is, according to Weiss, 'totally lacking' (Weiss, 2009a). In assessing the impact of the OSAPG it is necessary to again acknowledge the fact that preventative diplomacy by definition does not produce spectacular results. As Payam Akhavan noted, 'The Special Adviser has a thankless job. His success in early warning and prevention is necessarily measured in terms of what *does not* happen' (2005, p. 11). Additionally, behind-the-scenes diplomacy is not in itself inherently ineffective and clearly there is a place for just such a strategy, which is also by definition invisible. Yet, the Secretary-General and certain other UN offices and NGOs, particularly the Red Cross, arguably already fulfil this behind-the-scenes role. The OSAPG does not constitute an improvement of the information gathering capacity of the UN and hence its added value and potential utility lies in its capacity, as many NGOs argued, to fast-track information from other sources through the UN system. If the information handled by the OSAPG is quietly and unofficially disseminated then this impacts on its capacity to create a momentum in favour of action. Additionally, if the Security Council refuses to actually hear the OSAPG's warnings the office's capacity to fast-track information through the UN system is quite obviously of limited utility.

Deng acknowledged that states involved in activities deemed to be potentially genocidal, or likely to lead to genocide, are uncomfortable with discussing their situation in public for fear of external intervention, and he additionally noted that states with either the capacity to intervene or the mandate to take action – or both as in the case of the P5 – are also keen to bury bad news for fear that they will be called upon to take action. How then, will Deng's 'quiet approach' convince either the state involved in the deteriorating situation, or those states most likely to be called upon to respond, to take action to prevent an explosion of violence? None of the reports about the Rwandan genocide concluded that effective action would have occurred if the dire warnings issued before the genocide, by for example Ndiaye and Dallaire, had been relayed through the UN system in a 'quiet' manner. As Nicolas Wheeler notes, the eventual public clamour to do something when the scale of the carnage *was* made public, particularly in France, eventually led to action being taken, albeit disastrously late and possibly in a counter-productive fashion (2002, pp. 236–41). To discuss deteriorating situations – so grave that they bear the hallmarks of potential genocide – informally, behind closed doors and with a view to maintaining cordiality cannot by definition generate a momentum in favour of action. The explicit injunction within the OSAPG's mandate to act 'without excessive publicity' is, therefore, of detriment to its efficacy.

The efficacy of the OSAPG is also based on a dubious underlying assumption; the ostensible influence of the office is largely premised, not on a belief in the benevolence of statesmen, but rather on an assumption that they fear shame. Indicatively, Stavropoulou claimed that a formal report by the OSAPG becomes part of the public record and serves as a deterrent to inaction. She noted:

> if, God forbid, another Rwanda happens and if this office has done its job properly, then it must have been able to identify what was going on, what was coming ... it will have brought this to the attention of the Secretary-General and the Security

> Council and if no action is taken, then the responsibility and the accountability is very precisely located. (Stavropoulou, 2009)

Likewise, Castro Wesamba, Political Affairs Officer at the OSAPG, argued that a report from the OSAPG created 'obligations'. When pressed to identify what these 'obligations' were, given that there is no mention in the OSPAG's mandate of any obligation incumbent upon the Security Council to even listen to the Special Adviser let alone act on his recommendations, Wesamba argued that these were obligations in the sense that they created normative pressure rather than legal compulsions to act (Wesamba, 2009). Deng himself argued:

> [By establishing the OSAPG] we are sharpening our sensitivity to these issues and the resolve of the international community to act. Every time we say 'never again' and it happens again, the level of guilt rises and as the level of guilt rises, the level of resolve to do something about it before the next time increases. (Deng, 2009)

Given recent history this would appear to be a perspective born more from hope than experience. After the genocide in Rwanda, statesmen around the world lamented their response and 'Never Again!' was once again widely and loudly proclaimed. Yet, in his assessment of the response to the crisis in Darfur, Kofi Annan noted: 'We were slow, hesitant, uncaring and we had learnt nothing from Rwanda' (Fisher, 2007, p. 103). This assessment clearly doesn't support claims regarding the cumulative effects of shame. Indeed, former US National Security Adviser Anthony Lake observed, 'many people have learned to live with the thought that we haven't done enough in Darfur' (Reinold, 2010, p. 74). States appear to have little compunction about ignoring or equivocating about a looming or actual genocide unless they have significant national interests involved; this is explored in greater detail in Chapter 5.

The OSAPG may well constitute a tangible institutional innovation directly linked to the preventative element of R2P but it clearly suffers from a number of consciously constructed constitutional restrictions which limit its efficacy. The OSAPG does not enhance the information gathering capacity of the UN and thus cannot be cited as an improvement to the UN's early warning mechanism. While it may well act as a centralizing and coordinating focus for information gathered, the OSAPG's capacity to influence decision making with this information is limited by virtue of the fact that the terms of the OSAPG's own mandate commit it to behind-the-scenes work and the Security Council is empowered to ignore the Special Adviser – as indeed has happened. The incumbent Special Adviser's decision to adopt a 'quiet approach' certainly acts as an additional barrier to the OSAPG's profile and impact. Additionally, when the Special Adviser *has* sought to speak out he has been restrained by the Secretary-General and his statements have been invariably anodyne. The OSAPG has also been allocated meagre resources and even been ignored within the UN itself.

Therefore, for all the earnest statements issued by states and UN diplomats about the importance of prevention, the actual resources and powers allocated to the OSAPG suggest that prevention continues to be seen as a secondary issue. It is hard not to conclude, therefore, that the establishment of the OSAPG is mere window dressing. While the OSAPG's very existence can be cited as evidence of the practical application of the commitments routinely made to prioritize prevention, its restrictive mandate coupled with interference by the Secretary-General and a lack of cooperation from member states and even the UN system itself, suggest that the OSAPG is not expected to do much more than simply exist as a kind of showpiece. Regarding Deng and the OSAPG more generally, Weiss claimed that 'he's in a real comfort zone; the Secretary-General's not pushing him to do more, his [Advisory] Committee isn't pushing him to do more, states would just as soon he'd keep quiet' (Weiss, 2009a). While this is lamentable in itself, it should also serve as a wake-up call for those who eagerly advocate expansive preventative action as the primary means by which to address the problem of egregious intra-state humanitarian crises.

The last refuge of the unimaginative?

The increased championing of prevention as R2P's primary *raison d'être*, in tandem with the establishment of the OSAPG, constitutes a significant evolution in the history of R2P. The following sections argue, however, that far from constituting a means by which R2P can, in Bellamy's words, make 'a real difference', the contemporary emphasis on prevention is indicative of R2P's failure to effect real change with respect to reaction (2009, p. 3). Aside from this constituting something of a tactical retreat, the conceptual shift away from reaction to prevention additionally has limited potential as it adds little value to existing perspectives, theories and initiatives on prevention and is based on questionable underlying assumptions.

R2P's added value

The ICISS was not the first international commission to suggest that the discussions on how to deal with large scale intra-state crises should focus more on prevention than reaction. In tandem with the focus on responding to the many intra-state conflicts that achieved international attention during the 1990s, significant research was conducted and published on preventing these conflicts. To take but one example, the Carnegie Commission on Preventing Deadly Conflict was established in 1994 and prior to the establishment of the ICISS had published some 26 reports, ten books and, in 1997, the landmark study *Preventing Deadly Conflict*. At the international level, UN Secretary-Generals Pérez de Cuéllar, Boutros Boutros-Ghali and Kofi Annan were each proactive in this area prior to the ICISS report, and indeed previously, during the Cold War, Secretary-General Dag Hammarskjöld's innovative approach to peacekeeping led to a plethora of studies on preventative military deployment. Chapter VI of the UN Charter specifically deals with preventative diplomacy and Article 33 outlines a series of steps that should be taken to address any dispute, 'which is likely to endanger the maintenance of international peace and security'. The idea that conflict can be avoided through more holistic measures, such as the equitable distribution of resources, universal suffrage, improved education and equal opportunity, has been recognized, albeit not always implemented, for centuries. Research on conflict prevention may not receive the acclaim and attention it deserves but it is certainly not lacking.

Of course, because prevention has been championed in the past does not mean the ICISS's endorsement of the idea is outdated. The ICISS's recommendations, however, are problematic not so much because they address an often-discussed issue, but because they add nothing new to existing thinking on this issue beyond general recommendations. There is very little in the ICISS's chapter on prevention that could be cited as novel, let alone groundbreaking, and the claims and prescriptions advanced are so general as to be virtually devoid of real utility. The chapter is peppered with statements of the relatively obvious such as 'Effective conflict prevention depends on disparate actors working together strategically' (ICISS, 2001a, p. 25). There is little in the chapter with which one can disagree but this is due to its insipidity rather than convincing argument. Indeed, in a 2003 article, Bellamy criticized R2P's treatment of prevention noting: 'The need to pay more attention, and more money, to prevention and post-conflict rebuilding has long been identified' (2003, pp. 6–7). The chapter on prevention does nothing beyond restating that prevention is better than intervention and lacks detailed, or innovative, prescriptions as to how prevention may be best conducted, or more importantly, afforded the priority it deserves at the highest levels.

There is an obvious absence of meaningful theoretical engagement with the issue or deep understanding of the broader literature on prevention. There are, Hugh Miall observes, at least three theoretical approaches to conflict prevention; conflict management, conflict resolution and conflict transformation (2004, pp. 161–3) and yet the ICISS report acknowledges no such sub-categories but rather advances a generic, unmediated formulation. It is additionally noteworthy that the ICISS report, and its supplementary research volume, are both silent on the issue of self-determination. Despite the fact that self-determination and nationalism are routinely cited as primary causes of intra-state conflict in the post-Cold War era (see van der Stoel, 2004, p. 114), there is literally no reference to these catalysts in any of the sections on prevention in either of the ICISS's reports. The failure to deal with this seminal issue is illustrative of the superficial nature of the ICISS's prescriptions; prevention is presented as axiomatically good, and the contestation surrounding its various forms, strategies and broader context is simply ignored.

The longer essay in the ICISS's supplementary volume certainly provides more detail to support certain assertions made in the main report but again it is difficult to identify anything here that can be construed as innovative. The essay notes, 'Every step taken towards reducing poverty and achieving broad-based economic growth is a step toward conflict prevention' (ICISS, 2001b, p. 32). While this is difficult to refute it is arguably an unhelpful generalization. One could substitute 'conflict' in this sentence for a myriad of societal and international ills such as depression, anti-social behaviour, truancy, illiteracy, terrorism, drug abuse, etc. There appears, in effect, to be almost nothing, provided it constitutes a social good which doesn't positively contribute in some way to conflict prevention. Within ICISS's own essay there is an acknowledgement that over-generalization can be unhelpful. While, as noted, the essay asserts that there is a causal link between poverty and intra-state conflict, it later warns:

> Taking such a broad approach may divert attention away from the behavioural origins of violent conflict that are ultimately political. Too heavy an emphasis on structural causes of conflict is also empirically inaccurate – social inequalities and resource scarcity do not in fact always lead to deadly conflict. (ICISS, 2001b, p. 32)

As Michael Lund warns with respect to such expansive approaches: 'with so much varied activity now being lumped under conflict prevention there is also a risk it will lose its distinctive meaning' (2004, p. 122).

Likewise, while the 2005 World Summit *Outcome Document* reiterated the importance of prevention, it did little beyond rhetorically support prevention; the only practical aspect of the section on R2P was the commitment in paragraph 140 to the OSAPG which, as the previous section demonstrated, is itself of questionable practical utility. The chorus of states extolling the virtue of prevention during the 2009 General Assembly debate may have chimed with earnest resolve but in practical terms no new policy was agreed and the commitments were just that; promises to do better. The history of these non-binding commitments, however, is not encouraging; as Samuel Totten and Paul R. Bartop observe, 'all one needs to do is examine a short and incomplete list of the genocides that have been perpetrated over the past 50 years or so to see that talk has lorded over action almost every single time' (2009, p. 316).

If one was to endorse the idea that it is better to prevent conflicts than to intervene to halt them – obviously quite a logical proposition – and on this basis determine to seek out comprehensive, detailed, innovative and practical recommendations on how best to do so, then R2P would not be a particularly useful place to start, certainly when compared with the myriad alternatives. As Lund noted in 2004, 'conflict prevention has never been higher on the international political agenda'. Interestingly, the catalysts he identifies for this ascendency – international conferences organized by NGOs, policy statements by the UN and EU, the G-8 Okinawa Summit, the 2001 Report of the Secretary General on the Prevention of Armed Conflict and the work undertaken by various regional bodies such as the OSCE and ECOWAS – do not include the ICISS's report. Reflecting on the various initiatives launched in the post-Cold War era he notes, 'In sum, the policy "toolbox" on which prevention can draw is extensive' (Lund, 2004, pp. 120–1). The ICISS's discussion of prevention adds little of value to this 'extensive toolbox', while the 2005 *Outcome Document* and 2009 General Assembly debate constitute re-workings of the hundreds of broken promises made since the Holocaust.

It must be acknowledged, however, that it would have been remiss for the ICISS *not* to have briefly noted that prevention is preferable to intervention and likewise not to periodically reiterate this sentiment. The problem is, however, that this general restatement of existing clichés has been elevated from the periphery of R2P – where I contend it rightfully belongs – to its dominant *raison d'être*. The same concerns would arise if the Responsibility to Rebuild – itself a descriptive list of inoffensive observations – was elevated in the same manner. If R2P is now been marketed as primarily about prevention – as it surely is – then by virtue of the fact that it advances little of any practical utility, its future efficacy is in some doubt.

Underlying assumptions

No one can dispute the basic premise that on both humanitarian and financial grounds preventing mass atrocities is more desirable than halting them once they have started. Acknowledging this need to improve the international community's capacity to prevent mass atrocities should be tempered, however, by an attendant acknowledgement that preventative measures are highly unlikely to be 100 per cent effective, especially when it comes to man-made intra-state humanitarian crises. Human history is testimony to man's propensity for violence and aggression and is peppered with instances of inter- and intra-state violence, and indeed genocide (Hamburg, 2008, p. 2). Indeed, archaeological evidence suggests that the very evolution of man is a function of conflict between the Cro-Magnons and the Neanderthals leading Roland Wright to wonder whether as a species we are in fact the benefactors of genocide (2006, p. 25). In the past five hundred years, war has been present three times more frequently than it has been absent (Weltman, 1995, pp. 1–2). There is nothing in either our history or our contemporary condition which can reasonably be cited as evidence that we can contrive some means by which intra-state conflict can be prevented 'once and for all' as the subtitle of Evans' 2009 book suggests. As certain noted supporters of R2P realistically lament, 'Mass starvation, rape and suffering will reappear as global security threats, and humanitarian intervention will continue to smoulder on the public policy agenda' (Macfarlane, Thielking and Weiss, 2004, p. 986). There will always be, therefore, a pressing need to react to crises and thus the requirement to sharpen the international community's capacity in this area must be prioritized.

There is, additionally, a problem with borrowing the 'prevention is better than cure' slogan from the medicinal and health discourse. Conceiving of intra-state humanitarian crises as problems that can be eradicated before they erupt is to falsely conceptualize these events as something akin to a preventable disease. For example, given that there is a vaccine for smallpox, which if administered prevents the contraction of the disease, it is clearly sensible to focus primarily on the distribution of this preventative vaccine, rather than the treatment of smallpox. Smallpox is not comparable to intra-state conflict however; the disease has no consciousness and no desire to kill and is comprised of a limited number of identifiable attributes. Perpetrators of mass atrocities and war often display, however, 'a superabundance of analytic rationality' (Howard, 1984, pp. 14–15), as the mechanized slaughter of the Holocaust emphatically illustrated, and there are so many variables that contrive to convince an individual or group that the use of egregious force is prudent that it is surely impossible to contrive a universally applicable fail-safe preventative strategy. Certain strategies clearly contribute to alleviating the tensions that lead to violence and thus it makes sense to promote these policies but not without modest expectations; if history is a guide, as surely it must be, then gross acts of violence, perpetrated by individuals or states, are almost inevitable and we must, therefore, adopt a dual strategy which certainly comprises attempts to prevent and limit the occurrence such acts but also, crucially, to halt (and punish) them.

There are those, too, who argue that while prevention is an attractive idea, it is simply not possible to predict the occurrence of genocide and mass atrocity crimes with any kind of accuracy. According to Henry Huttenbach, 'the capability to predict wars, civil strife and revolutions, let alone specific genocides, with any kind of reasonable, rational certitude escapes even the most knowledgeable' (2008, p. 472). He argues:

> the best one can expect from the early warning approach is a compilation of global hot spots which number in the hundreds as we establish dangers in a conflict ridden world. The only means of distinguishing between crises, and of categorizing them as dormant, latent and imminent, is therefore, at best, educated guesswork. (Ibid, pp. 471–2)

It is not at all clear, therefore, that we can identify generic indicators of genocide or mass atrocities more generally. For example, the conflict in Rwanda seems in retrospect to have been obviously brewing for years but in hindsight, of course, conflicts always do; few remember today that in the 1980s Rwanda was hailed as the 'Switzerland of Africa' (Hintjens, 1999, p. 244). In the period immediately prior to the outbreak of genocide in Rwanda in 1994 'hard and fast early warning signals' simply did not exist (Huttenbach, 2005, p. 308). The International Panel of Eminent Personalities of the Organization of African Unity conducted a review which stated that by 1992 evidence suggested 'serious plans were afoot for ... appalling deeds', though they cautioned: 'That does not mean that the world knew that by 1992 or 1993, genocide was systematically being planned and organized' (Uvin, 2001, p. 91). The descent into genocidal violence can be traced to the negotiations surrounding, and the eventual signing of, the Arusha Accords in July 1993, and while concerns were raised by certain observers from 1990 on, the scale and speed of the genocide was a shock. Additionally, who predicted the outbreak of civil strife and state-sponsored violence in the Middle East in 2011? As Jennifer Welsh notes with respect to the conflict in Libya, 'Structural or root-cause prevention strategies would have had little to say about this particular country' (2011, p. 7).

Even if we reject the previous point and maintain that signals of looming genocide and mass atrocity crimes are identifiable, there is some dispute as to whether external intervention, even non-military intervention, is always positive. While many lamented the international community's 'failure to act' and the UN's inadequate preventative capacity in the context of the Rwandan genocide, others have argued that the lesson of Rwanda is actually that international preventative intervention, either in the form of peacekeeping, mediation or military intervention, far from helping to prevent violence may well catalyse it (Kuperman, 2001, pp. 109–10). The idea that the Rwandan genocide occurred because of a *lack* of international involvement is thus not an uncontested truism; Anne Orford notes that Rwanda has become emblematic of the 'need for early action' yet she argues that 'surprisingly little attention has been paid to the presence and activity of international institutions and agencies ... prior to the outbreak of violence' (2003, p. 85). The fact that the genocide was sparked by a number of external factors, such as the legacy of colonial rule, the structural adjustment programmes imposed by the World Bank and the IMF, the pressure put upon President Habyarimana, by the French in particular, to democratize, and the externally brokered Arusha Accords, suggested to some that international intervention was part of the problem and thus calls for *greater* international involvement were counter-intuitive (Collins, 2002; Williams, 2005, p. 113). The genocide was blamed by many observers on the unwillingness of the international community to become embroiled in Africa due to the absence of key strategic interests. Christopher Clapham argues, however: 'This claim can scarcely be made in the case of the Rwandan conflict, where the international community, led by regional states and the Organisation of African Unity, took an active role in attempting to negotiate a solution from a very early stage' (1998, p. 200), while James

Mayall notes, 'In many ways the pre-genocide Rwanda peace process was exemplary' (2006, p. 136). Similarly, Wheeler argued:

> It has become an accepted truism to claim that preventative diplomacy is always better than a belated intervention when things start to go wrong. However, the lesson of the Arusha process is that outside intervention aimed at averting a civil war can have unintended consequences that produce human wrongs on an unimaginable scale. (2002, 214)

Bruce Jones pointed to the fact that for at least three years prior to the genocide the international community was heavily involved in Rwanda. 'The ultimately catastrophic failure of those efforts', he suggested, 'should give pause for thought to those who believe that the appropriate response to Rwanda is to fashion an intrusive international regime of preventive intervention' (Jones, 1995, p. 226). Thus preventative diplomacy, as clearly practised in Rwanda from 1990–4, is not universally heralded as axiomatically good and necessary and this clearly has implications for the assumptions underpinning R2P, namely that early preventative intervention is good and that liberalism, in the form of democracy and capitalism, will ameliorate intra-state tensions. Indeed, the ICISS acknowledged, 'when sustained measures have been undertaken, results have been mixed' (ICISS, 2001b, p. 27). Lund in fact warned: 'the shift toward more political and economic openness that liberalism seeks, can, and often has, contributed to the intra-state instabilities in which violent conflicts have erupted' (2004, p. 124). Lund cites the violence which occurred in Croatia, Bosnia, Kosovo, Rwanda, Burundi, the DRC, Afghanistan, Tajikistan and East Timor in the post-Cold War era as examples and warns that the idea that the promotion of liberalism will negate societal tension, though empirically unsound, still informs a number of international missions today. With respect to these preventative missions and initiatives he warned, 'most of their activities are being carried out without much specific consciousness or scrutiny as to whether they are helping or hurting the larger process that is at stake in achieving liberalization without violence' (Lund, 2004, p. 127). The ICISS's promotion of liberalism, in the form of democracy and free markets, as a panacea

(2001a, p. 23), therefore, while not definitively erroneous, is not the truism R2P's advocates often suppose and suggest.

There are, therefore, predominantly two perspectives on prevention; there are those who believe that it is possible to predict the future occurrence of mass atrocities and that preventative intervention can work, and there are those who question the feasibility and efficacy of prevention and the accuracy of early warning systems. Neither perspective suggests that there is an absence of theoretical or empirical studies on prevention or a surfeit of early warning systems. Those in the latter category invariably lament the lack of political will to act on these early warnings and implement preventative measures. Hamburg, for example, argues, 'all the genocides of the twentieth century were clearly visible years in advance' (2008, p. 6). While this is not a universally agreed view, it is notable that his argument cites the lack of will as the primary reason why prevention hasn't worked. Championing the humanitarian and financial benefits of prevention has not, historically, always affected a change in the political will of those with the power to implement the necessary changes and policies. According to Hamburg the 'genocide' in Darfur 'could hardly have surprised international observers', thereby reiterating that the evidence was ignored, not that it was unavailable (2008, p. 2). As Weiss remarked:

> Logically speaking if you can't even get people mobilised to do something in the midst of a crisis, the idea that somehow even before you have a crisis, they're all going to align and put money into it seems to me to be against the nature of human beings and certainly against the nature of the interstate system. (Weiss, 2009a)

Of course, there are notable examples of effective international preventative action, such as the UN Preventative Deployment Force stationed on the Macedonian/Serbian border from 1992 to 1999. Yet, the history of the international response to intra-state crises undoubtedly suggests a reactive disposition despite the fact that it is widely acknowledged that proactive preventative action is not only likely to save lives but also significantly cheaper than action taken once violence has erupted (Fein, 2009, pp. 321–2). There is also, sadly, seemingly little political capital to be gained by acting before a crisis escalates; as Tom Malinowski of Human

Rights Watch stated in reference to the criticism raised against President Obama for taking action to prevent slaughter in Libya in 2011: 'Presidents get more credit for stopping atrocities after they begin than for preventing them before they get out of hand' (2011).

The ICISS's supplementary volume acknowledged that there has been, 'a wealth of theoretical and applied research ... generated since the 1950s' on prevention, but in assessing the record of the application of preventative measures it laments:

> many seemingly avoidable intrastate conflicts have inspired only token international efforts at prevention ... There are only a few unambiguous examples of successful preventative diplomacy in the post-Cold War era, while the catalogue of failed preventative action and missed opportunity is lengthy. (ICISS, 2001b, p. 27)

Simply extolling the virtues, both humanitarian and financial, of preventative measures and outlining various policies that *should* be undertaken, is, therefore, to avoid the key issue, namely the perennial lack of political will to act and the absence of an automatic, objective mechanism by which looming and actual crises are addressed (this is the focus of Chapter 8). Indicatively, the UN's enquiry into the Rwandan genocide claimed that the 'fundamental failure' was 'a persistent lack of political will' (Security Council, 1999, p. 3). As Chapter 5 argues, this question of political will is central to R2P's recommendations on both prevention and reaction and in each case R2P is ultimately predicated on, in my opinion, an erroneous notion that the disposition of states can be altered by force of argument.

Evasion?

As is clear, the evolution of R2P since the ICISS report in 2001 evidences a pronounced shift in emphasis towards preventing humanitarian crises rather than halting them. The original report did claim, as many supporters of prevention have noted, that prevention was 'the single most important dimension of the responsibility to protect' (ICISS, 2001a, p. xi). This assertion, however, is questionable as the report seems to contradict this claim by later stating: 'The 'responsibility to protect' implies *above all else* a responsibility to react to situations of compelling need for human protection' (ibid, p. 29). Indeed, Chapter 7 of the ICISS report, 'The Operational Dimension', refers briefly to prevention but primarily discusses reaction and in particular military intervention. Additionally, as Bellamy notes, it is strange that the chapter on prevention, despite its ostensible importance, constitutes only 9 of the 85 pages of the report (2009, p. 65).

The ICISS stated in the foreword to its report that it constitutes a 'response' to the question posed by Kofi Annan to the General Assembly in 2001, namely 'if humanitarian intervention is, indeed, an unacceptable assault on sovereignty, how should we respond to a Rwanda, to a Srebrenica – to gross and systematic violations of human rights that affect every precept of our common humanity?' (ICISS, 2001a, p. vii). Annan's question was inspired by the divisive debates on the interventions in Kosovo and East Timor in 1999 and his question – how should we *respond* – quite logically, refers explicitly to the issue of responding to, not preventing, intra-state crises. As the ICISS positions itself as a response to this question it is natural to expect this to be the focus. The ICISS report, for all its talk about the primary importance of prevention, and a chapter on 'the responsibility to rebuild', *does* predominately focus on the question of response; given the ICISS was established in response to Annan's question above, this is not surprising. What is surprising, however, is that the focus has gradually shifted from response to prevention since the report's publication. If R2P is now being championed as primarily aimed at *preventing* intra-state mass atrocities then this constitutes a significant alteration of its original *raison d'être* and an answer to a question that wasn't asked. Indeed, Evans acknowledges that the ICISS was established with the mandate 'to produce a guide to action on *responses* by the international community to internal, man-made, human rights violating catastrophes' (2009, p. 18).

It would appear that there is a desire to use the brand name 'R2P' when advancing proposals on prevention while radically changing the content of R2P's actual proposals on prevention. Bellamy's recent championing of prevention as the core idea behind R2P is interesting when one examines his views on the sections on prevention in the ICISS report. They are, he argued, 'brief, confused and unoriginal' and he asserted: 'I would go as far as to argue … that the commission should rewrite its chapters on prevention and rebuilding' (Bellamy, 2009, pp. 52–3). This desire to rewrite these aspects of the report is curious; if these sections are flawed how can it be that they constitute, according to Bellamy, the most important and potentially useful element of R2P? It is, as he stresses in his book, not the actual *prescriptions* that are so pregnant with potential, for he clearly believes these components are of limited utility, but rather the *principle* of prevention and rebuilding which is attractive. Discourse on conflict prevention is not the sole preserve of R2P, however, and it is unclear, therefore, why Bellamy, in seeking to prevent intra-state crises, feels it necessary to champion R2P when by his own admission the aspects of the report related to prevention are 'brief, confused and unoriginal'. Indeed, Weiss describes Bellamy's views on prevention as 'hard to fathom' (2011, p. 2).

Weiss described the ICISS's 'mumbling and stammering about prevention' as 'preposterous' and 'a superficially attractive but highly unrealistic way to try and pretend that we can finesse the hard issues of what essentially amounts to humanitarian intervention'. The concern with prevention, 'obscures the essence of the most urgent part of the spectrum of responsibility, to protect those caught in the crosshairs of war' (Weiss, 2007a, p. 104). The focus on 'better early warning systems', therefore, overlooks the fact that the lack of early warning has not been an especially significant issue. Historically, there has not been an absence of waning signs but rather an absence of political will to act on them. As Gregory Stanton succinctly observes: 'Early warning is meaningless without early response' (2009, p. 319). The ICISS report itself even noted: 'It is possible to exaggerate the extent to which lack of early warning is a serious problem ... lack of early warning is an excuse rather than an explanation, and the problem is not a lack of warning but of timely response' (ICISS, 2001a, p. 21). This statement clearly implies that the key focus must be improving the international community's response to these early warnings, not changing the international early warning mechanisms or focusing on other holistic preventative measures. As Secretary-General Ban Ki-Moon noted in a 2009 report, 'the crucial element in the prevention of genocide remains responding to concerns, once these have been communicated' (Human Rights Council, 2009, p. 17).

R2P's genesis was not the issue of prevention, it has added very little to existing theories on prevention, and it is, therefore, curious that R2P has been rebranded as primarily about prevention. According to Weiss, this shift constitutes 'evasiveness' and has been propelled to a significant extent by UN Secretary-General Ban Ki-Moon and his determination to avoid controversy (2011, p. 2). The focus on prevention is obviously attractive to some; it is a means by which R2P can be reinvigorated by refocusing it away from the infinitely more difficult, more real and more political issue of responding to actual intra-state crises. R2P's evolution in the area of response evidences a definite diminution of even the ICISS's modest prescriptions to the point that it is today devoid of legal basis or political utility. In the face of this obvious nullification of R2P's utility in this area, it is undoubtedly more attractive to claim that it was always, in fact, really about prevention and to retreat into this more theoretical realm where platitudes and normative recommendations are the prevailing currency. That preventing conflict is better than intervening to stop conflict is (relatively) axiomatic; that R2P constitutes a means of achieving this is not.

Conclusion: 'brief and unoriginal'?

Prior to the convening of the ICISS there was ample research on prevention; coherent theories on how prevention should be undertaken were not lacking and the ICISS was not charged with addressing this issue. The ICISS's own discussion of prevention, was therefore, understandably 'brief and unoriginal' (in Bellamy's words) given that the issue of prevention, though obviously relevant and important, was not the primary mandate or remit of the ICISS. The fact that R2P is today being rebranded as primarily about prevention is, therefore, obviously curious. There is certainly nothing inherently wrong with championing prevention but the attempt to utilize R2P to do so is disingenuous given that the section on prevention in the original ICISS report does not constitute a coherent, innovative set of prescriptions but rather a brief overview comprising general, and at times anodyne, suggestions. Michael Newman, in fact, charges the ICISS with paying 'inadequate attention to prevention' (2009, p. 190) highlighting the fact that the report is not a solid foundation for resolving the issues surrounding the lamentable failure to take timely and effective preventative action.

Since 1945, and with renewed vigour after the 1994 genocide in Rwanda, states have routinely issued statements extolling the virtues of prevention. The problem has been, however, that these statements and commitments have rarely translated into action; the establishment of the OSAPG and the declarations of support for prevention during the 2009 General Assembly debate are contemporary examples of this willingness to offer rhetorical rather than actual support to prevention. The fact that the OSAPG is mandated to act without excessive publicity and that the Security Council has the power to prevent the Special Advisor from attending its meetings suggests that the political commitment to prevention is shallow and that the various promises made in 2009 were made without cost or genuine commitment. Persuading states to commit themselves to prevention, both internally and externally, is therefore, not likely to affect real change if these commitments are predicated on the goodwill of states and do not involve meaningful political, judicial and institutional reform.

There are myriad studies on prevention and no shortage of political statements appealing for greater focus on this issue. These appeals invariably follow a fairly predictable format; an earnest endorsement of prevention as the most important aspect of the issue based on a reworking of the shibboleth 'prevention is better than cure', a lament about past cases (usually Rwanda) where ostensibly more could have been done earlier to stop carnage; the citation of studies demonstrating that addressing crises after they have erupted is financially more costly than doing so beforehand; a reference to the successful preventative mission in Macedonia; an assertion that early warning mechanisms need to be strengthened and finally, the articulation of a series of recommendations including the need to mobilize political will. It is, therefore, quite possible, and perhaps attractive, to retreat into this formulaic enunciation of 'shoulds' but ultimately of questionable utility, especially in the context of the actual existence of myriad conflicts which are taking place.

People obey laws either because they are convinced of their legitimacy, because they are forced to do so or because they fear the consequences of not doing so (Hurrell, 2005, p. 16). While we may be able to identify a large number of states, perhaps even a majority, that agree with the idea of respecting human rights internally and thus accept the legitimacy of a law on domestic human rights compliance, these are generally not the states which are going to commit egregious intra-state atrocities. It is those states run by governments which, for a variety of reasons, do not accept the legitimacy of international rules on intra-state human rights that are likely to commit intra-state mass atrocities. We are thus left with the latter two options with respect to dealing with this group, namely, coercion or compliance through fear of punishment. If R2P is increasingly weakening its emphasis on contriving a means of effectively halting mass atrocities then these two options are no longer available and thus the focus on prevention maybe, as Weiss claims, 'politically correct but counterproductive' (2011, p. 1). Those who reject the legitimacy of international human rights norms cannot possibly feel compelled to comply with these rights if there is no mechanism for enforcement. Thus, shifting the emphasis of R2P away from enforcement to prevention is not only idealistic but also liable to be ineffectual.

There is undoubtedly some merit to the argument that debates on humanitarian intervention often neglect to interrogate the international, regional and national contexts. In particular the fundamental international inequality which is behind much of the problems in so-called 'failed states' and 'trouble zones' is often overlooked and the violence appears to have erupted solely because of endogenous factors. Certainly, in broad terms any putative solution to the perennial cycle of large-scale intra-state crises must include provisions and recommendations for substantial reform of the international system (both economic and political) that would help prevent the societal tensions that lead to conflict. But while we await this theoretical panacea and its implementation, we must contrive an effective means of responding to crises once they have erupted.

Chapter 5

Political Will and Non-Intervention

To a striking extent, advocates of R2P have come to predicate its entire utility on changing the disposition of statesmen by pressurizing them into doing the right thing. R2P emerged at a time when the laws and institutions governing and regulating the use of force had lost credibility and there was a general mood amenable to the idea of reform. Rather than building on this widespread acceptance that the system required change, R2P has adopted a strategy which has ignored systemic reform in favour of moral advocacy. This strategy requires a focus on altering the collective political will and the humanitarian impulses of world leaders. In the words of the Global Centre for R2P the challenge is to create sufficient momentum to generate the 'will and imagination that will make mass atrocities a thing of the past' (2009a). This is quite obviously an extremely ambitious and onerous task. In this chapter, I argue that we must have reservations about R2P if it is this heavily dependent on something as transitory as political will and the disposition of statesmen.

I argue that, while it is perhaps comforting to think that eloquent appeals to governments to 'do something' will be effective, there is little empirical basis to suggest this will be the case given that since 1945 many grandiose declarations and slogans – most obviously 'Never Again!' issued in relation to the Holocaust and genocide more generally – have been of little practical utility. There has certainly been no lack of calls for a more humane disposition but this has not translated into a collective will to act humanly. The depressing litany of inaction, what Simon Chesterman describes as 'inhumanitarian nonintervention' (2003, p. 54), is a function of a *lack* of political will and this, rather than any political or legal restrictions, was the cause of the collective inertia in the face of the Rwandan genocide and arguably all other instances when the international community failed to respond to an intra-state mass atrocity. Why this reluctance to accept a responsibility for the welfare of people suffering egregious human rights violations in other states should now dissipate in the face of the emergence of R2P is unclear. Far from R2P having catalysed a change in the way intra-state crises are dealt with, the international response to the crisis in Darfur suggested that, as UN Secretary-General Kofi Annan claimed, 'we had learnt nothing from Rwanda' (Fisher, 2007, p. 103). The focus on 'generating political will' has led to the emergence of a plethora of NGO's specifically committed to promoting R2P and while these organizations have succeeded in raising the profile of R2P and cementing its place within the international political lexicon, it will be demonstrated that the capacity of such groups to affect real change is limited.

Additionally, I argue that the fact that states consider their own national interests when deciding whether or not to intervene in a particular situation is neither necessarily immoral or amoral, and certainly not surprising. Indeed, the primary duty of all states is to promote the welfare and security of their own citizens and it is not indefensible to determine that if particular intervention would imperil the citizenry's welfare, either financially or in terms of national security, it should not be undertaken. Thus, when advocates of R2P focus on moral arguments to pressurize states into taking action they are not engaging in a one-way moral discourse whereby 'acting morally' and 'doing the right thing' necessarily means intervening; states can advance strong, and indeed morally sound, arguments in defence of non-intervention. The notion that if states refuse to 'send in the troops' they are behaving immorally is not, therefore, axiomatic.

The centrality of political will

For all the furore and debate generated by R2P, its efficacy is ultimately dependent on one variable: political will. This central issue has often been obscured by the various debates about R2P's 'pillars', 'thresholds', and 'true meaning' and while there is genuine need for clarification on many of these issues, they are collectively and ultimately dependent on the exercise of political will.

Supporters of R2P have argued that the idea's most important innovation was to shift the focus from the international community's 'right to intervene' to the host state's 'responsibility to protect'. This realignment certainly changed the discourse and the terms of the debate and did much to consolidate the laudable notion that state sovereignty is not a right devoid of concomitant responsibilities. While this rejection of absolutist conceptions of sovereign inviolability is to be welcomed, no one has suggested that this reassertion of the state's internal responsibilities would in itself catalyse a new disposition amongst the world's states whereby, conscious of their responsibility, they would endeavour to protect their citizens from mass atrocities. If this was the expectation, then clearly there would have been no need to articulate guidelines on the international community's responsibility to protect when, in the words of the ICISS, 'the state in question is unwilling or unable to halt or avert [serious harm]' (ICISS, 2001a, p. xi). Therefore, there is an implicit acknowledgment within R2P's framework that all states will not abide by their domestic responsibility, either wilfully or through incapacity. The question of political will with respect to a state's internal policies is, therefore, (rightly) assumed to be transitory and of widely varying intensity; we may assume that Sweden, for example, has sufficient political will to exercise its domestic responsibilities but we cannot make similar assumptions about Myanmar, Zimbabwe, Israel or Iran. Since it is implicit in R2P that the political will to exercise domestic responsibilities is invariably lacking in certain cases, the question of political will is, therefore, most pertinent with respect to the prescriptions regarding the international community's response and it is this aspect of R2P – Pillar 3 in Ban Ki-Moon's 2009 formulation (2009a, p. 9) – that is the focus of this chapter.

'A discretionary entitlement'

Chapter 3 demonstrated that R2P has not altered international law or the means by which international law is enforced. The structural configuration and operational procedures of the UN remain unchanged and this means that compliance with, and the enforcement of, international laws and treaties is primarily a matter for states, as there are no international institutions analogous to the domestic police and judiciary. As Frank Berman noted, 'Faced with the truism ... that the international legal system lacks any general machinery to sanction breaches of its rules, the vital significance of patterns of voluntary compliance becomes immediately apparent' (2007, p. 157). This clearly has implications for the internal aspect of R2P – insofar as the protection of populations from mass atrocities may well be a responsibility but it is in essence voluntarily adhered to – but also in terms of the external aspect of R2P.

If compliance with international law is indeed a matter of 'voluntary compliance' then, one would assume, there must by definition be a lack of international mechanisms for enforcing international law. This is, however, only partially true. It is not the case that states can treat their citizens anyway they please safe in the knowledge that they will never face international sanction, executed in accordance with international law as opposed to unilateral vigilante-type intervention. As discussed at length in Chapter 3, the Security Council is empowered to take action to enforce compliance with UN law under Chapter VII of the Charter provided the P5 determine that a situation constitutes a threat to international peace and security. The problem, however, is that there is no obligation incumbent on the Security Council to do so. The P5 may choose to act under Chapter VII but this is dependent on their collective judgement. This of course begs the question; on what basis does the Security Council decide whether to take action? The answer, unfortunately, is political expediency; the P5's response to any particular alleged or clear breech of the law is entirely a function of their respective interests and there are no binding rules they must adhere to, apart from minor procedural regulations. In addition, there is no provision in the Charter, or supplementary international law, for initiating a juridical review of the decisions made by the Security Council (ICISS, 2001a, p. 50). The enforcement of the international laws outlined in the Charter, therefore, is essentially at the discretion of the P5 and thus the application of R2P is ultimately dependent on whether the P5 have a collective interest in – or are at least not opposed to – halting a particular looming or actual mass atrocity. This is manifestly not a propitious situation.

The creation of the Security Council was a conscious acknowledgement that power was a factor in international relations and one which had to be formally recognized in the new international legal system (Bosco, 2009, pp. 10–38). The UN system, of course, was designed by the victorious Allies, particularly the US, the UK and the Soviet Union, who reserved significant competencies for themselves, most notably the veto powers of the P5, described by Gerry Simpson as a form of 'legalised hegemony' (2004, p. 68). The powers vested in the P5 are the most obvious manifestation of Hedley Bull's assessment of legal systems, which, he argues will always, 'serve the interests of the ruling or dominant elements of the society more adequately than it serves the interests of the others' (2002, p. 53). The new organization could only function, it was suggested by the Great Powers in 1945, if it reflected, rather than sought to limit, the post-Second World War political hierarchy. As Herbert Briggs noted, the framers of the UN Charter sought to ensure that the new organization would 'work with, rather than in opposition to, the realities of power' (1945, p. 670). Likewise Dimitris Bourantonis notes that the permanent members of the Security Council were delegated a 'privileged position' and a 'superior status' on the basis that this was necessary to ensure these states would 'offer their political, military, technological and financial support' lest the organization as a whole collapse (2007, p. 6). The power of the Security Council at the zenith of the new system and the constitutional competencies at its disposal were particularly evident with respect to two features of the P5's power; their entitlement to sanction action under Chapter VII and the veto.

The structure of the new organization and the lack of judicial review of Security Council decision making meant that the provisions of Chapter VII were, in effect, a matter for the P5 to conceptualize and utilize as they saw fit. As Julie Mertus observed, 'the Security Council was left free to *interpret* what it meant to promote international peace and security' (2009, p. 98). The veto, additionally, ensured that each member of the P5 had the ability to block any other member's preferred response to a particular situation. It also, of course, served as a means by which the P5 acquired 'the legal and constitutional weapon with which they could defend their interests and position' (Bourantonis, 2007, p. 7). Given these powers, Nigel White's description of the P5 as 'a realist core in an institutionalist framework – a political core in a legal regime' is clearly accurate (2004, p. 666).

The Security Council does, of course, exercise its power within the Charter's stipulated framework. The Security Council's powers, therefore, technically, 'cannot be unlimited' (White, 2004, p. 646). In 1948 the International Court of Justice (ICJ) acknowledged the formal constraints acting upon the

Security Council; '[the] political character of an organ cannot release it from the observance of the treaty provisions established by the Charter when they constitute limitations on its powers or criteria for its judgments' (Gowlland-Debbas, 2000, p. 304). More recently in the 1995 Tadic case, the Appeals Chamber of the International Criminal Tribunal for the former Yugoslavia declared that the Security Council must only take action, 'within the limits of the Purposes and Principles of the Charter' (*Prosecutor* v. *Tadic*, 1995, p. 43). Nonetheless, despite these formal legal constraints, in reality the Security Council has acted as the principal interpreter of the Charter's rules and hence its own powers. During the negotiations on the establishment of the UN at San Francisco in 1945, Greece proposed that the ICJ be designated as the sole interpreter of the Charter but this was rejected. This has meant that, in practice, 'the Charter is what the principal organs do' (Franck, 2005, p. 206).

The vast corpus of human rights law lack independent enforcement mechanisms and are reliant on the Charter's provisions. These provisions, covered under Chapter VII, are essentially ill-suited to being applied to intra-state crises. Even if one maintains that Chapter VII, imperfect as it is, *can* be applied to intra-state crises there remains a key barrier to enforcement, namely the interests of the P5. Unless the P5 agree, no enforcement action can be ordered. An example is provided by the provisions of the 1948 Genocide Convention. Article 8 of the Convention states:

> Any Contracting Party may call upon the competent organs of the United Nations to take such action under the Charter of the United Nations as they consider appropriate for the prevention and suppression of acts of genocide or any of the other acts enumerated in article III.

In practice the 'competent organ' of the UN is the Security Council. Thus, if states believe that genocide is occurring and wish to stop it, the matter is referred to the Security Council which then decides what action, if indeed any, to take. By virtue of their veto power the P5 have the *discretion* to take action; there is no obligation incumbent on the P5 to act when a situation is deemed to constitute a threat to international peace and security and, therefore, the Security Council's response to a situation is the product of political calculations rather than legal principles or procedures. The international legal system's effectiveness is, therefore, necessarily predicated on political expediency.

As an illustration of the above, the crisis in Darfur which began in 2003 has been described as genocide by many NGOs and states (including the US) and referred to the Security Council. While the Security Council determined that the situation constituted a threat to international peace and security, and certain members agreed that the Sudanese government was orchestrating the atrocities, no action was mandated by the Security Council without the consent of the Sudanese government. Indeed, in 2004 in his testimony before the United States Senate Foreign Relations Committee, Secretary of State Colin Powell stated: 'genocide has been committed in Darfur and ... the Government of Sudan and the Jingaweit [sic] bear responsibility'. Yet, he subsequently added, 'no new action is dictated by this determination. We have been doing everything we can to get the Sudanese Government to act responsibly. So let us not be too preoccupied with this designation' (US Department of State, 2004). From a strict legal perspective, Powell was correct; his assertion that genocide was occurring only compelled the US to refer the matter to the Security Council – which they did – rather than to take further action. As Yoram Dinstein notes, 'no state acting alone (or even jointly with like-minded allies) has a legal option of resorting to force against another State, with a view to averting genocide or bringing it to an end' (2005, pp. 72–3). Thus, the US's justification for doing no more than referring the matter to the Security Council rather than acting to halt the 'genocide' was arguably legally sound given that the dominant legal view is that a state's acknowledgement of the occurrence of genocide does not require it to take direct action (Schabas, 2000, p. 495). The Security Council is not bound by either the Charter or the Genocide Convention to take any action and thus the routinely derided response to Darfur was the function of political calculations rather than a dereliction of a legal duty. Indeed, Chesterman argues that interventions do not take place simply because 'states choose not to undertake them' (2003, p. 54). The key determinant is, therefore, political will, especially amongst the P5.

The centrality of discretion, therefore, militates against consistency. The obvious solution to this is to reform the decision making process at the Security Council to limit discretion and introduce measures which would ensure an automatic response. Reforming the Security Council – both in terms of its composition and powers – however, has proved notoriously difficult, not least because of the P5's implacable opposition to any diminution of their power or constraints on their freedom. Indeed, Bourantonis notes that as the clamour for reform of the Security Council grew in the post-Cold War era the P5, 'reached a tacit agreement and adopted a common stance on the reform issue: to resist claims for reform and to do their utmost to prevent discussion on the subject in the UN' (2007, p. 35). The issue of reforming the UN system is the subject of Chapter 8; it suffices at this stage to be clear on two points. First, the Security Council is under no obligation to take action under Chapter VII, not because of a flaw in the constitutional design of the UN but because of a conscious decision to recognize the influence of power within international relations/law; second, R2P has not altered the prevailing systemic configuration and its effectiveness is, therefore, ultimately – and totally – dependent on the political will of the P5. The Security Council may well have included references to R2P in a number of resolutions since 2001 but, as Cheriff Bassiouni notes, 'For sure, many hortatory statements have found their way into preambles of Security Council resolutions … but no resolution posits the *duty* to act in order to protect or to prevent' (2009, p. 34). What action the Security Council takes, is, therefore, purely a matter of political discretion.

The need to mobilize political will

The centrality of political will has been acknowledged by many who have spoken in support of R2P. Evan's asserts that his belief in R2P is sustained by his conviction that 'good people, good governments, and good governance will eventually prevail over bad' (2008, p. 7). He acknowledges: 'Without the exercise of political will, by the relevant policy makers at the relevant time, almost none of the things for which this book has argued will actually happen' (ibid, p. 223). Likewise, Bellamy warns that if political will evaporates, R2P will falter (2009, p. 119). In a similar vein Lee Feinstein, effusively praised the 2005 World Summit agreement on R2P but warned that what was now required was, 'the political will to back it up' otherwise the *Outcome*

Document would constitute 'humanitarian hypocrisy' (2007). During the 2009 General Assembly debate on R2P, a number of states also acknowledged that the implementation of R2P was dependant on political will: indicatively, the Canadian ambassador argued that the efficacy of the concept was dependent on 'the goodwill of the states', Switzerland emphasized the need for 'political will at the right time', while the US ambassador ended her speech by extolling states to 'work to summon the courage of our convictions – and the will to act' (Canada, 2009; Switzerland, 2009, p. 6; United States of America, 2009, p. 2).

Given the acknowledged centrality of political will, supporters of R2P have argued that great effort must be made to 'mobilize' political will. According to Samantha Power, 'If R2P is to become an influential international norm, it will be because supporters of the concept understand that governments will rarely exercise their responsibility naturally – they will have to be pressured to do so' (2009, p. x). Likewise David Scheffer suggests that the message of R2P should be '[championed by] school children and their parents ... stamped on bumper stickers and broadcast through enlightened corporate sponsors' so that 'policymakers ultimately comprehend this siren call of their peoples' (2009, p. 95). Evans, acknowledging that political will is presently lacking in many quarters, reflected: 'we just have to express the fervent hope that even if leaders are not always born, and only on very rare occasions are elected, they can at least on occasion be made' (2008, p. 241). These arguments are predicated on two assumptions; first that states are susceptible to the blandishments of global and domestic civil society; second that the absence of political will to act in defence of oppressed peoples abroad is axiomatically ethically wrong. The following two sections critique each assumption in turn.

The false promise of benevolent internationalism

When the World Summit *Outcome Document* was agreed in 2005 Jack Straw, then UK Foreign Secretary, commenting on the provisions related to R2P, stated: 'If this new responsibility had been in place a decade ago, thousands in Srebrenica and Rwanda would have been saved' (Wheeler, 2005, p. 102). Aside from the obvious fact that it is impossible to state with this degree of certainty that past events would have occurred differently if certain variables had changed, Straw's claim is highly dubious. The implication of Straw's assertion is clear; the international response to the Rwandan genocide was lamentable because of the prevailing international norms/laws which prevented a timely and effective response. Now that these obstacles have been removed, we are assured, the altruistic impulses previously inhibited by international law can manifest. The underlying premise, therefore, is that law has finally caught up with morality. There is, however, scant evidence to support this.

The history of rhetoric

International history is replete with lofty declarations that have had little practical impact due to the fact that they were predicated on political will. Issues from climate change to poverty reduction have served as principles which world leaders have willingly endorsed but subsequently ignored safe in the knowledge that by virtue of the nature of the international law both compliance and enforcement were a matter of discretion. There has been, as Thomas Weiss noted, 'a dramatic disconnect between political reality and pious rhetoric' (2007b, p. 7).

The fate of the 1948 Genocide Convention is most illustrative of this trend; while the provisions of the Convention were lauded at the time, in 2001 UN Secretary-General Kofi Annan stated: '[the convention] has, for all practical purposes, remained a dead letter' (2001b). This was, of course, evident during the Rwandan genocide when states with the capacity to halt the massacres did little to help. As Romeo Daillaire noted, 'As long as these states procrastinated, bickered, and cynically pursued their own selfish foreign politics, the UN and UNAMIR could do little to stop the killing' (Shawcross, 2000, p. 119). The problem identified by Dallaire was not the absence of legal means by which the carnage could be arrested but rather the lack of will to utilize the means available. Indeed, Wheeler's analysis of the response to the genocide found that the idea that international law somehow prevented states from intervening – as suggested by Jack Straw – is simply untrue (2006, p. 36). The inaction was overwhelmingly a function of the absence of political will, particularly amongst the P5.

In the aftermath of the Rwandan genocide further iterations

of 'Never Again!' peppered memorial speeches for years, yet in the face of the next major atrocity to come near to the scale of the murder in Rwanda, the international reaction was sadly all too similar. Hugo Slim rightly described Darfur as the, 'test case by which to judge whether the international community has got any better at responding to genocide and crimes against humanity' (2004, p. 811). The evidence suggests the international community failed this test; indicatively, Lee Feinstein reflected, 'If Darfur is the first "test case" of the responsibility to protect there is no point in denying that the world has failed the entry exam' (2006, p. 38). Indeed, according to the UK Select Committee on Foreign Affairs, 'the international community's response to the events in Darfur has been slow and inadequate ... lives have been lost unnecessarily as a result' (Berdal, 2008, p. 184). John Mueller described the response as 'little more than huffing and puffing' (2005, pp. 122–3), while Dallaire argued that 'Western governments are still approaching it with the same lack of priority [as they did in 1994]. In the end, it receives the same intuitive reaction: "What's in it for us? Is it in our 'national' interest?"' (2004). Perhaps most illustrative of the shameful nature of the international response was that Sudanese President, Omar al-Bashir, was accused by the Special Prosecutor of the International Criminal Court of orchestrating genocide, war crimes and crimes against humanity yet, the international community, through the Security Council, refused to initiate any action on Darfur without his consent.

The fact that many states were willing to accept that the killings in Darfur constituted genocide and yet were unwilling to take effective action highlights the inherent weakness of the Genocide Convention. Evidently the legal advice received by the Bush administration in 2004 was that using the term 'genocide' 'would not obligate the US to anything beyond ... calling "upon the competent organs of the United Nations to take such action"' (Mayroz, 2008, p. 367). This willingness to acknowledge that genocide was occurring and yet still not take robust action was arguably more shameful than the reaction to the Rwandan genocide. As Weiss argued:

> At least in 1994 there was an attempt to maintain the fiction that no such horror was under way ... If we recognize the existence of genocide and do nothing ... the 1948 Convention ...

is literally not worth the paper on which it is reproduced. (2007a, p. 54)

The weakness of the convention stems from the fact that it is enforceable only when certain states, namely the P5, want to take action. It is hardly surprising then that at various times genocide has occurred largely unabated. This lends credence to Cherif Bassiouni's reflection on the efficacy of international human rights legislation: 'legal experience demonstrates that the enunciation of rights without concomitant remedies are pyrrhic pronouncements, and that remedies without enforcement are empty promises' (2009, p. 41). Given that R2P coheres with, rather than alters or amends, the existing legal architecture it logically constitutes the latest example of the 'enunciation of rights without concomitant remedies'. Ironically, Evans, perhaps the most vocal supporter of R2P, criticizes the Genocide Convention on the basis that it was little more than words; 'It was almost as if, with the signing of the Genocide Convention the task of addressing man-made atrocities was seen as complete: it was rarely invoked and never applied' (Evans, 2009, p. 17). Why R2P should somehow avoid a similar fate is unclear unless one is of the view that something has changed which today makes it more difficult for states to make empty promises.

R2P: a new normative force?

It seems largely irrefutable that the historical record shows that states have very often lacked sufficient political will to respond to egregious intra-state crises in the manner they previously promised to. While this is to be regretted it does not necessarily follow that this means they never will; we should be cautious about inferring future trends from history. It may well be the case that something *has* changed with the emergence of R2P which enhances the efficacy of this contemporary commitment to prevent and halt intra-state atrocities. This is certainly the perspective of many of R2P's most vocal proponents. Evans claimed that since the commitment to R2P in the 2005 World Summit there has been a 'reasonably steady trickle of good news' (2008, 50) while Bellamy has argued that there is a casual link between the 'international activism' generated by, and centred around, R2P and a diminution in incidents of mass atrocities

(2009, p. 2). R2P is, therefore, conceived as more vital than treaties or conventions by virtue of the fact that it is an evolving normative force as well as a political commitment. This force comprises the declarations made by states, such as two paragraphs in the 2005 World Summit *Outcome Document*, but also the constant vocal advocacy of NGO's specifically established to 'apply targeted pressure on key actors within governments ... about why R2P is important, why they should care and how it matters' (Considine and Sonner, 2009).

UN Secretary General Ban Ki-Moon addressed the issue of political will in his report to the General Assembly prior to the 2009 debate on R2P. Citing the international responses to the crises in Darfur, the Democratic Republic of the Congo (DRC) and Somalia, he reflected, 'It is true that we have yet to develop the tools or display the will to respond consistently and effectively to all emergencies relating to the responsibility to protect.' Yet, he subsequently claimed: 'Nonetheless, when confronted with crimes or violations relating to the responsibility to protect or their incitement, today the world is less likely to look the other way than in the last century' (Ki-Moon, 2009a, p. 24). In defence of this optimistic claim he cited the role of Office of the Special Adviser on the Prevention of Genocide (OSAPG) in defusing the crisis in the Ivory Coast in November 2004 when the then Special Adviser Juan Méndez warned the Ivorian government against the proliferation of hate speech. Following Méndez's intervention the inflammatory speeches ceased. Ban Ki-Moon also cited the international response to the crisis in Kenya following the presidential election in December 2007. When rioting broke out after the results were declared, resulting in up to 1,000 fatalities and over 250,000 displaced persons, Francis Deng, on behalf of the OSAPG, utilized the language of R2P and called for an end to the violence, warning political leaders they could be held accountable for violations of international law committed in response to inflammatory speeches. The result was the banning of live broadcasts during the crisis.

While these interventions evidently had the desired effect and the violence diminished they do not necessarily support Ban Ki-Moon's claim, 'today the world is less likely to look the other way than in the last century' or, more importantly, that the existence of R2P is a causal factor in this new disposition. Ban Ki-Moon, indeed, went on to acknowledge that the incitement of racial hatred was outlawed in the 1969 International Convention on the Elimination of All Forms of Racial Discrimination. R2P didn't, therefore, provide international actors with a previously unavailable tool with which to threaten the respective governments in either case. The Security Council mandated action against Libya in March 2011 was, of course, lauded as the most obvious manifestation of R2P's influence (Ki-Moon, 2011; Thakur, 2011). As I discussed at length in Chapter 1, however, that the Security Council mandated the intervention in Libya may have been both surprising and welcome but it does not necessarily prove the efficacy of R2P. While the term 'responsibility to protect' was certainly used during the course of the international engagement in these three cases, R2P can only be considered a casual factor in the outcome if the absence of the alleged 'norm' would have precluded international negotiators from applying pressure to the Ivorian or Kenyan authorities on the basis that they had a duty to halt the violence and hate speech, or from sanctioning military action against Gaddafi's regime. Clearly this is not the case; prior to the emergence of R2P, international pressure was brought to bear on governments implicated in internal conflicts and repression as evidenced by the Chapter VII resolutions sanctioned during the 1990s. Even during the Cold War there were a number of instances – though arguably too few – of UN-mandated action taken against internal repression, such as the action taken against the racist regimes in Rhodesia and South Africa in 1977. Thus, the evidence presented by Ban Ki-Moon to support his claim – 'today the world is less likely to look the other way than in the last century' – is not convincing. Indeed, in other contemporary instances when states have turned violently against their people, the absence of political will to robustly enforce R2P has been readily apparent. Steve Crawshaw of Human Rights Watch criticized the international community's response to the violence in Sri Lanka in 2009 noting 'there was a failure to address the Sri Lankan issue and that I think can be said to be indicative of where the gap between the words and the reality is' (2009). Likewise, Herbet Weiss's analysis of the curiously under publicized conflict in the DRC pointed to the protracted nature of the violence and the extent to which this could have been halted, 'if the will had been there, if the responsibility to protect had meant something substantial' (2009, p. 127). Of course, by far the most obvious counter to the claim that the disposition of states has altered significantly in the contemporary era, or even that states are more receptive to the advocacy of domestic and global civil society, was the response to the atrocities in Darfur.

The protracted violence in Darfur clearly challenges claims that the emergence of R2P has catalysed a change in political will and the way internal crises are addressed. The crisis, which began in 2003, was notable for both its savagery but also its duration; while the Rwandan genocide lasted some 100 days, five years after the crisis had erupted in Darfur a report drafted by 15 humanitarian NGOs found that in the first ten months of 2008 some 290,000 people had been displaced – 40,000 in September alone – while some four million required humanitarian assistance (Coalition of NGOs on Darfur, 2008, pp. 7–8). The UN Special Rapporteur on Sudan, Sima Samar, reported in September 2008 that extreme violence, including the systemic sexual abuse of women and children, was continuing, in her words, 'almost unabated throughout Darfur' (United Nations General Assembly, 2008, p. 12). Yet, despite these grim reports, in a paradoxical twist, certain supporters of R2P have defended the lack of robust international intervention in Darfur as somehow tragically prudent. Evans, while acknowledging the scale of the crisis and the governments' complicity in it, argued that more robust measures would have made the situation worse and called for 'the application of sustained diplomatic, economic, and legal pressure to change the cost-benefit balance of the regime's calculation' (2009, p. 61). The argument that coercive intervention would make matters worse – described by Evans as 'very strong' – is not universally endorsed, however. Bellamy argued that it would have been possible to use air power and light infantry to protect those huddled in camps and ensure the safe passage of humanitarian aid (2006b, p. 225). Similarly a report by the US National Defense University found that a military intervention would have achieved success (Gompert *et al.*, 2005, p. 26).

It has also been argued, however, that R2P *did* alter the international response by virtue of the fact that the P5 states regularly made public statements about Darfur and eventually made reference to R2P in a resolution which criticized the government in Khartoum and sanctioned the deployment of UN peacekeepers (Mayroz, 2008). Yet, the single mention of R2P in resolution

1674 was hardly a watershed, especially given the fact that the military force was not actually sanctioned for another year (Pace, Deller and Chhatpar, 2009, p. 224).

It is disingenuous to suggest that the crisis in Darfur somehow does not constitute evidence of R2P's limitations. According to Bassiouni, 'if the responsibility to protect existed' then troops would have been sent to Darfur, without or without the Sudanese governments permission 'long ago' (2009, p. 35), while Schulz describes Darfur as R2P's 'ground zero' (2009, p. 150). It is, therefore, difficult to sustain the claim that the international response to the greatest crisis to have erupted during R2P's lifetime is not illustrative of the efficacy of R2P.

The international response to Darfur is difficult to defend and most accept it was lamentable. This can be ascribed to the nefarious and/or anachronistic agenda of world leaders wedded to *realpolitik* and cited as evidence for the need for the mobilization of global civil society. This argument can hardly be made in the context of the situation in Darfur, however, without becoming counterfactual, given the massive international campaign launched to 'save Darfur' which forced the issue to the top of the international political agenda and the front pages of the global media (Hehir, 2008a, pp. 65–70). The logical assessment of the crisis in Darfur is that global civil society proved unable to significantly alter the disposition of states. To accept this, however, calls into question the entire normative edifice of R2P advocacy. To avoid this fate, many have articulated often contradictory analyses and prescriptions. For example, Samantha Power asserted: 'the stark reality is that little has been done to stop the slaughter in Darfur. Neither a finding of genocide by the US secretary of state nor a spirited affirmation of the responsibility to protect seems to have made a meaningful difference.' Yet, she later declared: 'the anti-atrocity movement … made it impossible for Bush to look away' (2009, viii–ix). If 'little has been done to stop the slaughter' what are we to make of the fact that NGO's 'made it impossible for Bush to look the other way'? That Bush looked and decided to do little? If forcing Bush to look results in the same response as him looking the other way one may well wonder whether there was any point in making it 'impossible to look the other way'. The defence routinely advanced by proponents of the public-outrage-compels-action idea, or the normative thesis, as I previously termed this view (Hehir, 2008a), is that while the tangible results of popular agitation were slight, the situation would have been much worse without the mobilization of this campaign (Mayroz, 2008; Simmons and Donnellan, 2009, p. 177). This is doubtless cold comfort to the hundreds of thousands of dead, injured and displaced and a statement that is easily made and almost by definition impossible to prove.

The campaign to pressurize states into taking more robust action – not necessarily military intervention – to protect the hundreds of thousands suffering in Darfur must, therefore, provide reasonable grounds for doubting the efficacy of R2P. Clearly states, particularly the P5, were largely unmoved by the mobilization of global civil society. If R2P is ultimately predicated on changing the political will of world leaders through the mobilization of global civil society, then it is evidently based on dubious assumptions as to the influence of global civil society. The ICISS research committee itself acknowledged that the 'soft-power' of NGOs 'is often exaggerated' (ICISS, 2001b, p. 31) which is not surprising given that the actual number of people involved in human rights-oriented NGO's is quite low. William Schulz estimates that in the US there are approximately 50,000 people active in such organizations which is less than 0.02 per cent of the total population, a figure dwarfed by those involved in other issues such as environmentalism and anti-racism (2009, p. 146). It is, therefore, far from clear that moral pressure advanced by global civil society can exercise sufficient leverage to compel states to alter their foreign policy priorities. Given that R2P is, as many of its key proponents accept, dependent on the political will of statesmen, this has obviously troubling implications for its future efficacy.

The moral defence of non-intervention

The debate about humanitarian intervention and R2P is often framed in terms of progressive moralism versus conservative (if not anachronistic) realism. That a state's decision not to intervene in response to a mass atrocity is morally wrong is often treated as axiomatic by proponents of R2P and the discourse on morality and intervention invariably presumes that for a state to be judged to have acted in a way that is morally correct, or at least defensible, in response to a particular intra-state conflict, some form of intervention must have taken place. Appealing to states to act morally is thus predicated on an implicit and often explicit assumption that this constitutes some form of intervention. The ICISS report, for example, talks of the need to 'produce arguments appealing to morality' (2001a, p. 72) while Bellamy argues that when crises reach a particular nadir the nature of the international response is dependent on 'the strength of individual leader's moral commitments' (2009, p. 3). In both cases the championing of moral action is implicitly held to denote intervention. Likewise, in his assessment of the role of morality in international relations, Chris Brown asserted, 'there is no viable moral rule that can tell statespersons what is the right thing to do in response to particular circumstances. They must exercise their judgement as best they can'. Despite this rejection of a extant universal moral code, Brown maintains, using the example of the Rwandan genocide, that the only way to prevent inaction in face of excessive internal state aggression is 'for those who have the power to act to develop the kind of moral sensitivity that will enable them to recognise what is the right thing to do in such appalling circumstances, and the strength of character to act upon this recognition' (2003, p. 47).

Many advocates of R2P place great emphasis on detailing various instances of deadly violence intermingling personal anecdotes with grim statistics. There is, in essence, a very obviously emotive character to many of the pro-R2P arguments. As an illustration, it is striking just how many books extolling the virtues of R2P have images of suffering – usually of black women and/or children – on the cover. The implication is obvious; no right-minded person would want such carnage to occur again; R2P is the only viable means to prevent and halt such atrocities and thus opposition to R2P is equated with callousness. There are two disconcerting aspects to this line of argument. First is the exploitation of the very victims these advocates seek to 'save'. Whether undertaken consciously or not, referring to the victims of mass atrocities to defend one's proposals constitutes a form of emotive bullying. This is a phenomenon critiqued at length by Ann Orford who decries the instrumental usage of 'the bodies of massacred women, children and men' as both cynical and ahistorical (2008, p. 218). Second, there is an inherently curious juxtaposition of a grim history of violence and apathy and a remarkably simple, yet ostensibly viable, solution. We are routinely told that 'something must be done' to halt the litany of atrocity and inaction but in the end we are assured that this 'something' demands – remarkably – no substantive institutional or legal change but rather just a change of heart. States *should* treat their populations better. If they don't the Great Powers *should* intervene. If the Great Powers don't want to 'we' *should* tell them to and if we are vocal enough they will (Scheffer, 2009, p. 95).

This section argues, however, that this presumed coherence between non-intervention and moral failure is fundamentally flawed; a state's decision not to intervene may well have a compelling moral basis. This has fundamental implications for humanitarian intervention and R2P, as recognizing the limited nature of a state's moral responsibility demonstrates that states cannot reasonably be expected to act as 'moral agents'. The implications of this serves as the basis for the proposal advanced in Chapter 8.

The most commonly articulated ethical defences of non-intervention are first, the claim that states should not engage in humanitarian intervention because it poses a threat to world order; second, that as human rights are not universal, external standards cannot be imposed on a sovereign state. As will be discussed in Chapter 6, these are not arguments I find compelling. Rather, the perspective advanced here in defence of non-intervention is that states are not moral actors in the international arena; the primary moral responsibility of states is to protect their own citizens and that there are times when to intervene to arrest a humanitarian catastrophe in another state would imperil domestic stability, security and welfare.

Moral duty?

In October 2001, Tony Blair stated that if a situation akin to Rwanda happened again 'we would have a moral duty to act' (Fisher, 2007, p. 102). This is both disingenuous and, more importantly, a principle which conflates moral cause with moral responsibility. Disingenuous because Blair himself previously admitted, quite understandably, in his famous 1999 Chicago speech made during the military intervention in Kosovo, that when weighing up how to respond to a particular situation he would consider whether, 'we have national interests involved' (Blair, 1999). This acknowledgement that national interests are considered before making a commitment to address a mass atrocity has been cited by some as evidence that humanitarian intervention is, in effect, inconceivable; intervention is always motivated by national interest (Chomsky, 1999). This implies that if a state, or group of states, has mixed motives for intervening, this precludes that intervention from being deemed humanitarian; I believe purity of motive is, however, an unreasonably onerous requirement. While I contend that for an intervention to be deemed humanitarian there must be at least a significant humanitarian motivation – in contrast to, for example, Wheeler (2002, p. 38) and Fernando Tesón (1998, pp. 106–7) – some degree of national interest surely does not fundamentally compromise the humanitarian credentials of a particular intervention (see also, Brown, 2001, p. 23; ICISS, 2001a, p. xii; Weiss, 2007a, p. 7). In essence, taking action to alleviate the suffering of others after considering your own national interests does not mean your action cannot be deemed humanitarian (Walzer, 2006, p. 26). Blair's assertion that he has a 'moral duty', however, by definition must be undermined by his previous claim that he would *choose* when to act. This explicit acknowledgement that he would *consider* taking action by definition means this is not in fact a *duty* he feels bound to fulfil. The fire brigade do not *consider* their interests when called to put out a fire; they are duty-bound to act. Blair's government's response to the crisis in Darfur, is indicative of this selective approach and a product of a deliberation process that compromises any notion of a 'duty'. Engaging in a deliberation process is not in itself amoral, however; it would be a dereliction of a governments national duty not to. As Schultz notes, 'the sad fact is ... even governments that care about human rights in the abstract are loathe to get their hands dirty if they see no direct tie to their strategic interests' (2009, p. 156). This is certainly a fact but whether it is a 'sad fact' is debatable.

States are normatively, and usually constitutionally, mandated to act on behalf of their citizens. While it is routinely stated in this context that states should always act in the 'national interest', what this constitutes is open to dispute and thus this prescription is of limited utility (Bull, 2002, p. 63). Obvious ideological, cultural and ethical differences exist with respect to the nature of the national interest and hence a state's responsibility to its own citizens. Nonetheless, all would at least agree with the general principle that states should ensure the welfare of their citizens and that this unquestionably comprises a primary aspect of 'the national interest'. Normatively, states are given this mandate by their citizens who entrust the government with this responsibility. Clearly, citizens of state A do not give their government a mandate to protect citizens in state B. They have no right to do so, only citizens of state B may ask state A to assume this responsibility, as indeed has happened through collective defence pacts such as NATO. Thus a functioning state is one which provides basic freedom from insecurity for its citizens, and a dereliction of duty in this respect rightly indicates state failure. We may certainly say that a state has acted morally if it intervenes to protect the loss of life abroad (provided of course that other criteria are met) but it does not follow that we can say that a state has not acted morally by not intervening. Intervention with positive moral consequences and impelled by moral impulses will by definition be morally laudable (though not necessarily prudent). Non-intervention, however, may also be a choice made on sound moral grounds and hence morally defensible. If, therefore, a state chooses a certain course of action (or inaction) on the basis of a balance of consequences judgement, that state has acted according to its moral responsibility. This may mean, in essence, that non-intervention is a morally defensible position. Thus, imploring a state to 'act morally' when faced with an intra-state mass atrocity is not necessarily synonymous, as some seem to imagine, with asking that state to intervene, militarily or otherwise, in the affairs of another state.

While an objective analysis of a particular intra-state crisis may determine that the actions of an oppressive regime or group are an egregious violation of another group's human rights, and hence halting the violence is morally defensible, it does not follow that parties external to the conflict must assume the responsibility to take the requisite moral action, unless this is their constitutional mandate. There is a fundamental difference between a situation demanding a response and demanding that a particular state respond.

Thus, if a state concludes that to intervene would imperil national security and/or domestic welfare it is entitled to decide not to do so and cannot reasonably be criticized for so doing. The state in question does not have the responsibility or duty to protect the citizens in the other states. We may say that certain human rights are inherent and inviolable; they are not awarded or regulated and individuals do not have to formally assume them. Rather, they constitute an unconditional, intrinsic facet of our humanity, as reflected in Articles 1, 2 and 3 of the UN Declaration of Human Rights. The same intrinsic quality cannot be ascribed to responsibility, however, which must by definition be assumed either as a consequence of one's actions or conscious choice. Legitimate responsibility for others, therefore, cannot be entrusted to an individual or an institution without their active consent. Unlike human rights, therefore, responsibility is a function of one's actions rather than an intrinsic quality. Thus, if we examine the international system in the context of human rights protection, we can clearly see that it comprises states that have formal responsibilities, but their primary responsibilities are to their own citizens. Therefore, in strictly positivist terms, there is no state with the formal responsibility to protect citizens in other states from genocide, war crimes, ethnic cleansing and crimes against humanity.

The only international actor which can plausibly be said to have a responsibility to protect citizens in other states is the UN Security Council. This is, however, a function of the new interpretation of Chapter VII which has emerged in the post-Cold War era rather than a constitutional provision within the Charter which mandates the Security Council to halt human rights abuses. Strictly speaking, therefore, the Security Council's mandate does not include a responsibility to protect citizens from abuse committed by their own governments, though it would be disingenuous for any permanent member of the Security Council to defend inaction on the grounds of having no formal responsibility to protect given the by-now widely understood expansion of Chapter VII's meaning. Nonetheless, the Security Council has been careful to invariably declare that their use of Chapter VII to mandate military intervention constituted an exceptional response rather than an act in accord with their understanding of their collective responsibility or duty (Chesterman, 2011a). This is a tacit acknowledgement that while the P5 have certain international responsibilities they do not necessarily trump their national interests and are thus neither obligations nor duties.

The key point, therefore, is that the primary responsibility of each state is to protect its own citizens. If a government determines that a particular intervention undertaken for the benefit of others would jeopardize the security or welfare of its own citizens, then its decision not to undertake that intervention is not necessarily devoid of moral justification. Intervention is necessarily expensive and dangerous and invariably demands a commitment to post-conflict reconstruction and stabilization which adds further costs to any putative intervention. Military mobilization, vast monetary expenditure, and long-term commitment, intrinsic to all interventions, by definition consume resources that would otherwise (ideally) be spent on national welfare. While the cosmopolitan ethic espoused by many of R2P's supporters is attractive, the world is divided into states with particular national responsibilities which, understandably, take priority. Demanding that states – whose primary constitutional and normative responsibility is to protect their own citizens – imperil their national security or expend vast monetary resources by coming to the aid of citizens in other states is, therefore, as well as being arguably naive, essentially unfair. Non-intervention is shameful only if it is absolutely clear that intervention would have resulted in very minor costs or if the responsibility to protect has been assumed by the third party to the conflict, or this third party was a catalyst for the eruption of conflict. The 2005 World Summit *Outcome Document* certainly includes a voluntary commitment on the part of the 'international community' to protect citizens in states where the host state is unable or unwilling to halt mass atrocities but the nature of this responsibility is nebulous. The key provision to 'take collective action ... on a case-by-case basis' clearly provides significant flexibility based on political calculations and does not constitute a general commitment to accept a responsibility to protect. It is difficult to imagine any national police force committing itself to respond to domestic violence 'on a case-by-case basis'. The police, normatively at least, are not mandated to choose when to exercise their responsibility; their *raison d'être* is to protect the weak and victimized regardless of the context or identity of the victims. States in the international system do not have anything like the same responsibility and are forced, by definition, to calculate the impact of any action they take externally on their citizen's welfare.

To illustrate, imagine that person X lives with his three children in an island country where there is no police and the only form of authority is a loose alliance comprised of the leaders of the five largest militias. This alliance is mandated to keep the peace between the five militias and prevent low-level conflicts from escalating. X knows that his neighbour beats his children; what should X do? X knows that the alliance will not intervene because they are not interested in domestic affairs and X's neighbour is not a member of their gangs. Should X take matters into his own hands and intervene? If X's neighbour is much weaker than X and he can easily restrain him when he beats his children then perhaps X should stop the abuse. If however, either X's neighbour is physically much stronger than him or has violent allies should X still intervene? To do so may imperil X's children as if X were to be killed, or so gravely injured that he could no longer earn a living, who would look after them? Even if X's neighbour is weaker than him is it really axiomatic that X should intervene? What happens after he stops the violence? Must he return every day to do so again? Should he stay in the house for an hour, a day, a week? Should X invite his neighbour's children to live with him? If so, for how long and does he have enough food to feed them and his own children? Clearly these are very difficult choices which comprise competing moral claims. If X was to decide that intervening would likely result in grave injury or death to himself, both of which would have negative consequences for his children, is it reasonable to criticize X for not doing so? I think not.

Some would disagree with my view, of course, and echo the sentiments of Saint Ambrose, who claimed, 'he who does not keep harm off a friend, if he can, is as much in fault as he who causes it' (Bellamy, 2006b, p. 24). Terry Nardin summarized, and defended, this position as, 'You shall not stand idly by, whoever you are, if you can provide effective assistance at reasonable cost and without neglecting other duties' (2003, p. 21). In the spirit of this enunciation, John Janzekovic claimed that we cannot criticize states alone for not stopping atrocities such as the genocide in Rwanda as 'We are all to blame for not responding directly and effectively to stop such activities ... Everyone is responsible for allowing severe violations of human rights to occur' (2006, p. 74). This may be an effective rallying cry but surely 'everyone' is an exaggeration; can children, the mentally ill, the imprisoned, and isolated groups such as the Amazonian tribes really be deemed responsible for allowing the

Rwandan genocide to occur? Leaving aside this exaggerated claim to return to the arguably more reasonable view espoused by Ambrose, it is important to note that his call for action does include the phrase 'if he can' thereby alluding to the possible existence of mitigating circumstances. One would reasonably assume that this denotes taking action that does not cost one's life or imperil the safety and welfare of one's dependants. Additionally, in the hypothetical example one need not conclude that X need literally do nothing; there are certain non-coercive measures he can, and perhaps morally should, take such as shunning his neighbour, alerting others to his neighbour's behaviour and providing comfort and support to his neighbour's children.

Thankfully this situation does not present itself in the majority of states in the West where if my neighbour beats his children I will ring the police. In this situation two actors have the key duties; my neighbour has the duty to protect his children, the police have a mandated duty to protect my neighbour's children in the event that he fails to do so. I, however, have no duty beyond ringing the police. If the police fail to halt the violence then they have failed to meet their duty on constitutional rather than moral grounds. Of course, there is nothing analogous to the police in the international system.

Using terms such as responsibility and moral imperative in the context of the system of sovereign states is, therefore, inherently problematic. Indeed, William Bain critiques the language employed by certain R2P supporters for conflating responsibility with obligation and duty. The latter constitutes an entirely different set of requirements from the former and demands the achievement of a more onerous set of justifications given the nature of 'obligation'. 'The idea of "responsibility"', Bain noted, 'does not of itself sustain the kind of action that the responsibility to protect norm demands' (2010, p. 26). Likewise Franck Berman asks 'if we are genuinely in the presence of a "right" ... where is the correlative obligation, and who has the legal quality to enforce it?' (2007, p. 160).

Proponents of R2P do not have a monopoly on morality; conceptualizing non-intervention as shameful, presupposes a responsibility or mandate when in fact no such mandate exists. Nonetheless, while states have no moral responsibility to imperil themselves for the benefit of citizens in other states, this can mean, and many times has meant, that mass atrocities have been committed while the world literally watched; this cannot be an acceptable state of affairs. In the hypothetical example above, while I contend that in this situation X does not have a responsibility to protect his neighbour's children to the detriment of his own, I do believe that X does have a responsibility to work towards reforming the system which has forced this difficult choice upon him by, for example, working to establish a legal code outlawing violence against children and a police force mandated to enforce this. To articulate the above rebuttal of states' responsibility to protect citizens in other states without subsequently advancing a means by which effective action can be undertaken by an authority constitutionally mandated to halt egregious intra-state atrocities is both unhelpful and, ultimately, an evasion of the pressing moral cause which demands some resolution. This alternative means of addressing intra-state crises is the focus of Part II of this book.

Conclusion: 'plus ça change, plus c'est la même chose'

If states honoured their commitments, then there would never have been a need for R2P. The myriad human rights treaties ratified since 1945 alone are sufficient to cover all potential humanitarian abuses; there is a surfeit of laws, commitments and promises. These various treaties and statements, however, have been routinely flouted. The Genocide Convention is an obvious example but so too is the 1948 UN Declaration of Human Rights which was compromised by the fact that it 'depended for its enforcement not upon any independent entity but upon the very governments who were guilty of its violation' (Schulz, 2009, p. 147).

We must conclude that states, left to their own devices, cannot be trusted to comply with these laws or honour their commitments. This is, essentially, implicit in R2P; the existence of the international community's responsibility to protect in addition to the host state's responsibility is an acknowledgement that states will not habitually abide by their pledge to accept their domestic responsibility to protect. Given this, why should we assume that states will abide by the latter, arguably more onerous, commitment to protect citizens of other states? Surely if we acknowledge that states lack the will to protect their own citizens it is even less likely that they will protect citizens of other states. The fact that R2P is ultimately dependent on political will is, therefore, its primary, and I contend fatal, weakness.

In assessing R2P's prescriptions Bassiouni reflected, 'Surely if a legally enforceable responsibility to protect existed, the Security Council would have the obligation to act whenever the conditions triggering such a duty existed' (2009, p. 32). Clearly, as discussed in Chapter 3, no such obligation exists and thus the Security Council chooses when and how to respond. This unsurprisingly has resulted in inconsistency – intervention in Libya but no intervention in Darfur – and it was precisely this inconsistency that led to the establishment of the ICISS in 2000 and ultimately the emergence of R2P. The fact that this *discretionary* entitlement remains cannot but be a major cause for concern as without change we are left with continuity, the result of which was the shambolic response to the catastrophe in Darfur. According to Schultz, the arguments against military intervention in Darfur are essentially spurious; while he argued that 'the path to protection is clear', he stated that 'the political will to follow it has thus far been largely missing' (2009, p. 153). This is indicative of many analyses previously cited, which identify the absence of political will as the primary reason for the lamentable, and manifestly ineffective, response to the state-sponsored violence in Darfur. The nature of the international response suggests, I contend, that the political will to undertake humanitarian interventions is shallow, and that global civil society, and the earnest advocacy of NGOs, have limited impact. Given that the entire utility of R2P is predicated on political will and, in its absence, the mobilization of political will via humanitarian advocacy, the prospects for R2P are surely limited so long as there is no vision beyond moral advocacy. The idea that the speeches of statesmen made to the General Assembly are somehow true reflections both of the state's intent and the state's vision of international law is itself questionable. A far more accurate means of discerning what states consider their legal obligations to be is by analysing *what states do* and on this basis R2P is not considered to be obligation incumbent on states. As Michael Glennon argues 'If the community of nations behaves as though rules do not exist, they do not exist, and if they do not exist, they are not binding' (2008b, p. 155).

There is additionally a further problem with the underlying assumption regarding the 'moral' obligations of states. Many appear to believe that if states 'do the right thing' in response to an intra-state crisis this will involve some form of intervention, military or otherwise. This is not necessarily the case; acting to prevent or halt a mass atrocity may well be moral but not doing so need not be amoral or immoral. The primary moral responsibility of all states is to the welfare of their own citizens and if a state determines that a particular course of action will imperil its citizen's security or jeopardize their welfare, then it is not indefensible for them to choose not to intervene. To reiterate, there is no ready conflation between a moral cause and the assumption of a moral imperative; one cannot reasonably be chastised for a dereliction of duty in the absence of a formal duty. The nature of many crises certainly provides sufficient grounds to justify intervention but this is often conflated with triggering a moral imperative for states to intervene. While states did agree at the World Summit in 2005 that the 'international community' has a responsibility to take 'appropriate measures' when an intra-state crisis reaches a certain nadir, this does not suggest that this responsibility trumps each individual state's responsibility to their own citizens. Attempting to operationalize R2P within the parameters of the current system is, therefore, likely to fail because the onus is on states to take risks to protect suffering strangers. This is a fundamentally untenable position.

The *status quo* is equally untenable, however. While the reliance on political will, the capacity of humanitarian advocacy and the presumption that states have a moral responsibility to protect citizens in other states collectively undermine the utility of R2P as presently conceived, this conclusion in itself is no more than a critique of a proposed solution; it does not address the underlying problem. This is the focus of the following chapters in Part II of this book.

Part II

Beyond R2P

Chapter 6

In Defence of Humanitarian Intervention and the Potential of International Law

R2P has come to dominate the discourse on humanitarian intervention and today serves as a unifying concept for those eager to 'do something' in response to intra-state atrocities. Advocates of humanitarian intervention now invariably champion R2P, though the category 'R2P supporters' is undeniably broad and heterogeneous. It almost seems, nonetheless, that if one is in favour of humanitarian intervention one must support R2P, whatever reservations one may hold about the idea. The fact that people with often conflicting perspectives find reasons for aligning with R2P is illustrative of the concept's virtual monopoly as *the* pro-intervention framework and evidence of R2P's dramatic ascendency.

Given the fact that the preceding chapters have advanced a critique of R2P, and a pessimistic assessment of its future efficacy, one may assume that I am opposed to humanitarian intervention. This is emphatically not the case. The purpose of this chapter, and indeed Part II of this book more generally, is to advance a defence of humanitarian intervention which is not allied with R2P. A reluctance to believe in the efficacy of R2P does not necessarily constitute opposition to humanitarian intervention.

The aim of this chapter is to justify two propositions which serve as the foundation for Chapters 7 and 8; first, that the use of force for humanitarian aims, namely to halt genocide, war crimes, ethnic cleansing and crimes against humanity perpetrated by states against their own citizens, should be facilitated rather than proscribed; and second, that international law is the only viable means by which humanitarian intervention can be effectively regulated.

In defence of humanitarian intervention

Many will no doubt contest the critique of R2P outlined in Part I of this book and there is certainly much scope for further debate on the issues discussed. Nonetheless, even if one *was* to conclude, 'I'm convinced; R2P cannot work' surely the next utterance would be, 'but what's the alternative?' In the absence of an alternative, critiques of R2P lose some credibility and can appear pedantic, pessimistic, ideological or perhaps even cynical. Either way, I contend, they are of limited utility. Critique in itself is certainly not without merit but there surely comes a point when one must put forward an alternative if one's contribution is to be constructive. This is the primary aim of this book and, in particular, Chapter 8. Before advancing an alternative, however, it is necessary to justify the underlying assumption motivating my support for humanitarian intervention.

Pacifism, relativism and realism

There are broadly three schools of thought or philosophical traditions that oppose humanitarian intervention on principle. The first is pacifism which, as Chris Brown notes, views the use of force – whatever the pretext – as 'unproblematically wrong' (2006a, p. 100). The use of force for ostensibly humanitarian aims is deemed especially contradictory. Indicatively, Fiona Terry argues, 'A "humanitarian war" is an oxymoron ... a humanitarian rationale cannot be invoked to justify killing one set of people in order to save another' (2002, p. 242). One must certainly have reservations about the utilization of often massive military force and its resultant casualties, in the name of humanitarianism. There have been many instances when the idea that it is necessary to cause *some* damage and inflict *some* casualties to prevent greater loss of life has been cynically employed. Nonetheless, in principle I believe the basic premise upon which the utilitarian position is based rings true; if using force and unavoidably killing ten people results in the prevention of the deaths of one hundred people then surely this is acceptable, if always lamentable. This does not mean that it is acceptable to use ten people to save a hundred; here the Kantian rejection of the instrumental use of individuals applies (Donaldson, 2002, pp. 136–9; Anscombe, 1981, pp. 78–9). Rather, if it is demonstrably impossible to avoid the deaths of ten to save a hundred then the use of force is defensible, though always regrettable.

The rich philosophical lineage of the just-war tradition provides ample grounds on which to justify this approach, and while this is not the place to engage in depth with this discourse, I believe that the fundamental principle underpinning the use of force as articulated through this tradition is more compelling, and certainly more realistic, than outright pacifism. Provided particular emphasis is placed on three criteria central to the just-war tradition's guidelines on the use of force – last resort, proportional means and right authority – then the use of force for humanitarian aims is, I believe, defensible (see Bellamy, 2006b; Evans, 2005). Indeed, in instances when force is justified on humanitarian grounds, there is a strong case for arguing that the criteria should in fact be more rigorously applied (Janzekovic, 2006, p. 109; Hayden, 2005, p. 90; ICISS, 2001a, p. 37).

It must be noted, however, that while the principle underpinning the just-war tradition's justification for the use of force is convincing, history is replete with examples of the abuse of this principle and the spurious and cynical invocation of 'just wars' (Bellamy, 2006b, pp. 46–7; Evans, 2005, p. 3). Without an objective means by which to determine whether the use of force is indeed just, all wars will naturally be deemed 'just' by their instigators. The just-war tradition cannot in itself, therefore, constrain aggressive war. Rather, it is better conceived of as a means by which to judge the legitimacy of the use of military force. Judgements will, of course, differ, therefore, as James Connelly and Don Carrick note, the just-war theory 'should not be thought of as an answer-generating machine operated by turning fact and value inputs into neatly minced outputs at the single turn of a handle. It is a way of reasoning, not a substitute for it' (2011, p. 45). This demonstrates the importance of the concomitant development of legal codes identifying a locus of authority and governing both the determination that force is necessary and the application of this force, lest the tradition's criteria lose all utility; this preference for positive law over 'natural law' will be dealt with in greater detail later in this chapter.

The conflation of humanitarianism and militarism is, nonetheless, certainly problematic and perhaps too readily assumed in contemporary discourse. David Kennedy argues that there has been a disturbing union between humanitarians and militarists whose objectives are the proliferation of a particular hegemony, with the latter essentially subsuming the former: 'Humanitarians and military officers now speak the same pragmatic language of legitimate objectives and proportional means. We have met the empire, and it is us' (2009, p. 151). Indeed, this would appear to be confirmed by statements such as that contained in the 2000 'Interagency Review of US Government Civilian Humanitarian and Transition Programs' which asserts: 'The line separating humanitarian stakes from our other key foreign policy goals has been erased: these issues have become deeply embedded in one another' (Feste, 2003, pp. 234–5). Accordingly, the neutral objectives of humanitarianism are often compromised by their association with the military (Barnett, 2010, p. 174).

The association between humanitarianism and militarism is, therefore, conceived, arguably correctly, as a corrupting one whereby humanitarian ideals are often cynically avowed to provide a cover for more nefarious, sectional aims. The attempt to portray the invasion of Iraq as a humanitarian intervention, for example, certainly adds credence to this claim. At the time of the invasion and occupation of Iraq, US Secretary of State Colin Powell, infamously described humanitarian NGOs as 'a force multiplier for us ... an important part of our combat team' which was illustrative of this manipulation of humanitarianism (Brauman and Saligon, 2004, p. 269). This is, however, a concern born from a sense that the agents of humanitarian intervention, namely national militaries, are driven by an agenda motivated by partisan objectives which necessarily conflict with objective humanitarianism. This melding of humanitarianism and militarism is a function, however, of the prevailing systemic architecture which necessarily compels advocates of robust humanitarian action to associate with agents of militarism. The fact that there is no independent international force mandated only to maintain international peace and security and enforce international human rights law means that the initiation and execution of a humanitarian intervention requires the mobilization of national armies or regional military organizations whose primary *raison d'être* is not humanitarian. Thus, if one concludes that on humanitarian grounds it is necessary to use force this leads one to necessarily lobby states and/or regional organizations to deploy their military forces (Campbell, 1998, p. 519; Hehir, 2008a, p. 92). It is perfectly reasonable, therefore, to have concerns about this conflation between humanitarianism and militarism but this is derived from the nature of the existing system rather than constituting a principled objection to the use of force. The proposal advanced in Chapter 8 seeks to overcome this particular reliance on national militaries, which by definition are motivated by sectional interests, to execute humanitarian interventions.

The relativist objections centre on a scepticism towards, if not an outright rejection of, the idea of universal morality. If moral norms are culturally specific then clearly intervening – which by definition involves external involvement – may constitute a clash between two sets of moral frameworks. If culture A believes in X but culture B does not, what right do agents from culture A have to impose X on culture B? There is clearly significant merit to this argument; cultural norms differ significantly throughout the world and in many cases what 'the West' considers to be axiomatically civilized/uncivilized is rejected in other cultures. Obviously, this has significant implications for matters of international law and universal jurisdiction. Additionally, due to the acceleration of globalization in the post-Cold War era the dramatic disconnect between the world's cultures has arguably become more manifest as integration and communication have increased, precipitating a number of often violent clashes.

Nonetheless, while this question is of profound importance with respect to a number of sensitive issues – not least the rights of women, children and homosexuals – in the specific context of humanitarian intervention it is less of an issue, at least since the 2005 World Summit. One fear prevalent in the 1990s regarding humanitarian intervention was that minor human rights violations, or violations of culturally specific norms, would be used by the major powers as a pretext for military intervention (Chandler, 2000). It was argued that in the absence of guidelines governing the transgressions that would legitimize intervention, violations of culturally specific human rights norms could be used to justify the use of force, as was routinely the case in the pre-Charter era (Ayoob, 2002). Many additionally felt that it would be impossible to achieve universal consensus on crimes that would legitimize intervention due to the inherently contested nature of moral norms (and the corresponding lack of legal expression).

This is, however, no longer a tenable critique; the 2005 World Summit *Outcome Document* reflects universal agreement that genocide, war crimes, ethnic cleansing and crimes against humanity are prohibited under all circumstances and in all places and are of sufficient gravity to legitimize external involvement, and possibly intervention. There is no culture, state, religion or national group which can claim that engaging in these acts is permissible according to their particular cultural moral mores. More accurately, anyone may make this claim, but it now universally and officially rejected. As Ramesh Thakur wryly noted, 'Relativism is often the first refuge of repressive governments' (ICISS, 2001b, p. 130). The debate about cultural imperialism and relativism can, and no doubt will, continue to rage in other areas but with respect to the particular crimes that may legitimize humanitarian intervention there is now universal agreement, and relativist arguments are anachronistic, so long as the debate, and the policies, are limited to the four crimes.

The realist critique is perhaps more dominant than either pacifism or relativism. To state the obvious, realism has a long history and is far from homogenous (Coicaud and Wheeler, 2008, p. 7). Nonetheless, Alex Bellamy's broad claim, 'The realist tradition opposes the norm of humanitarian intervention' is surely correct (2003, p. 10). The basis for this opposition to humanitarian intervention can be to traced to three key realist claims; human nature inclines us to compete (often violently) with the result that conflict is perennial and greed and egotistic impulses trump altruism (Boucher, 1998, p. 93; Donnelly, 2002, p. 86); states exist in an anarchical international system and are thereby compelled by this structural configuration to act in the pursuit of national interest, thus confining universal moral concerns to a secondary place in foreign policy (Waltz, 1991, p. 29; Morgenthau, 1954, p. 5; Hertz, 1957, p. 86; Spykman, 1942, p. 18); states that claim to act on the basis of morality are lying or worse, if genuine, constitute a threat to international peace and stability (Carr, 2001, p. 74; Kissinger, 1992, p. 5; Zolo, 1997, p. 15; Lyons and Mastanduno, 1995, p. 8). The preceding chapters in Part I in many respects closely adhere to these foundational assumptions. While there is, therefore, a strong correlation between the basis of my critique of R2P and realism, I depart from this perspective markedly with respect to the question of what to do in light of the fact that states are not reliable or suitable agents of humanitarian intervention.

The realist critique is certainly convincing within the context of the present international system, dominated as it is by states. As noted in Chapter 5, the argument that states have a moral responsibility to ensure the welfare of citizens of other states is not as axiomatic as many contend. This particular critique, however, does not solve the underlying problem of what to do in response to mass atrocities. While we may utilize realism to critique the proposition that states, or groups of states, will or should intervene for humanitarian reasons – which is the basic claim made by proponents of R2P – by doing so we have but determined that one particular putative solution to the problem posed by intra-state humanitarian crises is unworkable, and indeed possibly undesirable. The problem of course remains. It is unclear why, on the basis of an endorsement of the realist critique of humanitarian intervention by states, we should cease to explore alternative means by which we can prevent or halt mass atrocities within states. For example, as stated above and in Chapter 5, I endorse John Mearsheimer's claims that states do not act on the basis of moral concern for citizens in other states, and are unlikely to act at the behest of an international organization to intervene, if there are no significant national interests involved (1994). This need not constitute a rejection of humanitarian intervention *per se*, however. To view the realist critique as accurate and the end of the discussion is to mistakenly conflate an accurate critique of one form of humanitarian intervention with a critique of humanitarian intervention. Analogously, we can prove that fires cannot be put out using gasoline but does that prove that fires cannot be put out? Should we not seek alternatives given that the problem remains? Surely if the present system precludes humanitarian intervention the system should be changed. Rejecting this latter claim is only possible by adhering to the fatalistic assertion, as avowed by certain realists such as Christopher Layne, that the international structure is characterized by 'continuity, regularity and repetition' and therefore, 'probably unchangeable' (1994, p. 11). In light of the changes which have occurred even in the last twenty years this argument appears highly dubious. Indeed, Sir Arthur Watts argues precisely the opposite; his reflection on the evolution of the international legal system leads him to conclude that the changes in international law, both institutional and doctrinal, reflect evolving trends in the interests of *states*: 'The process is dynamic, not static: interests fade, existing interests change their emphasis, and new interests emerge' (2001, p. 15). Likewise, Henry Steiner, in identifying the weaknesses of the post-Charter laws on human rights, nonetheless argues that comparatively great progress has been made: 'However limited and inadequate those arrangements now appear, we should keep in mind how radical and politically implausible they would have seemed when the human rights movement was born' (2006, p. 757).

Of course, realists argue that cooperation between states is motivated by interest rather than benign pursuit of the common good (Mearsheimer, 1994, p. 9; Michalek, 1971, p. 387). Hence, the idea that states would voluntarily empower an international organization to engage in action – particularly military action – that could interfere with the state's interests is rejected. There is evidence that challenges this claim, however, with the establishment of the International Criminal Court, in particular, arguably constituting a manifestation of the very initiative realists deem impossible; this is dealt with further in Chapter 7.

The realist critique, however, goes beyond just a rejection of the possibility of regulating humanitarian intervention; it is held that by definition such action disrupts order and constitutes a threat to international peace and stability (Gray, 2001). Even if, therefore, an independent international military force mandated to maintain, enforce and protect human rights was established, such an entity would ostensibly disrupt international peace and stability. As I have argued in previous chapters, states engaging in humanitarian intervention *do* pose (though not always constitute) a threat to international peace and stability. It must be acknowledged, however, that it is conceivable that an intervention by a state or group of states may have, on balance, more positive consequences than negative. Nonetheless, if we seek to identify agents that will undertake humanitarian intervention consistently we should not look to states. To argue on the basis of the rejection of states as agents of humanitarian intervention that humanitarian intervention is itself a threat to international peace and stability is, however, an unsustainable extrapolation. An effective humanitarian intervention carried out for humanitarian motives by a truly neutral military force would either prevent or halt genocide, war crimes, ethnic cleansing and crimes against humanity. Such intra-state crises almost by definition pose a threat to international peace and stability. Even if one was to identify a particular intra-state atrocity that had implications only for the host state – though such a scenario is highly unlikely – a conception of international peace and stability that allows for genocide, war crimes, ethnic cleansing and crimes against humanity to take place within a particular state would be curious to say the least. This, in essence, boils down to the increasingly untenable claim that the international and the internal can be separated (Wight, 1966, p. 18). If the notion that the internal composition of states and the events within states had an insignificant bearing on the state's foreign policy was ever true it is surely no longer convincing (Lu, 2006, p. 50). Clearly the internal policies of states such as Israel, Iran and Burma have influenced their international repute, their foreign relations and regional stability. States which engage in atrocities or systematic oppression internally necessarily find that their relations with other states, and indeed increasingly powerful non-state international actors, are affected. Of course, the attendant consequences of such atrocities, such as refugee flows in particular, pose additional threats to regional stability, as was the case with respect to the genocide in Rwanda which had disastrous consequences for the surrounding region (H. Weiss, 2009). The idea, therefore, that mass atrocities within a state do not impact on international peace and stability is manifestly false.

Finally, it is worth noting that the textbook image of realism routinely advanced – whereby realists are portrayed as unconcerned with matters of morality, justice, human rights and the internal composition of states – is not necessarily accurate. Thomas Hobbes, for example, emphasized the state's duty to provide its citizens with the 'good life' and protection from harm (Jackson, 2006; Peters, 2009, p. 519). Likewise, Machiavelli's nefarious prescriptions have come to overshadow his normative advocacy of Republican constitutionalism (Brown, 2006a, p. 69). Realism has, therefore, often been unfairly caricatured by opponents and selectively read by proponents (Bain, 2006; Molloy, 2006; Williams, 2007). Normative prescriptions on improving intra-state conditions are not necessarily anathematic to realism.

The degradation of international law ... and humanity

In clarifying here why I support 'humanitarian intervention' I firstly defend the term itself and secondly justify the premise underlying the rationale for the argument advanced in Part II of this book. The defence below does not utilize the more common ethical arguments which stress our common humanity and the virtues of altruism. While I certainly concur with some of these sentiments, it is clear that they have consistently failed to sway key actors at key times. Additionally, as argued in Chapter 5, it is possible to advance a moral defence of non-intervention even if the cause is moral. Rather, this argument is based on a pragmatic assessment of the impact of what Simon Chesterman describes as 'inhumanitarian nonintervention' on the international legal and political system (2003, p. 54). Unfortunately, the moral arguments appear to have little impact and thus alternative means by which humanitarian intervention can be made a more established and consistently utilized option must be articulated (Hehir, 2008a, pp. 81–4). Chapter 7 argues that the reforms suggested – namely the establishment of a new judicial body and a UN military force mandated to undertake coercive humanitarian interventions – need not be an anathema to the majority of states. In fact, such reforms could be construed in positive terms.

In defence of 'humanitarian intervention'

Humanitarian intervention has become a term synonymous with controversy (Lang, 2003, p. 2). It has been discredited by the lamentable historical record, criticized by aid agencies, tarnished by association with the invasion of Iraq and become synonymous with Western interference and cultural imperialism. Proponents of intervention for humanitarian purposes now overwhelmingly frame their advocacy in the discourse of 'responsibility to protect' and there are few that continue to overtly champion 'humanitarian intervention'. Indeed, the International Commission on Intervention and State Sovereignty (ICISS) noted they 'made a deliberate decision not to adopt this terminology' due to its negative connotations and the range of objections raised against it (2001a, p. 9). Kofi Annan also warned against the use of the term, stating:

> [We must] get right away from using the term 'humanitarian' to describe military operations ... military intervention should not ... be confused with humanitarian action. Otherwise, we will find ourselves using phrases like 'humanitarian bombing' and people will soon get very cynical about the whole idea. (2000)

As noted in Chapter 4 there is now a campaign to reinvent R2P so that it is associated with prevention rather than the more controversial issue of intervention (Weiss, 2007a, p. 104).

While the term is certainly controversial I believe it is the most accurate description of the type of action under discussion. The objection to 'humanitarian intervention' advanced by the ICISS – '[the] use in this context of an inherently approving word like "humanitarian" tends to prejudge the very question in issue; that is whether the intervention is in fact defensible' (2001a, p. 9) – is, I believe, unconvincing. Those describing their military action as a 'humanitarian intervention' are certainly seeking moral approval rather than just an acknowledgement of the military necessity of their actions. The fact that the term has been misused, however, does not in itself constitute grounds for its abandonment. Any state may claim to have undertaken a humanitarian intervention but it is for others to judge; the fact that statesmen have claimed to have undertaken a humanitarian intervention when this was manifestly not the case – most infamously Hitler's invasion of Czechoslovakia in 1939 – should not necessarily render the term inherently corrupted. In fact, if a state claims that an action was a humanitarian intervention, they are raising the threshold by which the legitimacy of their action is to be judged as they are necessarily going beyond a strategic justification, which may cohere with subjective national interest into a discourse and necessarily implies universal applicability. If having examined the historical record, we duly conclude that there has never been a humanitarian intervention then that does not mean the term should be discarded. States always justify their actions as legal, and, generally, also to some extent as moral (Watts, 2001, p. 7). These are defences which can be rejected, not on the basis that that particular law or moral norm doesn't exist, but rather that the action itself did not cohere with an accepted understanding or definition of the law or moral norm in question. Indicatively, states often spuriously claim that a military action was an act of self-defence, this does not mean, however, that self-defence is an inherently corrupted term which should no longer be used (Gow, 2011; Hehir, 2008b).

Some have argued, however, that there is no agreed definition of the term 'humanitarian intervention' and hence it necessarily causes conceptual confusion. There are certainly myriad definitions but again this need not fatally undermine the term's utility. In a previous book, I reviewed the various definitions of humanitarian intervention and having identified key commonalities offered the following composite definition:

> Military action taken by a state, group of states or non-state actor, in the territory of another state, without that state's consent, which is justified, to some significant extent, by a humanitarian concern for the citizens of the host state. (Hehir, 2010a, p. 20)

The justifications for this definition need not be repeated here but it is important to note that it is certainly not impossible, and surely not inconceivable, that such an action could take place even accepting the depressing historical record.

The contagion of violence

The bigger issue with respect to justifying support for humanitarian intervention is the basic question 'why?' Why should the welfare of citizens of particular states be a global concern? Is it not the case that, while history overwhelms us with evidence of a government's propensity to kill their own citizens, this does not seem to have interrupted the technological and material evolution of humanity? In fact, perhaps violence is part of our genes and even a catalyst for scientific and technological innovation (Weltman, 1995, pp. 1–2). Perhaps the periodic eruptions of atrocities are unfortunate blips in the march of human progress, which, due to its necessarily uneven nature, creates jarring juxtapositions of ideas, systems and living standards which, like tectonic plates, periodically suddenly buckle and collide. War and violence, though unpalatable, could also perhaps be conceived of as necessary phases in the evolution of societies, a means by which old systems are replaced by new; a key tenet of revolutionary Marxism. If Europe is today largely peaceful and comprises states with generally settled borders then maybe this is a function of centuries of conflict which consolidated these borders and settled disputes.

While there is some sense to the basic premise that conflict has had some evolutionary benefits – in terms of societal rather than biological evolution, though the latter *is* suggested by some (Wright, 2006, p. 25) – it is difficult to apply this line of argument to the types of atrocities that, as previously noted, are today acknowledged as the only grounds for humanitarian intervention. Military conflict with fascism may well have been, despite the horrendous loss of life, a necessary evil given the ultimate defeat of that particularly odious ideology. Crimes such as genocide, however, do not have the same obviously beneficial end-result and are better conceived as egregious, gratuitous violence. One can, therefore, *possibly* endorse the premise that a world without military conflict would lead to stagnation and perhaps the perpetuation of anachronistic and ideologically driven destructive regimes without necessarily lamenting that, horrible though genocide is, it is a necessary phase in societal evolution. We may not be able to defeat certain ideologies and overthrow certain systems without recourse to force but we can surely do without genocide, war crimes, ethnic cleansing and crimes against humanity.

Arguably the most attractive argument for those keen to justify the need for humanitarian intervention to sceptics unconvinced by moral arguments is the security rationale; that is, intra-state crises cause internal instability which invariably spreads resulting in regional instability and ultimately, therefore, poses a threat to international peace and security. The argument that intra-state humanitarian atrocities pose a security threat is certainly convincing in many respects. A plausible argument can be made that intervention in Kosovo in 1999, for example, was a security imperative for NATO states. The problem with this argument, however, is that it logically leads to selectivity. If a crisis erupts in 2015 in Macedonia between the ethnic Albanians in the North and the majority Slav population then NATO states have a clear interest in halting the conflict, given its potential to destabilize the surrounding region and in particular embroil NATO members Albania, Greece and Turkey. Thus, in such a scenario advocates of intervention could stress the security argument to garner support though they may personally be primarily concerned with ending the suffering. If a similar conflict erupts in Fiji between the indigenous Fijians and Indo-Fijians, however, NATO has far less interest in becoming involved even if the casualties are greater. Unless one goes to extremes and deems conflict *anywhere* in the world to constitute a threat to one's security – as James Gow does with respect to 'the West' (2005, p. 60) – then intra-state crises are not always going to constitute a security imperative that demand intervention. In short, the security argument is compelling up to a point but, while it does constitute a potential means by which agents can be convinced to take an interest in a conflict, it cannot be utilized in all instances unless the concepts of 'security' and 'national interest' are stretched beyond breaking point. The logical end-point of the security argument is regional security organizations essentially policing particular areas. This naturally means that some regions will be better regulated than others, given the obvious disparity between, for example, the military capacity of NATO and the African Union. Additionally, within even these regional blocs, alliances naturally exists and selective intervention is thus inevitable.

To my mind the most compelling case for humanitarian intervention is the deleterious effect the occurrence of certain intra-state atrocities has on humanity and the international system. A violent society naturally impels its citizens to behave violently. The same is arguably true of the international arena; if we do not respond effectively to prevent or halt genocide, war crimes, ethnic cleansing and crimes against humanity, then this can only have a negative impact on our collective conception of the value of human life and the strategies we should adopt to 'survive'. The unabated occurrence of these four crimes can only facilitate the proliferation, consciously or otherwise, of a perspective on life which degrades the worth of our fellow humans and convinces us to behave aggressively in this evidently violent, indifferent and callous world. It clearly does not make sense to adopt a manner of living which is out of step with prevailing societal norms and hence if, by virtue of the periodic and unaddressed occurrence of genocide, war crimes, ethnic cleansing and crimes against humanity, we conclude that violence is a constant feature of our societies, and accepted as such, altruism is obviously folly and self-interest is paramount. This will, therefore, naturally impel us to behave in a particular way that will manifest aggressively both in the international arena and domestically. Not responding to these four crimes, therefore, has a domino effect which permeates throughout our collective consciousness and engenders a world view and disposition which has negative implications in all our affairs.

It is, perhaps, too much to seek a world where individuals, groups, and even governments do not occasionally decide that committing one of these four crimes is a prudent course of action. Sadly such decision making is not the preserve of lunatics or a function of the fog of war but often a calculated decision made in advance by ostensibly rational actors (Howard, 1984, pp. 14–15). While this in itself is a sobering feature of our species, it is mitigated to a large extent if we can contrive a means by which such abuses, if not prevented, are at least halted and/or punished. One murderer does not make his society murderous provided he is apprehended and punished. If that society tolerates the murderer, however, then the actions of this individual *do* impinge on that society's collective identity and repute. A reflection on even just the post-Charter era reveals a litany of inertia and indifference in the face of mass murder and naturally our perception of the contemporary system as a whole is tempered by these instances. Indeed, given the emotive nature of atrocities and the attention they receive, the lamentable reaction to their periodic occurrence has infinitely more impact on collective perceptions of the credibility of the UN than the thousands of routine, though unspectacular, improvements made in myriad areas since 1945.

So long as the 'international community' continues to be bound by a legal and political system which lacks a means by which atrocities on the scale of genocide, war crimes, ethnic cleansing and crimes against humanity are halted in an effective and consistent manner, I believe we must conclude that this is a failed system. The success of any legal and political system depends, to a significant extent, on how legitimate its citizens consider it to be. As Cherif Bassiouni notes, the efficacy of, and support for, a legal system is, to a significant extent, a function of its capacity to adhere to 'predictable and consistent outcomes' (2009, p. 37). International inertia in the face of these four crimes can only undermine perceptions of the efficacy of international law and the international system more generally and these negative perceptions encourage unilateralism, self-interest, aggression and the selective adherence to international laws and norms, all of which contribute to a more violent, adversarial and unstable international system (Bowring, 2008, pp. 39–60). The contemporary inability to respond effectively, objectively and robustly to the four crimes is like a malignant cancer that has, and will continue to, spread throughout the entire legal and political system with many extremely negative consequences; this indeed was the fate of the League of Nations, the manifest impotence of which undermined its credibility and precipitated its demise. This is especially the case with respect to humanitarian intervention due to the fact that questions regarding the basis for intervention were essentially clarified in paragraph 139 of the World Summit *Outcome Document*. The fact that these acts are universally proscribed and yet erratically addressed further erodes faith in the efficacy of international law. It is, indeed arguably worse to have a law that is inconsistently enforced than to not have that law.

An example of this is provided by the murder of ten Belgian peacekeepers in Rwanda in April 1994. The peacekeepers, serving as part of UNMIR were murdered by Hutu extremists on the 7 April, one day after the genocide is said to have begun. The intention of the perpetrators was to frighten Belgium, the UN, and the international community more generally into leaving and/or staying out of Rwanda to enable the genocide to occur (Wheeler, 2002, p. 215). This was based on the lessons garnered from the US's withdrawal from Somalia following the deaths of 19 soldiers during an engagement in Mogadishu in October 1993. The withdrawal from Somalia appeared to demonstrate that violence against external forces operating as part of a UN mission would compel the donor states to quickly extricate their troops with negligible negative repercussions (Docking, 2008, pp. 215–16; Prunier, 1997, p. 274). In other words, violence works. In a functioning domestic system such a calculation is inconceivable. If the use of violence achieves positive results clearly there is a great incentive to use it; this, therefore, demonstrates that the perpetrators of violence may be operating in a calculated, logical way. Any system that provokes such logic is surely deeply flawed.

The potential of international law

The proposal I advance for regulating humanitarian intervention clearly puts great importance on the capacity of international law to influence the behaviour of states. This proposal is outlined in detail in Chapter 8 but it is first necessary to defend the basic assumption underpinning it, namely that international law has the potential to solve the problem posed by humanitarian intervention. This is made all the more necessary given the fact that R2P advocacy invariably ignores international law, preferring instead to focus on generating 'moral norms', which ostensibly leverage states to behave in certain ways; indicatively, when asked whether she felt R2P required legal codification, Sapna Chhatpar Considine, Project Manager for the International Coalition for the Responsibility to Protect, replied: 'No, personally I don't feel that way ... I don't look at it as something that needs to actually become a treaty or international law ... my personal belief is that it doesn't have to become international law for it to work'. Rather, she argued, the better strategy was to work towards 'strengthening normative consensus' (Considine and Sonner, 2009). I do not share this widely held view and the following sections explain why.

Contemporary international law: chaos?

The attraction of international law for many International Relations specialists in the 1990s – particularly in the context of humanitarian intervention – was its ostensibly factual and objective foundations. Many craved the clarity they imagined it would bring by virtue of its ostensible freedom from political interference and moral subjectivity. Clearly this image of international law as definitive, as egalitarian, as a panacea even, does not equate with the reality; many expert analysts and scholars of international law are variously, and unashamedly, confused, critical, and at times outraged by the origins and tenets of international law and its propensity to support the proliferation of hierarchy, inequality and oppression while maintaining a veneer of emancipation and fairness (Koskenniemi, 2001, p. 166; Orford, 2009; Simpson, 2004).

There exists, in fact, a very real existential crisis amongst many scholars of international law with questions often raised about the very notion that there is such thing as 'international law'; as Hilary Charlesworth and David Kennedy note, 'There turns out to be more than one international law'. They argue that as a result of this 'legal pluralism', 'what had seemed legal judgements come into sharp relief as personal decisions'. International law thus becomes 'a series of professional performances rather than an edifice of ideas and doctrines' (Charlesworth and Kennedy, 2009, pp. 404–5). The international legal system is, therefore, characterized by inconsistencies and the influence of power, leading Dan Danielsen to describe it as 'chaos' (2009, p. 99).

There is, additionally, a dramatic disconnect between the myriad laws and the various resolutions passed at the UN and the actual practice of states. If the legal system itself is politicized and characterized by 'chaos', then the efficacy of international law is further undermined by the extent to which those laws that do exist and those institutions that proscribe action on the basis of them, are simply ignored. As Michael Glennon observes:

> canvassing the words of a state's official diplomatic representatives in a forum such as the Security Council may reveal only a small slice of indicia of its intent; the scope of the rule to which it consents must be gleaned from the words of numerous policymakers throughout pertinent organs of its government. When all those words and deeds are weighed, the results may not be encouraging for those who believe in the rule of law. (2008b, p. 162)

This combination of institutional 'chaos' and à la carte adherence to positive law understandably led, and continues to lead, many to dismiss international law and find either solace in natural law or reluctantly accept the perennial influence of power. If some of the most damning critiques of international law come from its practitioners and most qualified analysts, it is perhaps not surprising that writers from other disciplines have disregarded it as a potential solution to the problem posed by humanitarian intervention.

The fact that critiques of international law abound, and contemporary international relations seems replete with examples of international law's impotence, certainly makes the task of defending the utility of international law challenging. The prescriptions advanced in this book, however, are based on a belief in the *potential* of international law which clearly needs to be justified.

In the first instance, it is important to note that the contemporary lamentations about international law's redundancy are not new; rather, concern, if not outright scepticism, about international law is arguably the norm, even amongst legal practitioners. As Charlesworth and Kennedy concede:

> international lawyers specialize in crises. Our sense that we are living through a momentous period in history is permanent. We will always feel as though there is something peculiarly challenging and significant about this moment in international law and that the core of our discipline is somehow under threat. (2009, p. 405)

Thus, while the contemporary 'crisis' may appear uniquely ominous, international law has demonstrated resilience in the face of near perennial crisis and, crucially, a capacity to change and adapt even after enduring seemingly fatal blows (Neff, 2006). The many contemporary critiques of international law, catalysed in particular by the controversies surrounding both humanitarian intervention and the 'war on terror', are not, therefore, definitive proof that international law has finally lost its power and viability as the 'gentle civiliser of nations' (Koskenniemi, 2001). The challenges posed by these contemporary problems are not necessarily insurmountable provided international law demonstrates flexibility, as it has done many times (Byers, 2005a; Gow, 2011). Indeed, some argue that international law, particularly with respect to state and individual responsibility for genocide and crimes against humanity, has entered a new era characterised by 'resurgence' (Milanović, 2006, p. 554). Nonetheless, supporting its amendment demands a justification for its potentiality.

International law or universal morality?

Frustration with international law and the institutions which are charged with its regulation – specifically the Security Council – led many supporters of humanitarian intervention to champion 'natural law' as an alternative framework for the regulation of human rights enforcement (Onuf, 2003). This was arguably most apparent during NATO's intervention in Kosovo in 1999. Indicatively, at the time, the then President of the Czech Republic Václav Havel stated:

> Although [NATO's intervention] has no direct mandate from the UN, it did not happen as an act of aggression or out of disrespect for international law. It happened, on the contrary, out of respect for a law that ranks higher than the law which protects the sovereignty of states. (Robertson, 2002, p. 407)

This preference for 'a law that ranks higher than the law', that is, natural law, permeated throughout much of the discussion on humanitarian intervention in the 1990s and, in essence, held that law was temporal and a function of political expediency while morality was universal and timeless and thus a preferable means by which to judge and regulate the use of force (Nardin, 2003, p. 19). This view has a certain compelling rationale; if the existing laws are demonstrably immoral or illegitimate is it not obviously legitimate to subvert them? When confronted with a legal system which proscribes and prevents legitimate action, such as humanitarian intervention, surely morality and 'natural law' offer an alternative framework? This disconnect, seemingly evident in the 1990s, between law and legitimacy – famously and succinctly captured by the Independent International Commission on Kosovo's conclusion that NATO's 1999 intervention was 'illegal but legitimate' (2000, p. 4) – heralded a challenge to international law which, as Havel's earlier quote attests, did not stem from a frustration with law's constraining influence on the exercise of power but rather its inability to defend the weak and hence, this was ostensibly a morally legitimate critique. If the existing legal system is anachronistic then, the argument follows, we should not be bound by it. According to Michael Walzer:

> [The UN's decrees] do not command intellectual or moral respect except among the positivist lawyers whose business it is to interpret them. [They] have created a paper world, which fails at crucial points to correspond to the world the rest of us still live in. (2006, pp. xx–xxi)

This may be true but this constitutes a critique of the *present* legal system rather than the efficacy of international law generally; it does not prove international law cannot work but merely that as presently organized it does not work.

Attractive as the natural law argument may be when juxtaposed with the seemingly recalcitrant purveyors of *realpolitik* on the Security Council, positive law arguably still constitutes a preferable means by which international relations are regulated, particularly with respect to humanitarian intervention. The problem is, essentially, that while natural law claims to adhere to a politically neutral and pre-existing framework, it is clear first, that there is a plurality of moral codes and second, and more importantly, the absence of an arbitrator with the authority to judge between competing moral claims militates against the utility of natural law and facilitates it potential abuse. The issue of intervention, Martin Wight wrote, 'raises questions of the utmost moral complexity: adherents of every political belief will regard intervention as justified under certain circumstances' (1979, p. 191). Given this plurality, how can morality or natural law possibly constrain the use of force? Obviously, as stated earlier in this chapter, there are no religious or cultural systems which could, or would, claim that any of the four crimes proscribed at the 2005 World Summit are morally defensible but, of course, for this to have broader applicability we must be clear as to what, for example, 'genocide' and 'war crimes' actually are, when they have occurred and the agreed means by which we should address such acts; hence the need for legal codes.

Laws do not, however, spontaneously appear; morality certainly informs our understanding of right and wrong and these understandings determine the existing legal codes, at least they should, and can. Law and morality, therefore, need not be construed as mutually exclusive systems operating in isolation, or indeed in opposition, to each other or, as Havel suggested, on different tiers in a hierarchy. Rather, morality informs law and indeed regulates it; if laws lag behind moral evolution, then this is (generally) readily apparent and the legal system should change rather than be abandoned, temporarily or otherwise. Positive law, therefore, is important precisely because it has the potential to reflect existing common morality and, crucially, to, in essence, give it teeth. As Martti Koskenniemi observes, 'we do not honour the law because of the sacred aura of its text or its origin but because it enables us to reach valuable human purposes' (2006, p. 65). Thus 'the law' is not an abstract set of codes but, ideally a reflection of moral norms, and indeed pragmatism. '[W]hat distinguishes the rules and principles of international law from "mere morality"', Peter Malanczuk notes, 'is that they are accepted in practice as legally binding by states in their intercourse because they are useful to reduce complexity and uncertainty in international relations' (2006, p. 7). Natural law and moral reasoning lack an agreed basis and detail and hence necessarily create the 'complexity and uncertainty' Malanczuk speaks of.

Additionally, morality without legal expression suffers from a lack of clarity regarding duties; while we may use morality to determine that individuals have particular inalienable rights, for these rights to have meaning beyond the abstract there must be clarity regarding the actor charged with defending and enforcing these rights, lest these 'rights' be trampled with impunity by the powerful. If we construct a system where morality informs our understanding of the rights of the individual, and the justifiability of protecting these rights, without sanctioning a particular actor with the duty or obligation to protect, then we have created both a permissive system whereby actors can unilaterally determine that they have the right to defend the rights of others but also a system that necessarily must lead to the inconsistent defence of these rights as the lack of specificity regarding who has a duty to defend these rights will naturally lead to occasions when no-one will (Bain, 2010). Morality without legal expression, therefore, cannot ensure either consistent protection for rights bearers or guard against the subjective, and spurious, utilization of universal morality for selfish objectives. With respect to this latter point Samuel von Pufendorf stated:

> We are not to imagine that every man, even they who live in the liberty of nature, has a right to correct and punish with war any person who has done another an injury ... [for it is] ... contrary to the natural equality of mankind for a man to force himself upon the world for a judge and decider of controversies ... Any man might make war upon any man upon such a pleasure. (Nardin, 2003, p. 16)

Crucially Pufendorf's warning does not focus on the status of the actor or the nature of the violation as the basis for his critique but rather the deleterious effects the unconstrained enforcement of rights has when there is an absence of a defined (and objective) actor charged with a duty or obligation to protect certain rights; if there is no agreement as to the locus of authority and duty then violent instability follows. Moral reasoning, therefore, is capable of determining who has rights and what these rights are, and when it is right to defend them – though in each case subjective perspectives cannot be discounted – but less able to clarify who has the *duty* to do so. Rights without protection in the form of agreed codes and actors with a duty to protect are in practice meaningless, as is moral reasoning without legal expression.

Finally, beyond the theoretical, history suggests that natural law without legal expression leads to disorder and more frequent recourse to conflict including spurious 'just' wars. Indeed, as Bellamy asserts, 'Positive international law ... derived as a response to the endemic abuse of natural law' (2004b, p. 141). Powerful states naturally have an interest in a system based on moral rather than positive law as the former is by definition more malleable and hence susceptible to the influence of power. The fact that the most powerful states today have sought to move beyond the restrictions imposed by positive international law has, therefore, occasioned little surprise among many cognisant of this historical trend (Reus-Smit, 2005; Byers and Chesterman, 2003).

Thus, the idea that we can regulate human rights, inter-state relations and issues such as humanitarian intervention through moral reasoning rather than positive law, is based on an arguably erroneous conception of the two as incompatible and a misplaced faith in the capacity of morality to regulate the behaviour of states. In fact, natural law itself is dependent on positive legal expression to have any real-world effect while positive law cannot exist without 'natural law' underpinning it. Where there is a disconnect between law and morality, as I maintain is manifestly the case with respect to humanitarian intervention, we must use moral reasoning to lobby for positive legal reform, but not assume moral reasoning can act as a viable long-term substitute for positive law.

A further point in favour of the argument that positive law constitutes a necessary means by which natural law and morality can become an essential element in the calculus and behaviour of states is that regarding the binding influence of law. As Costas Douzinas notes, law functions as more than simply a means of maintaining order and (normatively) dispensing justice; it serves an additional, and crucial, function, namely, as a means by which communities constitute themselves. Through the exercise of power, the application of law and the bequeathing of authority to a particular sovereign acting over, and on behalf of, a particular community, the community is constituted and bound together by virtue of the actions of, and the conceptual identification with, the recognised authority figure. Douzinas writes that the people subject to law and the proclamations of the lawgiver, 'become community by receiving the law and by recognizing in the law the ground of their commonality ... The voice that speaks the law comes to personify the community in its sovereignty'. The establishment of a locus of legal power and the legal rulings articulated by this authority, 'transforms sovereignty from an expression of plural beings together into that of a singular body politic' (Douzinas, 2009, p. 44). The manifestation of community, integral to the adoption and implementation of moral norms, is thus predicated on the existence of an authority figure or group capable of, and constitutionally entitled to, interpret and uphold 'the law'. Thus to speak of an 'international community' and the existence of influential moral norms within that community in the absence of centralized authority is arguably a misnomer. The expectations and prescriptions – the various '*shoulds*' – expressed by supporters of R2P are framed in a discourse of community, responsibility and ethical claims, yet, without a concomitant acknowledgement of the need for a fundamental restructuring of the international legal architecture – to both dispense justice on the basis of a legal constitution with widespread legitimacy and to additionally serve as a binding source of communal identification – these expectations are destined to be unfulfilled.

International law, power and the need for change

Citizens living in Darfur would doubtless find the preceding defence of international law curious. Neither Sudanese nor international law provided them with much protection from oppression by the powerful during the 'reign of terror' which engulfed the region in 2003 (United Nations Economic and Social Council, 2004, p. 3). This, and myriad other cases not peculiar to the 'developing world', demonstrates the extent to which power in its various forms influences both the law itself and its enforcement. The preceding preference for law over morality, therefore, should not be read as a blanket endorsement of law but rather a defence of its normative character.

There is, to my mind, no doubt that the present international legal system arguably fails to fulfil the two key criteria for any legal system; to protect the weak and constrain the powerful. One may here note, however, that the UN system was designed to enshrine the primacy of the powerful and, while the Charter makes vague commitments to human rights, it places little coherent emphasis on protecting the individual from oppression (Cassese, 2005, p. 319). Thus, we cannot be surprised that this system has more often than not failed to provide security for the weak – such as the oppressed in Darfur – given this was arguably not its *raison d'être*. Yet, as discussed earlier, while there are certainly grounds for the contention that the international legal system established through the creation of the UN should primarily aim to maintain peace between the major powers and thereby avoid a potentially cataclysmic third world war, this preference for a narrow understanding of the Security Council's mandate to act to protect 'international peace and security', as per the wording of Chapter VII of the Charter, is arguably untenable today. We can identify a clear shift in global expectations of international law with the UN increasingly called on to respond to intra-state crises and humanitarian disasters. It is also possible to say with some confidence that states, including those in the developing world, are amenable to the involvement of international actors in 'internal' affairs provided certain criteria are met; this is explored in greater detail in Chapter 7. We have, therefore, reached a point where, in the specific context of humanitarian intervention, consensus exists on the atrocities that constitute grounds for external intervention yet the international legal architecture has not evolved to facilitate consistent action on the basis of this consensus. The obstacle to the necessary evolution of the legal system is institutional, namely the powers vested in the Security Council, a point developed further in Chapter 8.

It is certainly true that laws are obeyed when they are enforced. Nonetheless, a legal system which commands compliance with its rules on the basis of coercion alone is weak (Armstrong and Farrell, 2005, p. 5). Ideally, law reflects societal norms and thus members of that society are naturally predisposed to adhere to positive law as it reflects their moral codes (Armstrong, Farrell and Lambert, 2007, p. 22). Thus, legal systems should display two characteristics; first, laws which reflect societal norms that are, in fact, derived from these norms;

second, a means by which these laws are consistently enforced. With respect to humanitarian intervention, there is much evidence to support the premise that we have agreement on the impermissibility of certain acts namely the four crimes outlined in the 2005 World Summit *Outcome Document* and an acceptance that, if these crimes occur, external intervention *of some kind* is permissible. If there continued to be disagreement about the basic crimes which could warrant intervention, then any talk of enforcing humanitarian intervention would be hopelessly premature. As Hedley Bull observed, the absence of consensus between states in the seventeenth and eighteenth centuries as to what the human rights of their citizens actually were precluded the formation of any rules and (logically) enforcement procedures related to human rights, hence these matters were left to the discretion of each state (2002, p. 146). This inability to agree on what constitutes the impermissible violation of one's citizen's rights no longer exists, yet there has been no concomitant institutional or legal reform which reflects this important new consensus.

Thus, the obstacle to the consistent enforcement on the prohibition of the four crimes listed in the 2005 World Summit *Outcome Document* are the powers vested in the Security Council and the procedures governing its deliberations, rather than any significant outstanding disagreements about either the crimes, which are universally prohibited, or whether international action to halt such crimes within states is legitimate. As discussed in Chapter 5, the Security Council is a political body the members of which – unsurprisingly – judge how to react to cases on their agenda with their national interests to the fore (Cassese, 2005, pp. 320–1). Thus, the Security Council's discretionary powers and its individual national interests militate against consistency. This has undoubtedly had a corrosive effect on perceptions on the efficacy of the UN as a whole – if not, in fact, international law itself – and, of arguably greater importance, has been the cause of inertia in the face of mass atrocities. This is an untenable state of affairs and a legal model which is at variance with the normative principles underpinning legal design. As Koskenniemi writes:

> The very ideas of treaty and codification make sense only if one assumes that at some point there emerges an agreement ...

> a standard that is separate from its legislative background ... The point of law is to give rise to standards that are no longer merely 'proposed' or 'useful' or 'good', and which therefore can be deviated from if one happens to share a deviating notion of what in fact is useful and good. (2006, p. 69)

The 'deviation' Koskenniemi here warns about can be seen to manifest, in the specific case of humanitarian intervention, with respect to the discretionary powers of the P5, which, by definition, facilitates political selectivity that is destructive of the original law.

As Kennedy notes with respect to the Security Council, 'What began as an institutional effort to monopolize force became a constitutional regime to legitimate justifications for warfare' (2009, p. 145). Today the Security Council, in effect, acts as a means by which interventions can be essentially laundered (Hurd, 2007, p. 129). States seek Security Council approval for their actions to boost the perceived legitimacy of their actions and, as evidenced by the 2003 invasion of Iraq, are prepared to proceed without Security Council authorization if necessary. Indeed, at its Fiftieth Anniversary conference in April 1999 NATO announced: 'Even though all NATO member states undoubtedly would prefer to act with such mandates [from the Security Council] they must not limit themselves to acting only when such a mandate can be agreed' (Caplan, 2000, p. 31). As decisions of the Security Council are a function of politics, political machinations, rather than legality or humanitarian need, determine the 'UN's' reaction to intra-state crises. A legal system so heavily dependent on the political whims of its five most powerful states – though Thomas Weiss argues it is in fact the US rather than the P5 which ultimately determines when military force is used with UN sanction (2009b, p. 5) – is an affront to the basic principle that the enforcement of law should be divorced from politics.

Thus, the international system is hampered by the inconsistent enforcement of existing laws (Hakimi, 2010, pp. 350–2). This means, therefore, that the current international legal system is, as Hans Kelsen's observed, 'primitive' (1945, p. 338). Crucially, however, Kelsen considered this predicament to be but a stage in the evolution of the international system, a necessary step towards the development of a legal order that would ensure global peace (Kelsen, 1972). As the historical development of international law amply demonstrates its capacity to evolve, and given that the current system has arguably reached the limit of its applicability, it is prudent to discuss future systems. In this vein, Bassiouni, reflecting on the inadequacies of the contemporary international legal order, contrasts the present system with the normative structure and functioning of domestic legal systems and suggests what a more evolved – and hence more effective – legal structure would comprise:

> The modern *civitas maxima* must, therefore, be subject to an international rule of law that includes both binding legal norms that transcend domestic norms as well as international legal processes that are similar to national legal processes, but which also apply to state action. (2009, p. 37)

In this conception the evolution from the current 'primitive' system to the '*civitas maxima*' comprises not simply new laws but rather new mechanisms for enforcing these laws, a point I develop further in Chapter 8.

The UN, Weiss, remarked, is 'remarkably ill-adapted to the times' (2009b, p. 1). While Weiss identifies a number of problems with the UN system beyond the Security Council, he is clear as to the deleterious impact of the Security Council's primacy, specifically in the context of human rights; the primary institutions of the UN, he asserts, 'do almost nothing to help address life-threatening problems' (ibid, p. 220). This is a situation which demands change on prudential as well as moral grounds. As Frank Berman observed:

> In any society the correlation between compliance and enforcement is fundamental to the functioning quality of its system of legal rules ... given that enforcement ... is such a rare occurrence on the international plane, special attention must necessarily be given to the appropriate circumstances for it to happen. (2007, p. 157)

Hence, the functioning of any legal system is dependent on its capacity to enforce its laws; the fact that the enforcement of international law is dependent on the Security Council, especially in relation to the enforcement of the proscription against genocide, war crimes, ethnic cleansing and crimes against humanity, means that, so long as this corrupt system exists, we are consigned to erratic enforcement, which is corrosive of international law as a whole. The institutional architecture, therefore, upon which international law is presently based, particularly with respect to the powers vested in the Security Council, must function inconsistently. This does not mean, however, that international law can never be effective; as Kelsen argues, we must see international law as indispensable for the achievement of a peaceful world, but also as a fluid system which, as presently constituted, demands reform.

International law *can* regulate humanitarian intervention provided the legal system and its institutions are reformed. Already much has occurred that can facilitate this reform. The international community of states have reached agreement as to the crimes that potentially warrant external intervention and there is, certainly compared to thirty years ago, a new disposition which is amenable to the basic idea that states are prohibited from treating their citizens in certain ways; Cassese, indeed, describes this 'new ethos' prevalent today as a akin to a 'Copernican revolution' (2005, p. 333). Thus, the consensus and the laws both exist, and the remaining problem is the institutional design of the UN and specifically the Security Council.

Conclusion: 'elementary situations'

That human rights violations on the scale of genocide, war crimes, ethnic cleansing and crimes against humanity should be halted may appear axiomatic given the human tragedy involved. There have been, however, a number of objections raised against humanitarian intervention which are more nuanced than simply a callous disregard for human life. Additionally, even if the moral appeal of humanitarian intervention is compelling, the practice must be regulated by legal codes and implemented by impartial authoritative bodies. As Jean Cohen argues, 'Only international law can mediate between the moral and the political so as to establish clear limits and rules while affording legality and legitimacy to appropriate action' (2004, p. 23). Thus, simply stating 'something must be done' is insufficient.

This chapter has argued that in principle humanitarian intervention is defensible. Yet, as discussed in Chapter 5, moral appeals to 'do something' appear to carry little weight and moral norms and natural law in themselves do not provide a sufficiently robust framework to both prevent abuse and ensure consistency. The international legal structure, as presently constituted, has also proved to be inherently deficient – specifically in terms of consistency and the influence of power – and thus there is a very real problem. In light of these key institutional and constitutional failings, a security rationale has been articulated which seeks to demonstrate that intra-state atrocities constitute a threat to peace and stability beyond the state in which they occur. While there is certainly evidence to support this, this rationale can only ever compel states to act in certain circumstances where a particular intra-state crisis is deemed to threaten their particular national interest and security. The security imperative argument additionally suffers from the fact that states can shield themselves from external intervention by virtue of their geographical location – that is when their geostrategic importance is slight – or by aligning themselves with a powerful ally, such as is arguably the case with respect to the relationship between Sudan and China and the US and Israel. Thus, given the above, it is my contention that the only viable means to solve the problem posed by humanitarian intervention is the reform of international law.

The consequences of this problematic structure of the current UN system remaining unresolved, I have argued, go beyond the obvious human suffering and regional insecurity generated by unabated intra-state crises. If the international legal and political system cannot halt intra-state crises on the scale of genocide, war crimes, ethnic cleansing and crimes against humanity, then the entire system will be degraded both in terms of its actual functioning and its perception. There are, Mats Berdal notes, 'elementary situations' which regardless of the context 'demand total consistency in response' (2008, p. 193). If, such a situation – which he argues include egregious human rights violations – occurs without remedy, then this has profoundly negative repercussions both for humanity and the international legal system. Spectacular abuses of human rights necessarily led to cynicism about international law's efficacy and can encourage unilateralism and an à la carte approach to law generally which causes disorder and a belief in the necessity of individualism in the form of violent 'self-help' and vigilantism (Koskenniemi, 2006, p. 65).

It stands to reason that the unabated occurrence of the four crimes proscribed in 2005 suggests to observers, be they states or non-state actors, both that protection must be provided by one's own military capability and that violence can be employed against internal opposition with near impunity, provided one cultivates allegiances with the very states charged with enforcing international law.

The key argument of this chapter is that the existing laws prohibiting the four crimes cited in the 2005 World Summit *Outcome Document* can only be effective if they are consistently enforced. As Bassiouni writes, these laws are based on an assumed universality; that is that they apply in all cases and at all times. This certainly imposes certain restrictions on states but also logically must create a concomitant set of duties; the effective implementation of these laws, he argues, 'cannot be achieved without the existence of an internationally binding legal obligation to act whenever gross violations of human rights and humanitarian law occur' (Bassiouni, 2009, p. 40). At present, enforcement is dependent on the P5 and thus advocating that state practice regarding humanitarian intervention be guided by existing international law is neither an attractive, or prudent solution. There is, in essence a compelling need to reform the international legal structure in such a way as to remove, to a great if not exclusive extent, politics from the determination as to when and where to launch a humanitarian intervention. This has obvious implications for sovereignty and the existing institutional design of the UN and these issues are each the focus of the following two chapters.

Chapter 7

Understanding the Tension between Sovereignty and Intervention

Sovereignty has always been a 'contested concept'. According to Lassa Oppenheim:

> there is perhaps no conception the meaning of which is more controversial than that of sovereignty. It is an indisputable fact that this conception, from the moment when it was introduced into political science, until the present day, has never had a meaning which was universally agreed upon. (2006, p. 129)

This is particularly evident with respect to the debate on humanitarian intervention and R2P, as reconciling humanitarian intervention with state sovereignty, 'represents a profound moral and political challenge' (Danish Institute of International Affairs, 1999, p. 34). Addressing this challenge, this chapter argues that the creation of a right of humanitarian intervention does not necessitate the abandonment of sovereignty – understood broadly as comprising two principles, inviolability and equality – nor, I contend, should it.

Proponents of humanitarian intervention and R2P have often presented a singularly negative image of sovereignty to the extent that today 'sovereignty has become a dirty word and an endangered concept' (Douzinas, 2009, p. 35). These critiques of sovereignty are, however, often erroneous and derive from an – at times seemingly wilful – exaggeration of sovereignty. On the other hand, many of the most vocal critics of R2P have themselves advanced precisely this image of sovereignty as comprising an absolute proscription on external interference. The debate is, therefore, dominated by two opposing views which, in fact, both share a mistaken understanding of the meaning of sovereignty. This is, Sibyelle Scheipers argues, indicative of a broader tendency in International Relations literature which seeks to, 'establish dichotomies ... thereby obscuring the constructedness of these dichotomies ... Two concepts are not only depicted as antithetic, but the relationship between them is determined by the prevalence of one concept' (2009, p. 17). It is the aim of this chapter to demonstrate that the negative image of sovereignty is a caricature based on an absolutist conception which has very minimal real-world applicability. The idea of total sovereign inviolability is, I argue, morally, empirically and theoretically untenable, and indeed, rarely invoked in the contemporary era by states and certainly far less prevalent than critics of sovereignty suggest.

While this book's proposal – outlined in Chapter 8 – is undeniably ambitious, it is not, I contend, necessarily anathematic to 'sovereign' states, particularly, as is often the contention, those in the developing world. If one could demonstrate that the developing world remains wedded to an absolutist conception of sovereignty and, on principle, these states oppose all forms of external intervention, then clearly the reforms suggested in Chapter 8 would be rejected out of hand and the proposal would be impossible to realize. This chapter suggests, however, that the often vocal scepticism in the developing world towards humanitarian intervention stems not from an endorsement of an absolutist conception of sovereignty but rather from an intrinsic, and understandable, opposition to *unilateral* humanitarian intervention due to the possibility that this type of action can be easily abused. The divisive debate about sovereignty, therefore, is theoretically flawed and too often obscures the issue of authority, which is the real source of the scepticism and opposition to humanitarian intervention.

The sovereignty myth

According to Gareth Evans, the debate on humanitarian intervention involves those arguing for the primacy of humanitarian values and those 'defenders of the traditional prerogatives of state sovereignty, who insist that internal events were none of the rest of the world's business' (2008, p. 3). Sadly he may be right;

the dominant opposing voices in the debate on humanitarian intervention, at least within academia, have too often been those who demonize sovereignty and their opponents who inflate both its legal status and normative underpinnings.

The myth of Westphalian absolutism

The violent implosion of a number of states in the early 1990s and particularly the genocide in Rwanda, led to calls for 'something' to be done in the face of the 'tidal wave' of humanitarian crises (Wheeler, 1997, p. 9). The desire to 'do something' appeared to clash with the existing tenets of international law and specifically the rights of non-intervention afforded to sovereign states. The sovereign inviolability of the state, as stipulated in Article 2.1 and more specifically Article 2.7 of the Charter, thus became widely portrayed as both anachronistic and morally unconscionable and there began, 'a revolution against unfettered sovereignty' (Hoffman, 2003, p. 22).

Sovereignty has since been routinely cited as a causal factor in the proliferation of numerous humanitarian crises; Jarat Chopra and Thomas Weiss indicatively argued, 'One word explains why the international community has difficulty countering [human rights] violations: sovereignty' (1992, p. 95). Sovereignty is held to 'reward tyrants' (Tesón, 1996, p. 342), to constitute 'a plastic term, allowing a government to justify almost any action' (Gow, 1997, p. 155), while to respect sovereign inviolability is, 'to be complicit in human rights violations' (Linklater, 2000). Evans, co-chair of the International Commission on Intervention and State Sovereignty (ICISS), has been one of the most vocal champions of this reading of sovereignty. He claims 'since [the Treaty of Westphalia in] 1648 the view has prevailed that, to put it bluntly, sovereignty is a license to kill: what happens within state borders, however grotesque and morally indefensible, is nobody else's business' (2009, p. 16). Assessing the pernicious influence of 1648 on the post-Charter era he stated: 'What most inhibited action throughout the post-war years was the perceived constraint imposed by the UN Charter' (Evans, 2006). To bolster his claims that sovereignty is responsible for the litany of inaction in response to intra-state atrocities, Michael Newman cites a particularly emotive quote from Leo Kuper; 'the sovereign territorial state claims, as an integral part of its sovereignty, the right to commit genocide, or engage in genocidal massacres against people under its rule, and ... the United Nations for all practical purposes, defends this right'. Kuper does subsequently acknowledge: 'To be sure, no state explicitly claims the right to commit genocide ... but the right is exercised in under other more acceptable rubrics' (Newman, 2009, p. 37). Here again is the suggestion that the UN is somehow complicit in genocide by virtue of its Charter's provisions, most particularly those relating to non-intervention contained in Chapter 1, Article 2. This view is pervasive and there are myriad examples of similar negative interpretations of sovereignty (Booth, 2001, p. 65; Held, 1995, p. 268; Kegley and Wittkopf, 2006, p. 542).

The notion that the legal system ushered in by the establishment of the UN was somehow responsible for non-intervention and the generally lamentable response to internal oppression during the Cold War is curious to say the least. If this were true, then one would need to demonstrate that there were occasions when states decided that a particular intra-state atrocity was so grave that they were willing to intervene to stop it but were prevented from doing so by the restrictions imposed by the Charter and international law more generally. As noted in Chapter 5, however, this has simply never happened (Chesterman, 2002, p. 236). Perhaps most indicatively, the international inaction in response to the genocide in Rwanda was a function of a lack of will and not in any way a consequence of the international community's respect for Rwanda's sovereignty and unwillingness to violate international law by intervening (Wheeler, 2006).

Jarat Chopra and Thomas Weiss argued that the Treaties of Augsburg and Westphalia imbued the state with historically unprecedented power and 'transferred to nation-states the special godlike features of church authority. Nation states inherited the pedigree of sovereignty and an unassailable position above the law that has since been frozen in the structure of international relations' (1992, p. 104). This is perhaps an exaggeration. It would certainly be wrong to view Westphalia as ushering in an era of respect for sovereign inviolability. While the recognition of the external sovereignty of states meant that no national or international entity could legitimately interfere in the activities of another state, state practice after 1648 was not conducted in accordance with this principle. The concept of sovereignty manifest under the 'Westphalian System' was an inconsistently honoured norm. Indicatively, from 1648 to 1815 the number of states actually declined, as large states forcibly absorbed smaller ones (Bull, 2002, 17). The eighteenth, and especially the nineteenth, centuries were characterized by the rise of nation-states asserting the *cuius regio, eius religio* principle, yet the more powerful European states systematically ignored the notion of self-determination and sovereign inviolability especially in their colonial quests through '*terra nullius*' – no man's land (Clapham, 1999, p. 522). According to Jean Cohen this legal arrangement, *jus publicum europaeum* (public law of Europe), was a conspicuously contingent norm which paradoxically facilitated colonialism (2004, p. 12). The interests of the 'Great Powers' of the eighteenth and nineteenth centuries – Great Britain, France, Prussia, the Austrian Empire and Russia – were the primary factor in international relations at this time and certainly of far greater influence than nebulous principles regarding sovereignty. Nonetheless, despite the historical evidence, sovereignty continues to be portrayed by many as an absolute and influential proscription on external intervention and thus an unconscionable barrier to humanitarian intervention.

As noted in Chapter 2 the establishment of the ICISS was a direct result of the question posed by Kofi Annan in 1999; 'if humanitarian intervention is, indeed, an unacceptable assault on sovereignty, how should we respond to a Rwanda, to a Srebrenica – to gross and systematic violations of human rights that affect every precept of our common humanity?' (ICISS, 2001a, p. vii). Annan's question portrays the controversy as a clash between sovereign inviolability, as ostensibly codified in international law, and humanitarian necessity. The implicit assumption is clear; the occurrence of contemporary atrocities has been a function of the fact that the principle of non-intervention takes precedence over external intervention to prevent or halt massive human rights violations. The two cases cited by Annan are, however, questionable choices. In both cases foreign troops under UN command were present on the ground at the time of the massacres, UNAMIR in Rwanda and UNPROFOR in Srebrenica. In each case, these UN contingents lacked sufficient manpower and arms, and were hamstrung by a restrictive mandate given to them by the Security Council. They were, in effect, left to watch as the infamous massacres unfolded. These were not, therefore, cases where violence erupted within particular states and the international community were unable to react because international law, with respect to sovereignty, prevented external intervention. There is, in short, no evidence that the desire to respect sovereignty exercised any influence on the reaction to Rwanda and Srebrenica. Calls for a diminution of sovereignty in light of these incidents would only make sense if external actors did not intervene because they did not want to break international law. This, however, was not the case. As Nicholas Wheeler notes in relation to Rwanda, no state at the time cited Rwanda's sovereign right to non-intervention as the basis for their inaction (2006, p. 36). The ineffective response of the international community to both Rwanda and Srebrenica inarguably derived from a lack of interest and will on behalf of those with the capacity to intervene rather than any commitment to uphold a tenet of international law that precluded intervention.

Likewise, no-one argued at the time that, awful though these massacres were, they constituted an exclusively domestic concern and that the states involved were entitled to perpetrate them by virtue of their sovereign rights. Prior to both Rwanda and Srebrenica, the Security Council had sanctioned the use of military force in a number of states – such as Somalia and Haiti – citing humanitarian imperatives and thus by the time of each crisis it was established that sovereignty could be supplanted in accordance with the Charter if – and as noted in Chapter 5, this is a big if – the Security Council collectively agreed. The problem in each case, therefore, *did* have its roots in international law though not, as many seemed to conclude, with the law of sovereign inviolability but rather the powers vested in the P5.

To argue, therefore, that sovereignty has acted as a barrier to humanitarian intervention has very little basis in fact. States accused of egregious human rights violations have certainly routinely claimed that the conflict or crisis constituted an 'internal matter'. This reflected, however, an attempt to portray the violence as something the government can control and halt, not that it is permissible under international law; when has a state ever stated 'we are committing genocide but we are permitted to do so because we are sovereign'? If sovereign inviolability was as robust as its critics claim then this would be the obvious refrain invoked to reject external intervention. Cohen notes that for its critics, sovereignty signifies 'a claim to power unrestrained by law and a bulwark against legal, political, and military action necessary to enforce human rights'. She contends, however, that the arguments presented by many of sovereignty's critics can only be sustained by presenting an absolutist conception of sovereignty which, Cohen maintains 'has long since been abandoned' (2004, pp. 12–13). The image of sovereignty presented by its opponents is, therefore, very often a caricature.

Defending the myth

Despite the fact that the argument against sovereignty can be challenged on legal and historical grounds, perhaps the most vocal retort has been, paradoxically, to defend this mythical notion of sovereignty. Humanitarian intervention, it is routinely claimed, is by definition incompatible with sovereignty. As sovereignty is a means by which the weak are protected against the strong, by definition humanitarian intervention is bad, so bad in fact it is a modern rendering of colonialism.

Stanley Hoffman describes proponents of this perspective aptly as 'sovereignists' (2008, p. xiv) and the view they espouse is a defence of the extreme version of 'negative sovereignty' identified by Robert Jackson as initially pervasive among newly decolonized states (1996, p. 25). While there is no doubt that many General Assembly Resolutions and declarations, such as the ten point *Declaration on World Peace and Cooperation* agreed at the Bandung Conference of 1955, advanced a perspective on sovereignty that precluded external intervention, there is also evidence which points to an acknowledgement amongst the developing world that absolute sovereign inviolability is untenable; this is discussed in the next section. Nonetheless, opponents of humanitarian intervention have ignored the nuances of sovereignty and the position of the developing world in favour of an altogether more extreme rendering of the concept.

Indicatively, according to Jon Holbrook, 'Sovereignty is a quality that a state either has or does not have. Either a state makes and enforces its own laws or it does not' (2002, p. 147). Sovereignty is a principle worth defending, he argued, for three reasons: 'it is a bulwark against the abuse of international power ... it enables those who exercise power to be accountable for it, and ... it permits power to be exercised in a way that is seen as legitimate' (ibid, p. 147). The discourse of humanitarian intervention is, in effect, a means by which power can trump sovereign equality; 'a right of humanitarian intervention gives the powerful states of the world an unfettered ability to intervene in less powerful states as and when they like' (ibid, p. 147).

Holbrook's arguments, illustrative of a broader discourse (Mamdani, 2009; Chomsky, 1999; Thomas, 2003), belie an evident misconception that humanitarian intervention is by definition characterized by two features; first, it is absolutely incompatible with sovereignty, second it is something the powerful spuriously invoke to subjugate the weak. The view 'either a state makes and enforces its own laws or it does not' is out-dated and simply untrue; there are countless examples of situations where states do not independently make and enforce the laws which pertain in their respective jurisdictions. The EU's transnational powers over its member states is an obvious case in point. The existence of the International Court of Justice and the International Criminal Court (ICC) also highlight the fact that 'sovereign states' can, and do, submit to a higher judicial authority without immediately losing their sovereignty. Such arrangements do have profound implications for sovereignty, but are indicative of an evolving understanding whereby the voluntary acceptance of external control has increasingly become a means by which a state's internal and external sovereignty is actually increased (Peters, 2009).

While there is ample evidence which can be cited to bolster the second point made by Holbrook regarding the nefarious influence of power, there is a mistaken conflation inherent in this perspective, which views humanitarian intervention as necessarily comprising *unilateral* humanitarian intervention, that is, intervention by a state or group of states without Security Council authorization. There is little, if indeed any, engagement with an alternative conception of humanitarian intervention which seeks to regulate the practice so that unilateral intervention is proscribed but, crucially, not at the expense of protecting people from slaughter at the hands of their governments, as advocated in Chapter 8. The choice is presented starkly; maintain sovereign inviolability or facilitate Great Power domination which is deemed both morally unacceptable and a source of global instability.

While many on the political left quickly moved to the centre in the wake of the demise of the Soviet Union, others went in an altogether different direction, finding comfort with their heretofore 'class enemies' (Newman, 2009, pp. 39–42). These groups and individuals cultivated relationships with various European conservative parties and pressure groups who also advanced an opposition to liberal internationalism (albeit for sometimes different reasons). A case in point was the UK online-only magazine *Spiked*. Many of the writer's are former members of the Revolutionary Communist Party who previously wrote for *Living Marxism*. Today *Spiked* champions 'liberty, enlightenment, experimentation and excellence' (*Spiked*, 2011) and the ethos is one of wilful provocation and the championing of 'libertarianism'. The evolution of thinking from socialism/communism towards libertarianism – characterized by the conservatism exemplified by *Spiked* – is indicative of a trend in left-wing conceptions of the international system which have definite implications for humanitarian intervention.

The notion that sovereignty has protected small states from external intervention has little basis in fact and is contradicted by the many instances, even since 1945, when sovereign inviolability received its most concrete legal expression, where powerful states have invaded weaker ones. Perhaps more problematic is the fact that this extreme view of sovereign inviolability wilfully ignores the fact that the primary threat to the lives of people in the twentieth century came from the governments of their own states (Lu, 2006, p. 54). Holbrook's idea, therefore, that sovereignty 'enables those who exercise power to be accountable for it, and ... permits power to be exercised in a way that is seen as legitimate' (2002, p. 147) overlooks the myriad cases where citizens have been persecuted by their own tyrannical governments. Championing the sovereignty of states on the grounds that so doing affords protection to the weak does not make sense if wilfully oppressive states benefit from the protection afforded to them by virtue of their 'sovereignty'. Anne Peters usefully contrasts the rights, and normative rationale for these rights, of individuals and states. While the legal personality of an individual can correctly proceed from an understanding of their intrinsic 'right' to freedom and non-interference, the same starting point cannot be ascribed to states which by definition exist to serve their people. She argues:

> the starting point of analysis must be the needs of human beings, notably of potential victims of mass atrocities. Therefore, the examination of the rules on intervention should not begin ... with an eventual exceptional right of states to intervene in extreme cases, but with the need of human beings for help. (2009, p. 535)

The question posed by intervention and sovereignty is certainly concerned with protecting the weak but it is weak *individuals* rather than states.

To advocate a right of humanitarian intervention to address cases of state-sponsored violence does not imply, as the 'sovereigntists' suggest, delegating exceptional rights of intervention to the Great Powers to be used at their discretion (Fake and Funk, 2009). Clearly, the history of humanitarian intervention suggests that great powers have abused the term 'humanitarian intervention' but it is strange that this litany of misuse by states and groups of states should convince these defenders of sovereignty that humanitarian intervention is thus *always* wrong; there are alternatives to unilateral intervention and given the fact that intra-state atrocities have been of such an egregious scale, it is surely incumbent on us to think creatively about ways to reconcile sovereignty and intervention. It is certainly patently unhelpful to champion sovereign inviolability given the obvious implications this has for the millions of people suffering daily oppression and attack at the hands of their host state. Where, indeed, is the alternative strategy? Such absolutist perspectives articulate a passionate critique but rarely advance a solution. Evidently, this perspective is orientated more towards decrying imperialism than advancing constructive strategies for improving the lives of millions of people. As William Bain argues, while we must always be cautious about altering sovereignty, static conceptions of the norm are untenable: 'To hold stubbornly to an abstract principle ... in the face of great human suffering is to refuse to make contact with the real problems of the real world' (2003, p. 75).

It seems that many of sovereignty's self-appointed defenders derive their opposition to what they characterize as the negation or diminution of sovereignty from an inherent enmity towards the primary agents of (both prospective and real) intervention, namely Western capitalist states (Chomsky, 1999,

76). Cognizant of the imperial excess and humanitarian hypocrisy of the colonial era and Cold War *realpolitik,* many appear constitutionally predestined to oppose all Western military interventions (Anghie 2006; Amin 2008; Mgbeoji 2006). Opposition to humanitarian intervention is, therefore, seemingly a function of an immutable article of faith which brokers no discrimination. In the absence of the Soviet Union, and with communism a discredited ideology, these critics have latched onto sovereignty as the venerable bulwark against the march of Western capitalism (Gibbs, 2009; Thomas, 2003; Ali, 2000). This largely instrumental relationship with, and utilization of, sovereignty has led to the emergence of a truncated rendering of sovereignty and a curious nostalgia for a bygone era when sovereignty 'meant something'. Ignoring a number of inconvenient facts – namely that sovereignty has periodically been violated by major powers even after 1945, the rapid acceleration of international human rights law since 1945, the willingness of states to cede certain elements of their sovereignty by joining regional organizations such as the African and European Unions, and the fact that sovereign inviolability has been lauded most vociferously by oppressive totalitarian states – champions of sovereign inviolability have proliferated an exaggerated conception of sovereignty that the Burmese Generals would shrink from publicly defending. Advancing a selective reading of the now somewhat anachronistic works of Jean Bodin, sovereignty is portrayed as unalterable and indivisible, despite the overwhelming evidence to the contrary; sovereignty is cited as a progressive enabler of self-determination, a notion the Kurds, Palestinians and Tamils would doubtless find curious; sovereignty is lauded as a bulwark against aggression by the great powers, despite the many instances of aggression in the past 450 years. The works of scholars such as Hedley Bull, E.H. Carr and Carl Schmitt are touted as constituting a theoretical basis for sovereign inviolability derived from an evidently highly selective reading of their works. In short, the very loud and often very public critique emanating from the disillusioned and disaffected left is morally, empirically and theoretically untenable, and, in utilitarian terms, ultimately unhelpful.

Relative sovereignty

Building on the previous critique of the pro- and anti-sovereignty perspectives, which have come to dominate the debate, this section makes two points; first, sovereignty is not static and its meaning at any given time is ultimately dependent on prevailing laws and norms. In this sense it is relative rather than fixed. Second, while those aspects of sovereignty that enshrine equality and proscribe external intervention by states or groups of states are certainly principles worth preserving, their preservation need not preclude humanitarian intervention in all circumstances.

The contingent nature of sovereignty

In the course of the debate on sovereignty, particularly with respect to the international administration of post-conflict territories such as Bosnia and Kosovo, it has been noted that 'you can't be a little bit pregnant'. The implication being that sovereignty is also an either/or quality (Peters, 2009, p. 517). The analogy is flawed with respect to sovereignty, however, because, unlike pregnancy, what it means to be 'sovereign' changes. Sovereignty, as Chopra and Weiss describe it, is 'a quality of a fact', rather than a fixed and immutable amalgam of specific tenets (1992, p. 103). The reason sovereignty is mutable is primarily a function of its relativity; a state's sovereignty only exists insofar as the external community recognizes that state as sovereign and this community, rather than any individual state, determines what 'sovereignty' comprises at any given time (Brown, 2006a, p. 36).

While a key aspect of sovereignty is the principle of inviolability, this does not isolate the individual state from the international system; it arguably never has. As Carsten Stahn observed, 'in international law the state has never been exclusively considered a self-referential entity ... Ever since the seventeenth century, attempts have been made to grant individuals and groups international protection from arbitrary exercise of state authority' (2007, p. 111). Sovereignty is, in fact, dependent on a number of external factors. 'It is relative' according to Gerry Simpson, 'in that this form of sovereignty must constantly treat with the sovereignty of other states'. It is also relative, he notes, insofar as it is 'constrained by the existence of international law itself' (Simpson, 2004, p. 41). This is a view similar to that of Bull who, though an advocate of the principle of sovereign inviolability, did not conceptualize sovereignty as synonymous with absolute isolation or complete internal autonomy. He wrote:

> Whatever rights are due to states or nations or other actors in international relations, they are subject to and limited by the rights of the international community. The rights of sovereign states, and of sovereign peoples or nations, derive from the rules of the international community or society and are limited by them ... the idea of sovereign rights existing apart from the rules laid down by international society itself and enjoyed without qualification has to be rejected in principle. (1984, pp. 11–12)

Bull is clear, therefore, that there are definite limits to the extent to which sovereignty can be equated with absolute independence and indeed inviolability. Indeed, being 'sovereign' is by definition a function of external recognition; for example, Chechen rebels may well declare Chechnya to be a state but it is only through international recognition that Chechnya's statehood, and hence sovereignty, has any practical utility. Thus the 'sovereignty' of Chechnya is determined by factors other than just the disposition of the Chechens and Russia and is conditional on external actors.

International law itself formally recognizes this relativity; the 1923 ruling of the Permanent Court of International Justice in the Case of the *Nationality Decrees in Tunis and Morocco* remains a landmark judgment with respect to the relationship between sovereign states and the international system. In its findings, the court declared: 'The question whether a certain matter is or is not solely within the jurisdiction of a State is an essentially relative question; it depends on the development of international relations' (Doehring, 2002, p. 156). Thus, while at one particular juncture external involvement of one kind may constitute a violation of sovereignty, this does not necessarily constitute an immutable proscription as 'the development of international relations' ultimately determines what sovereignty comprises and may come to mean that a particular form of external interference is acceptable.

In the nineteenth century it may have been inconceivable that a sovereign state would submit to the laws of a transnational actor and still be considered sovereign but this is now a routine occurrence. Cherif Bassiouni observes that in comparison to the Westphalian concept of sovereignty, the current international legal system 'evidences a significant change ... reflected in the many changes that have occurred in the legal system ... particularly with respect to multilateral decision making and limitation on state sovereignty' (2009, p. 40). If one adheres to a nineteenth century, or even a 1950s, understanding of sovereignty, then the ICC and the EU, for example, fundamentally compromise sovereignty. But in the modern era, we know that states can (and do) remain sovereign *and* delegate significant powers to external bodies. Sovereignty is, therefore, obviously a fluid concept which evolves, as it has always done, in tandem with the fluctuations of international norms and laws (Walker, 1993, pp. 9–11; Reus-Smit, 2001).

A new norm or law regarding sovereignty – such as the permissibility of intervention to prevent or halt genocide, ethnic cleansing, etc. – need not, therefore, necessarily undermine sovereignty as some have suggested. It would certainly *alter* our understanding of sovereignty but alterations have occurred many times since the fabled Treaty of Westphalia in 1648. There is, importantly, no contradiction between this conditional or relative character and sovereign equality (Peters, 2009, p. 529). International law determines what sovereignty is and international law is itself fluid and a reflection of evolving moral norms, though law does not always match the pace of this moral evolution. Hans Kelsen argued forcefully that the sovereignty enjoyed by states is itself a function of a higher legal order and not, as some suggest, a preformed intrinsic characteristic (Zolo 1998, p. 313). International law, therefore, though it imposes constraints on what states may do internally and externally, is the essential means through with states can enjoy a degree of freedom of action which would otherwise be impossible (Lu, 2006, p. 157). Without the constraining influence of international law, states may certainly have more freedom but this freedom will necessarily be repeatedly violated by the free reign afforded to the powerful and thus a world without international law, for the individual state, is 'chaotic, incomprehensible' whereas with an international legal system in place, states are 'lifted from the tyranny of subjective interests and preferences' (Koskenniemi, 2006, p. 69). The significance of law, Martti

Koskenniemi asserts, 'is that it expresses the universalist principle of inclusion at the outset, making possible the regulative ideal of a pluralistic international world' (2006, p. 69). Law can, therefore, been seen as something of a trade-off; clearly there are occasions when adherence to law interferes with one's interests but, providing the process of law formation is inclusive, its judges impartial, and its application consistent, law is obeyed precisely because, on balance, we have an interest in the stability it brings. As Sir Arthur Watts argues, '[International law] provides for stability in international relations. That stability is in turn the necessary basis for the pursuit by States of their national interests' (2001, p. 7).

Specifically addressing the argument advanced by defenders of an immutable, absolutist notion of sovereignty who claimed that the creation of rules and institutions charged with regulating human rights within states would fundamentally undermine sovereignty, Kelsen argued, 'it is a misuse of the concept of sovereignty to maintain that it is incompatible with the sovereignty of the States as subjects of international law to establish an agency endowed with the competence to bind' (1972, p. 40). He elaborated further:

> Neither the fact that a treaty establishing a legislative agency restricts the freedom of action of the contracting States, nor the fact that the community constituted by such a treaty is more centralized than other international communities are, justifies the argument that the establishment of a legislative agency is incompatible with the nature of international law, or, what amounts to the same, with the sovereignty of the States. (Ibid, p. 41)

In this respect, if states voluntarily agree that an international body can regulate their internal behaviour the fact that this necessarily constitutes external interference does not also necessarily mean the sovereignty of the contracting states has been compromised, but merely that it has been altered. It is, therefore, perfectly possible, and in keeping with historical precedents, that an evolution, and perhaps even a sudden change, in international norms regarding the balance between human rights and state sovereignty can be reflected in international law through an inclusive, consensual process, which delegates powers and privileges previously enjoyed by states to an international body without these states signing away their sovereignty.

The fear of unilateral intervention

The evolution of sovereignty has much to do with the capacity of the state to protect itself – by which I mean its resources, culture and people – from external aggression. While the notion of the state as an organic expression of national consciousness inflates its genesis, the capacity of the tenets of sovereignty, as defined by the UN Charter, to prohibit external interference constituted a major attraction for those determined to extricate themselves from colonialism. The codification of sovereign equality and inviolability in the Charter can thus been conceived, at least to some extent, as progressive developments insofar as they constituted the means by which entitlements, previously almost exclusively enjoyed by Western powers, were universalized and codified, though certain institutionalized hierarchies clearly remained. Indicatively, in an address to the General Assembly, Abdelaziz Bouteflika, President of the African Union, described sovereignty as 'our final defense against the rules of an unjust world' (Weiss, 2007a, p. 16). Support for the prohibition on external interference thus derives from the dubious record of benevolent interventionism and the normative notion that citizens should be free to determine the political system within their state without external interference, rather than 'evil attempts to block the efforts of good humanitarians' (Lang, 2003, p. 2).

The effect of the codification of sovereign equality in the Charter and subsequent international legislation, in particular the 1960 General Assembly Declaration on the Granting of Independence to Colonial Countries and Peoples, was that, 'it no longer made sense to speak of a hierarchical society of states in which rights of membership and participation were granted in proportion to a society's development and capability' (Bain, 2003, p. 66). Contemporary moves towards recognizing a hierarchy of states, are therefore, according to Bain, 'fundamentally irreconcilable with a universal society of sovereign states ordered according to the principle of universal equality' (ibid, p. 75). Thus, the two key arguments advanced by many defenders of sovereignty against humanitarian intervention are first, that sovereignty is a means by which the weak are protected from the strong and second, that the creation of any permissive right of intervention would open the floodgates to egregious great power interference. There is, however, a problem with this argument; while sovereignty may well be a principle worth preserving on the basis that it enables militarily weak political communities to exist, legalizing humanitarian intervention does not necessarily mean giving individual states, or indeed groups of states, new expansive powers of intervention, or the creation of a sovereignty hierarchy with rights of intervention bestowed only on certain states. Developing world states, unsurprisingly, extol the virtues of sovereign inviolability in large part because of their experiences of colonial interference and subjugation. It is still possible (in theory), however, to enable external intervention without increasing the scope for the powerful states to abuse this if the new law on intervention is regulated by an international, independent body rather than individual states (Feste, 2003, p. 61). Louis Henkin highlighted the nuances inherent in the codification of sovereignty, arguing that those principles of international law that prohibit unilateral humanitarian intervention

> do not reflect a conclusion that the 'sovereignty' of the target state stands higher in the scale of values of contemporary international society than the human rights of its inhabitants to be protected from genocide and massive crimes against humanity ... rather they reflect, above all, the moral-political conclusion that no individual state can be trusted with authority to judge and determine wisely. (1999, pp. 824–5)

The fact that 'no individual state' can be trusted with this authority does not, of course mean that no *entity* can ever be trusted such authority.

Additionally, while advocating special rights of intervention for 'enlightened states' (Glennon, 1999, p. 2) clearly replaces sovereign equality with a hierarchy, this is not the only means by which humanitarian intervention can be realized as some seem to believe. Indicatively, David Chandler criticized the principle of humanitarian intervention and the notion of conditional sovereignty because he maintained it

> replaces an enforceable equal standard of state sovereignty with an abstract universality that can never be realised within

> the confines of contemporary society [which at worst will lead to] the legitimisation of a new more divisive international framework based on economic and military power. (2002, p. 36)

This is true only insofar as the regulation of this conditional sovereignty is reserved for some ostensibly enlightened states; certainly this *is* inherently problematic. The fact that a hierarchy of states, comprising an enlightened elite determining whether other states meet certain benchmarks, is objectionable, does not mean that by definition conditional sovereignty is objectionable or divisive. The principle that sovereignty must be justified according to prevailing norms and laws is, Peters notes 'not new' and it has long been accepted that sovereignty, 'must be grounded in other, higher-order values, which sovereign states are thought to realize' (2009, p. 518). Chandler's own view on this has also evolved and he now suggests that the idea of a 'responsibility to protect', rather than facilitating intervention, actually enables non-intervention by delegating the 'responsibility to protect' to the host state and it is, therefore, used by Western states to justify non-intervention (2009). Indeed, Bellamy has identified this as an aspect of the UK's response to the crisis in Darfur (2005, p. 45). This is described by Carsten Stahn as the 'complementarity trap'; as R2P recognizes that the host state has the primary responsibility for the protection of its citizens, there is the danger that so long as the host state claims to be attempting to resolve a particular crisis, external actors are essentially unable to act (2007, p. 116). This, of course, becomes less of a trap and more of an excuse if external actors are aware that the state is lying.

In principle, therefore, conditional sovereignty would undermine neither sovereignty nor sovereign equality if the regulation of a state's adherence to domestic human rights laws was a function of a collective delegation of competencies to an international, independent authority. This would constitute a development which would necessarily reflect universal consensus, and the non-partisan enforcement and regulation of this new understanding of sovereignty and intervention would not usher in a new era of Great Power domination. Whether this is likely to happen is certainly debatable but in principle such a change would not fundamentally undermine sovereignty and sovereign equality.

Indeed, at present the absence of an impartial means by which humanitarian intervention can be regulated and executed arguably increases the scope for the very type of unilateral, nefarious intervention defenders of sovereignty seek to avoid. Given that the regulation of humanitarian intervention is presently a competency vested in the Security Council, states can, and indeed have, justified unilateral intervention on the basis that the P5 veto is an unreasonable barrier to justice. Indeed, this was the refrain repeatedly advanced in defence of NATO's intervention in Kosovo in 1999 (Bellamy, 2002, p. 212; Stromseth, 2005).

We can, therefore, refute the notion that humanitarian intervention is by definition an assault on sovereignty, which ushers in a hierarchy fundamentally incompatible with the principle of sovereign equality. The remaining obstacle, therefore, is practical, rather than theoretical; it is claimed that states, in particular the developing world, will never accept such a reform. The following section seeks to prove that this may not be as axiomatic as some suggest.

Understanding the developing world's concerns

'Africans and Asians', Ramesh Thakur observed, 'are neither amused nor mindful at being lectured on universal human values by those who failed to practice the same during European colonialism and now urge them to cooperate in promoting "global" human rights norms' (2004, p. 197). There is no doubt that the developing world – perfectly reasonably – fears a return to pre-Charter colonialism when the Great Powers intervened at will, often citing humanitarian motives when clearly more nefarious aims were the true inspiration (Bull, 1984, p. 6). During the period of colonialism, the currency of *jus publicum europaeum* ensured that vast areas of the globe, and the inhabitants therein, were denied collective and individual rights to liberty and freedom, with disastrous results for indigenous culture and human welfare. In this sense, as noted by Anthony Lang, 'the restraints of sovereignty and the structures of international law that support those restraints serve a moral purpose: the promotion of a community inside clearly defined borders' (2003, p. 2). The fact that 'sovereignty as responsibility' echoes the discourse of colonialism has thus understandably led to deep suspicion as to the implications of this norm for sovereignty, itself deemed vital to national security and, ultimately, the preservation of identity and culture (Mamdani, 2009, p. 274). The developing world, therefore, quite rightly, has no desire to usher in a new hierarchical system with special discretionary rights of intervention reserved for powerful states. Such rights would, history shows, be used inconsistently and for national interest rather than humanitarian ends.

Additionally, beyond the concerns of the developing world there is the more general fear that legitimizing intervention would threaten international peace and stability. As Bull warned:

> Particular states or groups of states that set themselves up as the authoritative judges of the world common good, in disregard of the views of others, are in fact a menace to international order, and thus to effective action in that field. (1984, p. 12)

There is certainly evidence which suggests that a system based on a hierarchy of states, rather than sovereign equality, and regulated by this hierarchy in accordance with its collective subjective moral determinations, is more disorderly and violent than the present system based on positive international law and sovereign equality (Bellamy, 2004b, p. 141). It is eminently logical that a weakening of the restraints on the use of force, particularly on the basis of the ostensibly higher moral rectitude of a few, would precipitate an increase in the use of force. The US-led campaign during the 'war on terror' to reinterpret 'self-defence' so as to legitimize a more expansive range of permissible actions was a clear attempt to stretch a legal concept to facilitate a new policy choice (White, 2004; Chesterman, 2011b). The fallout from this particular case clearly adds credence to the view that loosening restrictions on the laws of war increases warfare even if the champions of exceptional rights claim to be acting for the global good.

Again, while these concerns are no doubt valid, they are relevant only to a particular type of intervention, in this context *unilateral* humanitarian intervention. These concerns can arguably be assuaged if the practice is regulated and implemented not by states but by a universally legitimate, independent international authority as proposed in Chapter 8. Indeed, an examination of the perspectives advanced by the developing world shows that these countries are opposed to unilateral humanitarian intervention rather than the very principle of external intervention for the purpose of preventing or halting egregious human rights violations.

Grounds for optimism?

Cathal Nolan's analysis of the evolution of sovereignty highlights the extent to which, post-World War II, sovereignty evolved in a way which, in legal terms at least, challenged the previous norm whereby sovereignty was a function of deference to the Great Powers. Yet, even those states which had recently emerged from decolonization accepted limitations on their sovereign inviolability, and Nolan noted: ' "Westphalian fundamentalism" (in the form of claims to a radical right of non-intervention in one's "internal affairs") is seldom invoked' (2006, pp. 82–3). The occasional espousal of absolutist conceptions of sovereign inviolability proffered by, for example, Myanmar, North Korea and Zimbabwe cannot be taken as a general disposition amongst the developing world. As Antonio Cassese notes it is clear that the overwhelming majority of states now agree on five key principles related to human rights; that the dignity of human beings is a basic value states must protect; that states must aim to achieve the fundamental rights of groups and peoples; that racial discrimination is intolerable; that states cannot legitimately violate human rights in a systematic manner; and, importantly, 'when these large-scale violations are perpetrated, the international community is justified in "intervening" ' (2005, p. 375). This latter point – the permissibility of intervention – though often overlooked in many of the debates on sovereignty and intervention, is illustrated in the following sections.

If there existed a significant global constituency opposed to humanitarian intervention, in all circumstances, then the prospects of forging consensus around the issue would obviously be negligible. Such a disposition would also bolster the arguments presented by the defenders of sovereign inviolability discussed earlier. Absolute sovereign inviolability is not, however, a widely held view. Following its global consultations on the subject of humanitarian intervention and sovereignty the ICISS found, 'even in states where there was the strongest opposition to infringements on sovereignty, there was a general acceptance that there must be limited exceptions to the non-intervention rule for certain kinds of emergencies' (2001a, p. 31). This amenability to intervention in certain circumstances is further proven by the research carried out by the Institute for Global Policy which found little opposition to the principle of humanitarian intervention in the developing world. They did find, however, significant concerns as to the authorization of such action (Institute for Global Policy, 2009, pp. 7–8). This suggests that there isn't widespread opposition to the principle of the international community having a role in upholding universally agreed human rights domestically. Indeed, Article 4(h) of the Constitutive Act of the African Union recognizes 'the right of the Union to intervene in a Member State pursuant to a decision of the Assembly in respect of grave circumstances, namely: war crimes, genocide and crimes against humanity'. Intervention by the African Union still constitutes intervention and thus, if this provision exists, the argument that African states champion absolute sovereign inviolability loses credibility. Bellamy also notes that the developing world's reaction to NATO's intervention in Kosovo, which was predominantly critical of NATO for not acting in accordance with the Security Council, actually 'revealed a broad constituency of states that were prepared to acknowledge that sovereignty did not give states a blank cheque to treat their citizens however they liked' (2010, p. 38). Thus, while the G-77 condemned NATO's intervention, this did not constitute a blanket condemnation of humanitarian intervention or external interference more generally. Rather, the fact that NATO acted without Security Council authorization constituted the key concern – even if in this case the cause was deemed by many to have been genuinely legitimate – and the fear that such unilateral intervention could become a new norm reserved for the militarily powerful which would inevitably lead to abuse. Adam Roberts argued that the developing world's response to Tanzania's intervention in Uganda in 1979 is also illustrative of this disposition; while there were few who openly supported Tanzania's intervention, few actually criticized it as it was manifestly good for Uganda and the wider region. Thus in this case the principle proscribing unilateral intervention was upheld though the particular intervention was tacitly endorsed (Roberts, 2006, p. 80). The support of the Gulf Cooperation Council, the Organization of Islamic Conference and, albeit to a lesser extent, the Arab League for the Security Council-mandated military action against Libya in March 2011, of course, provided a more contemporary and emphatic example of this willingness to countenance external intervention (Bellamy, 2011, p. 1) This was definitive evidence that sovereign inviolability is not a sacrosanct principle in the developing world (Weiss, 2011, p. 5).

While certain developing world despots have advanced extreme views on non-intervention, and generated much publicity in so doing, many rational voices have articulated an altogether different perspective. At an Organisation of African Unity (OAU) summit in 1998, Nelson Mandela declared, 'we must all accept that we cannot abuse the concept of national sovereignty to deny the rest of the continent the right and duty to intervene when behind those sovereign boundaries people are being slaughtered to protect tyranny' (Hutchful, 2000, p. 218). Francis Deng *et al.* make the point that while certain African states have advanced a defence of the inviolability of the state and its primacy, this is out of step with cultural norms in Africa. They observed:

> The protection of every individual member of is as important to the group as the group solidarity is a source of security to the individual ... Under those circumstances, the primacy of the community's interest is not that of an abstract notion of the state, but of the higher value of the greatest number of individuals who constitute or represent the collective interest of the whole. (1996, pp. 4–5)

This view essentially suggests that there is a significant disjuncture between African norms and the norms espoused by certain despotic African leaders. The inviolability occasionally espoused by figures such as Robert Mugabe and the late Muammar Gaddafi, therefore, can be seen to reflect the particular interests of self-interested despots rather than a reflection of societal norms in Africa or the developing world. Indeed, the ICISS's research consultations in Africa noted that participants reported that 'the sovereignty of most African states has become superficial and not deeply rooted in society' and thus there existed a 'crisis of legitimacy' (2001b, p. 364). The representativeness of those vocal proponents of sovereign inviolability is thus dubious. What we actually hear, therefore, when certain leaders articulate a defence of sovereign inviolability, is not an objective reflection of societal concerns and cultural norms but rather a cynical attempt by those who have oppressed their own people to shield themselves from justice by invoking nationalism and (ironically) international law (Thakur, 2001, p. 19).

As discussed in Chapter 2, the 2009 General Assembly debate on R2P also revealed general agreement that states had a duty to protect their population from grave harm and that external interference to redress a dereliction of this duty was potentially legitimate. There were, however, significant concerns raised as to the authorization of intervention and the form it would take (Hehir, 2011). This unease at the inconsistency and evident politicization of the Security Council's decision making suggests that this institution is not regarded as an impartial judge that can be trusted to consistently apply a right of military intervention for humanitarian purposes (Cassese, 2005, p. 347; Roberts, 2006, p. 71). This was evident during the negotiations on the Rome Statute of the ICC when the non-aligned bloc opposed any significant role for the Security Council in the new body (Weller, 2002). Additionally, in the wake of the Security Council's authorization of intervention against Libya in 2011, a number of states argued that it was Libya's oil and geostrategic importance, rather than humanitarian concerns, which prompted the Security Council, and particularly the US, the UK and France, to act.

As detailed in Chapter 5 the response of the international community is dependent on the will of the Security Council and this will is heavily contingent on political exigencies. Indeed, as the Benin ambassador noted during the 2009 General Assembly debate:

> The real problem does not relate to the existence of a legal basis for United Nations enforcement action, but rather to the inconsistent practice of the Council. We know the reasons for this. It is because of geo-strategic rivalries that have paralyzed the work of the Council and that have made the Council incapable of taking the decisions that were expected of it in circumstances that called for its decisive action.

Without substantial reform of the decision making process within the Security Council, the Benin ambassador argued, R2P would be a 'mere scarecrow' (Benin, 2009). Again we see that the key cause for concern is not the violation of the principle of non-intervention but rather the inconsistent application of this right either by the Security Council or unilaterally. This concern is certainly not new; in 1992 the Secretary General of the OAU, Salim Ahmed Salim, stated that the OAU should be empowered to militarily intervene in its member states as 'otherwise it cannot be ensured that whoever acts will do so in accordance with African interests' (Deng *et al.*, 1996, p. 15). Here, well before the emergence of R2P, we see a perspective strongly in favour of military intervention, and by definition conditional sovereignty, but one determined to regulate the authorization of this action without the interference of the Security Council. The ICISS found through its African consultations in Mozambique a general recognition, 'that sovereign states can and do mishandle their responsibilities as governing authorities and are therefore not immune from intervention' (2001b, p. 364). The ICISS consultations in Egypt reported that there existed a belief that 'the mechanisms and procedures of the intervention process must be subject to objective international regulation' (ibid, p. 375). Likewise in Latin America, participants did not articulate an outright rejection of intervention but did express concern that political interests would continue to impact on the consistent authorization of intervention if the present system was not reformed (ibid, p. 372).

The idea, therefore, that the developing world is wedded to absolutist conceptions of sovereign inviolability is not a true reflection of the more nuanced objections voiced by many developing world states to the current trajectory of the debate on humanitarian intervention. In essence, the politicization of humanitarian intervention is the problem, not the fact that it undermines sovereignty and constitutes, by definition, unacceptable external interference. If states trust an international authority, they appear to have no major compunction about delegating to it significant competencies previously deemed the exclusive preserve of sovereign states. The establishment of the ICC arguably backs this up given that it was an initiative primarily driven by smaller states against the wishes of the powerful (Armstrong, Farrell and Lambert, 2007, p. 62). Indeed the US, Russia and China have yet to fully submit to the court. The nature of the initial contestation surrounding the establishment of the court also did not evidence a particular concern about the negation of sovereignty. According to Scheipers, this debate:

> did not take the form of a conflict between adherents of competing norms – advocates of sovereignty on the one hand and proponents of human rights on the other. Rather, the debate evolved from competing concepts about the configuration of sovereignty and human rights. (2009, p. 7)

Thus the sharp bifurcation for and against sovereign inviolability held to characterize the debate on humanitarian intervention did not have a significant impact on the establishment of the ICC, despite the similarity of the issues at hand. By any marker the ICC necessarily impacts on the sovereignty of those who submit to it; indeed Marc Weller argued that the establishment of ICC constituted a development whereby 'human rights and humanitarian law, in particular, had undermined state-centric thinking' (2002, p. 695). And yet, 'sovereign' states created this institution. This clearly shows that, under certain circumstances, sovereign states are willing to cede aspects of their sovereignty to a higher authority. The key determinant as to whether this voluntary abdication of certain sovereign rights takes place appears to be perceptions as to the legitimacy and independence of the higher authority. With respect to humanitarian intervention, the absence of a legitimate higher authority has meant that states have been reluctant to support a more interventionist Security Council as, mindful of the interests of the P5, they fear such power will be abused (Chesterman, 2011b; Roberts, 2006). This does not mean, however, that states are implacably opposed to humanitarian intervention; the establishment of a higher authority to regulate such action could well be possible.

This question of reform links to the proposals I advance in Chapter 8. While the idea of creating an alternative source of authorization may seem fantastical to some, it was actually a recurrent theme during the ICISS's consultations. In Latin America, 'suggestions were made for a modification of the UN Security Council and creation of a tribunal or other body within the General Assembly to make pronouncements upon the gravity of human rights abuses and the related necessity or otherwise of an intervention' (ICISS, 2001b, p. 372). The ICISS reported that participants in Egypt believed, 'the mechanisms and procedures of the intervention process must be subject to objective international regulation' but that the Security Council was not sufficiently objective (ibid, pp. 375–6). To ensure intervention was, 'objective, nonselective and free from double standards' the participants called for reform of the Security Council's powers: 'It was suggested that an international body of eminent persons be created to make recommendations to the President of the Security Council or to the Secretary General as to when collective intervention might be required' (ibid, p. 377). In India there were calls for, 'an international independent body established outside the UN in order to make sure that standards and conditions are met by interveners' (ibid, p. 389). These calls from the developing world for the regulation of humanitarian intervention by an international body clearly contradict the two dominant perspectives on sovereignty discussed earlier and illustrate the subtlety of the concerns expressed by the developing world. It is precisely the existence of this subtlety that gives grounds for some hope that reform of the international legal and political architecture, as advanced in the following chapter, is possible.

Conclusion: 'a judicial climate change'?

This chapter has primarily sought to demonstrate that the idea that sovereignty and humanitarian intervention are fundamentally irreconcilable is simply not true. Not only is this of historic interest, it is a principle which should guide future thinking. Indeed, Cohen argued that *both* must be preserved; 'Without a global rule of law that protects sovereignty as well as human rights', she argued, 'any talk of "cosmopolitan" right, especially and above all the alleged right to intervene militarily to enforce human rights, is inherently suspect' (2004, p. 4). The rejection of humanitarian intervention on the grounds that it constitutes an unacceptable violation of sovereignty is an untenable position. It is unfortunate that a position so lacking in theoretical and empirical support should have become so prominent a voice in the debate. That it is a position avowed by many ostensibly on the political left is tragically ironic given this group's foundational avocation of universal solidarity. One may oppose Western interventionism, or more emotively Western 'imperialism' (Gibbs, 2009, p. 10), without necessarily opposing external intervention *per se*. The idea that in the immediate aftermath of the Cold War the US and its allies, determined to craft a rhetoric façade with which to shroud their nefarious global expansion, happened upon humanitarian intervention as an appropriate ruse, surely exaggerates their desire to undertake overseas military operations.

The preceding analysis suggests that the status of sovereignty at any given time *should* reflect the general will of states and changes in this status *can* occur if the international community agrees. Sovereignty is in essence, as Brown reflects, a condition that is, always has been, and by definition must be, determined by the external world:

> the idea that states are constrained by the existence of forces outside their control is by no means simply a feature of this age. States have always existed in such a context – only states without an 'outside' could be genuinely and purely 'self-determining'. (Brown, 2006b, p. xii)

Humanitarian intervention necessarily impacts on sovereignty and if it becomes an accepted norm then naturally this challenges and changes existing conceptions, both legal and normative, of sovereignty. Sovereignty, however, has always changed and is by definition fluid, buffeted as it is by the fluctuations in prevailing political and moral exigencies. Therefore, amendments to the law governing humanitarian intervention, derived from an inclusive process and with the consent of all states, would certainly constitute an alteration of the status of sovereignty but would be based on general agreement rather than a unilateral initiative and thus potentially acceptable. The normative concept of sovereignty and its current legal status, do not, therefore, preclude collective intervention authorized by an internationally recognized body.

It is very clear that the developing world *do* have significant objections to the discourse of humanitarian intervention and R2P, but this is not, as some suggest, because they adhere to a conception of sovereignty as absolute inviolability. Rather their fears stem from the potential for the misuse and inconsistent use of any 'right' of intervention (Welsh, 2010, p. 429). Unilateral intervention is unsurprisingly rejected, while it is also evident that few have much faith in the capacity of the Security Council to act as impartial judge of such a sensitive issue, though they prefer the Security Council to unilateralism. Thus, given that the two dominant solutions proffered to facilitate humanitarian intervention – the idea of a sovereignty hierarchy and R2P – do not allay but in fact arguably exacerbate this fear by virtue of ensuring, albeit in different ways, that there is a link between power and authority, both are unlikely to appeal to states in the developing world. Paradoxically, as evidenced by the pronouncements on reforming the procedures for authorizing intervention cited above, far more extensive reform may be more palatable.

There is evidence that reform, particularly reform which delegates greater power to independent non-state international bodies, could be acceptable. Watts argued that it is today possible to identify a 'judicial climate change' which he claims constitutes 'a gradually greater willingness on the part of the international community to impose strong judicial structures on itself, but also a greater readiness on the part of states to accept that increased strength' (2001, p. 14). Bassiouni also argues that globalization has, 'enhanced the acceptance of external obligations, while at the same time nurturing confidence among states that the relinquishment of individual decision making is not without its concomitant benefits' (2009, p. 39). There is, therefore, some evidence that sovereign states – even in the ostensibly recalcitrant developing world – are cognizant of the benefits of international regulation and willing to delegate powers to international bodies. Thus, it may not be too fanciful to imagine the establishment of a new authority with power to regulate, and execute humanitarian intervention; indeed some argue there is no choice but to establish such an entity as it is the only way sovereignty can be preserved (Cohen, 2004, p. 3). The next chapter builds on this belief in the potential reconcilability of sovereignty and intervention and advances a proposal which would, I believe, allay the fears of the developing world by retaining a meaningful conception of sovereignty while ensuring genocide, war crimes, ethnic cleansing and crimes against humanity are halted in a timely and consistent fashion.

Chapter 8

Grasping the Nettle: The Parameters of Viable Reform

As stated in Chapter 6, to only critique existing proposals for dealing with intra-state humanitarian crises is of limited utility. There is, obviously, some merit in critique, as this potentially improves existing proposals or highlights flaws that may ultimately undermine policy. Nonetheless, it is my contention that an alternative strategy to that currently proffered by advocates of R2P does exist and that those interested in regulating humanitarian intervention should explore innovative means by which the structure of the international system can be reformed, as indeed some have already done (Buchanan and Keohane, 2011; Pattison, 2010). The aim of this chapter, and this book more generally, is to articulate the parameters of viable reform in the hope that the focus can be orientated away from R2P-type moral advocacy towards specific legal reform. That is not to suggest that the proposal advanced here is sufficiently detailed to be operable or that it is beyond critique, but rather that it constitutes an alternative to systemic *status quo* and moral advocacy.

Ultimately, this proposal is informed by two underlying principles discussed throughout this book; first, that humanitarian intervention is occasionally necessary and should be regulated to ensure consistency. Second, that the trajectory of the debate on how to achieve consistent humanitarian intervention, which has moved via R2P towards moral advocacy, is inherently problematic and there is, therefore, a pressing need to return to discussing legal and institutional reform.

This chapter begins by advancing a critique of the powers vested in the Security Council. The hegemony exercised by the P5 is old news to anyone even vaguely familiar with international relations. The pernicious implications of this structural configuration are discussed in detail to explode the fallacy that we can somehow circumvent this profound institutional and legal corruption at the heart of the contemporary system. Lee Feinstein described R2P as a 'revolutionary principle' (2007) and yet, remarkably, it is deemed capable of 'revolutionary' change without any change in international law or the system established over 65 years ago to regulate it. Attempting to introduce radical proposals on humanitarian intervention – for that is essentially what R2P is – without seeking to amend the power of the P5, is, I maintain, unlikely to achieve significant success; as Susan Meyer argued, 'without major changes in the UN, R2P will go the way of the Genocide Convention' (2009, p. 56). The chapter then proceeds to offer a proposal comprising two major innovations; a new international judicial body charged with judging the most appropriate response to intra-state crises, and a standing UN military force.

Catherine Lu's sadly accurate metaphor, 'Historically, the society of states has often acted like the drunken friends who desert the scene when violence breaks out' (2006, p. 10), illustrates arguably the key feature of the existing UN system: the absence of duties. The need for reform of the existing legal structure, and in particular the Security Council, is widely acknowledged and the subject of myriad books, articles and UN commissions. These reforms range from voting procedures to membership; there is, I believe, something qualitatively different about reform in the context of humanitarian intervention. Again, this view is not unique; as Andrew Hurrell argues, 'The degree to which international society is affected morally and practically by humanitarian catastrophe means that we need new rules on humanitarian intervention' (2005, p. 30). The discretionary nature of international law, at both domestic and international levels, was discussed in Chapters 5 and 6 and this feature of the system is keenly evident with respect to humanitarian intervention, perhaps more so than any other issue. The Security Council *can* intervene to prevent or halt mass atrocities, but it has no *duty* to do so. So long as this discretion is codified in international law, the decision to intervene will be dependent on the political will of the P5, which I have argued throughout the book will always be fickle and hence some cases, which demand intervention, will be ignored. Thus, as Allen Buchanan and Robert Keohane observe, 'The central problem with the Security Council is, therefore, not what it does, but what it fails to do' (2011, p. 51). The chapter's third section outlines the key advantages of this proposed structural reform and addresses a number of criticisms routinely articulated in opposition to such reform.

This proposal builds on the conception of international law's potential advanced in Chapter 6 and draws on the work of Hans Kelsen and Martti Koskenniemi to defend reforms which conceive of, and employ, international law in a proactive rather than a reactive way – compelling rather than restraining intervention. It is a proposal which attempts to preserve the ethos of the UN and the principle of sovereign equality and one motivated by a desire to see an end to the unedifying juxtaposition of images of carnage and political obfuscation which too often characterize intra-state atrocities.

The Security Council and national interest

The end of the Cold War clearly changed the dynamics within the Security Council and led many to hope, if not assume, that a new era had dawned. In 1991 the then UN Secretary-General Pérez de Cuéllar stated:

> The extinction of the bipolarity associated with the cold war has no doubt removed the factor that virtually immobilized international relations over four decades. It has cured the Security Council's paralysis and helped immensely in resolving some regional conflicts. (1991, p. 2)

The view notion that the end of the Cold War had 'cured the Security Council's paralysis' proved false.

The great illusion

As Michael Barnett notes, the end of the Cold War witnessed a proliferation of reports and commissions which, 'wax eloquent about the transformational possibilities for global politics and about the role of the UN as the prospective global deliverer'. These optimistic predictions, he notes, were 'overtaken by events' as the UN found itself very quickly dealing with situations which were 'descending into chaos if not hell' (Barnett, 2010, pp. 21–2). This belief in the imminence of a new era for the

UN, what Mats Berdal described as 'the great illusion' (2003, p. 9), was widely held and predicated on an assumption that the new character of the P5, derived from the recent systemic change, would be more amenable to the protection of human rights and the enforcement of international law (Chesterman, 2011b, p. 2).

Security Council activism did increase, and certain Security Council mandated Chapter VII interventions in the 1990s were heralded as examples of this new humanitarian disposition. Yet, there was – and indeed in the context of the Libyan intervention in 2011 still is – a tendency to assume a moral motive when a moral cause has been addressed or a moral outcome achieved, and also that this is indicative of a new disposition. Alex Bellamy, for example, wrote, '[The Security Council mandated interventions in] Somalia and Haiti were particularly important because in both cases the Security Council identified human suffering and governance issues as threats to international peace and security, and therefore legitimate objects of intervention' (2004a, p. 232). In these cases perhaps the right thing to do was to intervene but, though this made an arguably pleasant change, neither case necessarily meant that the Security Council had moved beyond a focus on their respective national interests, or that their conception of their national interests had changed dramatically; what the Security Council cite in resolutions as being their justification does not necessarily reflect reality. Simon Chesterman, in fact, demonstrated that such cases constituted a coincidence between humanitarian suffering and the interests of the P5 thereby suggesting continuity rather than change; while agreement at the Security Council was now more common, intervention, and proactive action more generally, was still predicated on the interests of the P5 rather than the flowering of a new humanitarianism (2002, p. 1655). In addition, as discussed in Chapter 3, throughout the 1990s, the Security Council consistently declared in every resolution sanctioning action that their application of Chapter VII was an exception. As the Danish Institute of International Affairs (DIIA) notes, 'This approach reveals an unwillingness on the part of the Security Council to set precedents for humanitarian intervention in internal conflicts' (1999, p. 74). The Security Council has, therefore, deliberately avoided justifying any measures it took in a way that may have been cited as precedential so as to 'retain discretionary power'; and because the

Security Council 'tends to avoid explaining the nature of the link and the reasons for its action' with respect to employing Chapter VII, the result is a record of intervention that 'lacks consistency and turns out to be selective' (Cassese, 2005, p. 347). In effect these resolutions highlighted that the Security Council *could* intervene but, crucially, not that they *would* (Kuhrt, 2011, p. 97).

The positive view of the UN in the new era appeared to overlook two salient features of the post-Cold War Security Council; first, the continued presence of China on the P5. While the implosion of the Soviet Union may well have removed the largest state on one side of the Security Council's East–West divide, China retained its seat and its inherent opposition to interference in the domestic affairs of states. China's slaughter of its own people at Tiananmen Square in 1989 certainly constituted graphic evidence that it retained a less than enlightened view of human rights and, so long as it retained its veto power, the absence of the Soviet Union was of less importance than it may have seemed given that the achievement of Security Council unanimity was still extremely difficult. The Chinese view of R2P as articulated during the 2009 General Assembly debate on the issue, points to a definite, principled objection to the key tenets underpinning the concept. During the debate China stated:

> the implementation of the responsibility to protect should not contravene the principle of state sovereignty and the principle of non-interference in the internal affairs of States ... There must be no wavering with regard to the principles of respect for state sovereignty and non-interference in the internal affairs of states. (China, 2009)

Quite how R2P can be implemented without challenging 'the principle of non-interference in the internal affairs of states' is unclear. Indeed, Theresa Reinold argues that the Chinese position, supported by a number of other states, which holds that R2P should only be exercised in a way which complements traditional notions of non-interference 'would render the idea of R2P entirely meaningless' (2010, p. 65). The Chinese statement in 2009 went on to declare with respect to the legitimate authorization of intervention: 'no state must be allowed to unilaterally implement R2P' and 'the Security Council ... must make judgments and decisions tailored to specific circumstances and must act prudently. Here it must be pointed out that the responsibility entrusted to the Council by the Charter is the maintenance of international peace and security' (ibid). Thus, China continues to recognize the primacy of the Security Council and accepts no obligation either to intervene or protect human rights. With respect to even the use of R2P as a means by which moral pressure can be applied to offending states China warned, 'states must avoid using the responsibility to protect as a diplomatic tool to exert pressure on others' (ibid). Given this statement it is difficult to see how the rise of China can be viewed as anything other than calamitous for R2P.

Second, the presumption that the Western powers amongst the P5 were straining at the leash to protect human rights across the world was, and is, ahistorical and utopian. As detailed in Chapter 7, the Western members of the P5 – the US, the UK and France – have never accepted a legal *duty* to protect universal human rights and a strong argument can be made to defend the claim that they do not have any moral duty to do so. These states clearly have a view of 'the good society' which differed, and differs, substantially from the Soviet Union/Russia and China, but evidence to suggest that the protection and promotion of human rights trumps their respective national interests is simply lacking. Their respective willingness to actively support known human rights abusers, such as Israel, Saudi Arabia and Pakistan to name but three, clearly compromises the notion that compliance with international human rights legislation is a *sine qua non* for Western support. Unsurprisingly then, the hoped for 'age of enforcement' and new era of 'ethical foreign policies' failed to materialize and the Security Council's record continued to be erratic and a function of national interests. Leaving the system as it is will surely perpetuate this trend. The increasing power of Russia, but especially China, can only limit the possibility that R2P will be utilized by the Security Council.

'A political body dominated by the Great Powers'

As discussed in Chapter 5, the existing international legal framework is not an egalitarian regime created via an inclusive pluralist process designed to preserve equality and neutralize asymmetries of power. The international legal order, as represented by the UN, has been consciously constructed so as to privilege certain militarily and economically powerful states. As Antonio Cassese notes with respect to the UN, 'from the outset the new Organization was envisaged as a political body dominated by the Great Powers' (2005, p. 319). The Security Council was created as a means by which the victorious allies could consolidate their power after the Second World War and from its inception, as Ian Hurd notes, constituted a 'political pact among the Great Powers ... [which] ... was never intended to stop Great Powers from intervening in smaller states ... [The Charter] contains no obligation of collective action except when the permanent members choose it' (2007, p. 191). The Security Council is thus, very obviously, a political organ which dominates the legal framework in which it exists (White, 2004). It is thus naive to imagine that power is not an ongoing barrier to the effective implementation of existing international laws and international legal reform.

The Security Council's determination as to the 'legality' of a particular use of force is dependent on a coincidence of variables of which legal doctrine is but a minor one. As Hilary Charlesworth and David Kennedy warn, in the context of a world characterized by economic inequality, the capacity of powerful states to apply 'economic coercion' to bully others into agreeing to declare that their policies are legal raises significant concerns and creates ample scope for 'legal but illegitimate' action (2009, p. 407). The illegality of the 2003 Iraq invasion – at least the unwillingness of the Security Council to sanction it – was a function, not of custodians of the law bravely upholding its tenets, but of a particular set of states – France, Russia and China – making a political decision not to endorse the invasion. Thus, the inherently politicized and subjective nature of the legality of the invasion evidences the extent to which upholding or protecting 'the law' has very little influence over the decisions made by the P5. Had the French agreed to support the invasion, as they had agreed to support the military action against Yugoslavia in 1999, and had Russia and China abstained from using their veto, then questions regarding the legality of the invasion would have been largely assuaged, though some have argued that the P5 cannot do whatever they like (White, 2004). The fact that the invasion could have been deemed legal, if different attitudes and political calculations had prevailed in Paris, Moscow and Beijing, demonstrates quite clearly the extent to which 'legality' in this context is a reflection of what states support rather than an objective judgement of what states do (Rengger, 2005). Of course, even in the absence of Security Council authorization the P5 still use force, as evidenced by the invasion of Iraq. This à la carte approach to the Security Council cannot be deemed peculiar to the Bush administration; William Cohen, US Secretary of Defence under President Clinton, described Security Council authorization as 'desirable, not imperative' (Voeten, 2008, p. 52).

As Bruce Cronin notes, it is important to distinguish between the Charter and international law more generally. The Security Council is charged with overseeing the rules contained in the Charter rather than international law as a whole. In this sense, the scope of the Security Council's powers are limited (Cronin, 2008, p. 61). Additionally, the Security Council does not have the power to create law but rather 'simply interprets and applies existing law' (de Brichambaut, 2000, p. 275). Under Articles 24.1 and 24.2, the Security Council is charged with acting on behalf of the members of the UN and in accordance with the purposes and principles of the Charter. Even a cursory glance at the history of Security Council decision making shows, however, that the P5 have never acted as a collective body with the interests of the 'international community' as their priority, nor can they be said to have consistently honoured either the purposes or the principles of the Charter (Bosco, 2009). The problem is compounded by the fact that 'there is no provision for juridical review of Security Council decisions and, therefore, no way that a dispute over Charter interpretation can be resolved' (ICISS, 2001a, p. 50). The key obstacle to achieving the lofty aims set out in the Charter's Preamble and Article 1, and specifically to addressing intra-state humanitarian crises effectively, consistently and impartially is, therefore, the Security Council. Yet R2P – despite the claims made by its many advocates – does not address this central issue and its utility is thus necessarily limited. As Buchanan and Keohane note:

> R2P may ultimately lead to broader international agreement on the conditions under which humanitarian intervention is justified, but it does not resolve a crucial issue: whether, if the Security Council refuses to act due to the exercise of a Great Power veto, other means may legitimately be used to authorize the use of armed force. (2011, p. 42)

There is, in effect, what Anne Peters describes as 'a missing link' in R2P with respect to the responsibility of the 'international community' to act when a state is unable or unwilling to do so (2009, p. 535). For this residual responsibility to have effect it must, surely, take the form of an obligation. Given that the powers currently vested in the Security Council amount only to a discretionary entitlement and its record in responding to intra-state crises, I believe the present system must be reformed.

Two major failings

On a number of occasions since the end of the Cold War, the international response to intra-state crises has, I contend, demonstrated two major failings with the current international system, namely the influence of politics on decision making at the Security Council and the lack of a standing military force capable of being deployed to intervene. Both are interlinked, as the following examples illustrate.

The response to the genocide in Rwanda in 1994 has been discussed elsewhere in this book but here I wish to emphasize the confluence of the two failings highlighted above. In 1999 UN Secretary-General Kofi Annan asked:

> If, in those dark days and hours leading up to the genocide, a coalition of States had been prepared to act in defence of the Tutsi population, but did not receive prompt Council authorization, should such a coalition have stood aside and allowed the horror to unfold? (Krieger, 2001, p. 451)

This question is especially pertinent with respect to R2P's contemporary manifestation. As Annan noted, in 1994 the Security Council were unwilling to intervene, which of course begs the question 'why?' The argument that the P5 didn't know how bad the situation on the ground actually was is simply implausible (Carroll, 2004; Weiss, 2007a, p. 54; Power, 2001). The reality was that those with the capability to act did not want to; according to Samantha Power, 'staying out of Rwanda was an explicit US policy objective' (2001) while the International Panel of Eminent Personalities established by the Organisation of African Unity to review the Rwandan genocide concluded that once the genocide began, 'the US repeatedly and deliberately undermined all attempts to strengthen the UN military presence' and that when a more robust UN force was eventually sanctioned, 'the US did all in its power to undermine its effectiveness' (Organisation of African Unity, 2000, p. 7). Clearly the problem at the time was the Security Council's – and particularly the US's – unwillingness to intervene, as indeed was noted by the UN's own official enquiry (United Nations, 1999, p. 3). Given that Annan claimed that the international reaction to the crisis in Darfur demonstrated that 'we had learnt nothing from Rwanda' this disposition is arguably still pervasive (Fisher, 2007, p. 103). This has to have profound implications for R2P which is predicated on Security Council authorization.

The additional point raised by Annan's question links to the second failing identified above, namely the lack of a standing military force. If, and this is a big if, a coalition of states, appalled by the Security Council's refusal to respond to the situation in Rwanda, decided to intervene unilaterally to stop the slaughter, would they have had sufficient military capacity? Perhaps states could have mustered sufficient troop numbers but what about lift capacity and the appropriate military equipment? According to the Carnegie Commission on Preventing Deadly Conflict, '5,000 troops could have averted the slaughter of a half-million people [in Rwanda]' (1997, p. 6). But these troops had to be airlifted and armed and of course placed under a competent unified command. Such capacity, absent P5 support, was simply lacking in 1994, and arguably still is today with respect to interventions of that scale. The lack of military response derived in no small part from the fact that the UN lacked, and lacks, the capacity to launch an intervention without the support of the Security Council and the willingness of member states to supply troops. Michael Barnett, who had first-hand experience of the deliberations at the UN at the time, reflected that while there was 'a brief discussion' about the possibility of UNAMIR intervening to halt the escalating violence, 'I was (and still am) unaware of a single member state who offered their troops for such an operation' (1997, p. 559). Calls for intervention made by states with modest military capacity in 1994 were, essentially, calls for other states with the necessary military capacity – namely the P5 – to take action. The difficulty faced by those smaller states, such as New Zealand and the Czech Republic, who called for military intervention, was, as Nicholas Wheeler noted, 'they wanted to volunteer the soldiers of other states for UN intervention' (2002, p. 227). Even if these smaller states had been willing to volunteer troops, as indeed Ghana and Senegal eventually were, they lacked the capacity to actually deploy their troops and were reliant on major states to provide the finances and logistical support. Indeed, Power argues that in addition to refusing to send it its own troops the US, 'aggressively worked to block the subsequent authorization of UN reinforcements' (2001), a point also made by Chesterman (2002, p. 145).

Both these failings were again evident with respect to the Security Council's response to the situation in Darfur. In April 2004, the UN High Commissioner for Refugees (UNHCR) blamed the Government of Sudan for the violence which sparked the humanitarian crisis in Darfur and stated: 'It is clear there is a reign of terror in Darfur ... [our] mission identified disturbing patterns of massive human rights violations in Darfur perpetrated by the Government of the Sudan and its proxy militia' (UNHCHR, 2004, pp. 6 and 22). It is worth emphasizing this finding; the UN's own report into the situation in Darfur reported that the Sudanese government were engaged in a 'reign of terror'. There is no equivocation here and yet the response of the P5, as discussed in earlier chapters and in myriad books and articles, and acknowledged by UN Secretary-General Kofi Annan, was lamentable. Again, the interests of the P5 appear to have contrived against effective action, in particular China's close links with Khartoum and the US's strategic interests elsewhere. Eventually, Security Council Resolution 1556 mandated the deployment of an African Union peacekeeping mission (AMIS) but the force 'lacked adequate personnel and equipment to do its job' (Schulz, 2009, p. 153) and within months Kofi Annan described it bluntly as 'not working' (Bellamy, 2006b, p. 224). Security Council Resolution 1564 in September 2004 recognized that the Sudanese government had failed to honour Resolution 1556 but did not impose any punitive measures. The resolution established the International Commission of Enquiry on Darfur which published its report in January 2005 detailing a litany of extreme violence and widespread sexual cruelty perpetrated by 'The Government of Sudan and the Janjaweed' (2005, p. 3). Various subsequent resolutions were passed; AMIS's mandate was extended, a 'panel of experts' was established to oversee and report on the crisis, the matter was referred to the

International Criminal Court (ICC) and targeted sanctions were imposed. These were not insignificant, but as Thomas Weiss remarked, 'the chasm between the magnitude of the suffering and the international response could hardly have been greater' (2007a, p. 55).

It has been argued elsewhere, however, that R2P *did* alter the international response by virtue of the fact that the Security Council made reference to R2P in a condemnatory resolution – 1674 in April 2006 – aimed at the government in Khartoum and subsequently deployed peacekeepers (Mayroz, 2008). Yet, as R2P advocates William Pace, Nicole Deller and Sapna Chhatpar more realistically noted, the single reference to R2P in resolution 1674 was just that – a reference – and the force was not actually sanctioned for another year and then not deployed for another five months (2009, p. 224). Security Council Resolution 1706 in August 2006 authorized the deployment of 17,300 troops and 3,300 civilian police to replace the 7,000-strong AMIS contingent. Once again, however, this action was taken only with the consent of the Sudanese government, previously accused by a series of UN reports as orchestrating the carnage. The Report of the UN High-Level Mission in March 2007 advised that the steps taken by the international community in response to the crisis in Darfur 'have not proven adequate' (Human Rights Council 2007: 22). The UN Special Rapporteur on Sudan, Sima Samar, reported in September 2008 that 'violence and sexual abuse of women and children ... continue almost unabated throughout Darfur' (United Nations General Assembly, 2008, p. 12). All this occurred in the full glare of the world's media and under the nose of the Security Council.

The response to Darfur was, as is clear, shameful, and again the P5's disinterest must be cited as *the* major causal factor. Linked to this, of course, was the absence of a standing military force that could have been deployed. The troops sent into Darfur were manifestly ill-equipped to deal with the situation and constituted a hastily assembled force hamstrung both by a restrictive mandate, insufficient personnel and poor equipment, all of which could have been rectified by the P5. In a report to the Security Council in November 2007, UN Under-Secretary General Jean-Marie Guehenno stated that the UN peacekeeping force lacked sufficient helicopters due to the fact that pledges made by member states had not been honoured (Reinold, 2010,

p. 71). This dual reluctance to take robust action and also to provide sufficient troops, once a military deployment has been sanctioned, is evident with respect to many other situations. The ICISS noted that the UN peacekeeping mission sent to Sierra Leone in 1998 constituted 'an inadequate response' because the troops were 'poorly armed' (2001b, p. 109). In the context of the often overlooked international response to the slaughter in the Great Lakes region Herbert Weiss reflects:

> if the will had been there, if the responsibility to protect had meant something substantial, it might have been possible to reverse this horrific and deadly tide, but that would have required an international force many times the size of MONUC. Yet, there was no will to send an appropriate number of troops. (2009, p. 127)

This twin problem – the lack of will and the absence of sufficient military resources – has been responsible for arguably all those cases where the international response to a particular crisis has been lamentable. They have, Robert Johansen argues, been responsible for 'many of the atrocities that have killed millions of civilians, wounded millions more, forced tens of millions from their homes, destroyed entire economies, and wasted hundreds of billions of dollars' (2006, p. 23). Kofi Annan's weary summation of the process highlights the obvious failings:

> Where the will is not there and the resources are not available, the UN peacekeepers will arrive late. It takes us on the average 4–5 months to put troops on the ground because we have no troops. The UN doesn't have an army. We borrow from our governments. So we can put on the ground the troops the governments offer. And only as fast as they come, and not always with the equipment they promised. (Langille, 2002, p. 2)

In 1994, the UN Standby Arrangement System (UNSAS) was established to provide the UN with information about the forces and capabilities of member states willing to supply troops to peacekeeping missions. While this was undoubtedly a progressive development, to date less than half of UN members states have signed up to UNSAS and, crucially, member states retain a veto over the deployment of their troops. The Panel on UN Peace

Operations described UNSAS as 'yet to become a dependable supply of resources' (United Nations, 2000, p. 14). The panel also reported, 'few of the basic building blocks are in place for the United Nations to rapidly acquire and deploy the human and material resources required to mount any complex peace operation in the future' (ibid, p. 34). Thus, the voluntary national army contribution system is clearly not working. This was particularly evident with respect to the UN peacekeeping operation in Rwanda in 1994; as the genocide unfolded, states began to worry about the safety of their troops seconded to UNAMIR and issued instructions which compromised the UN force on the ground. Romeo Dallaire's account of the political interference on the day the genocide began clearly highlights this problem:

> the contingents were, over the course of the day, getting more and more communications with their international capitals, who were becoming more and more restrictive in what they wanted their guys to do because the risk was too high ... so we entered this arena where I had troops but I didn't have troops ... as the day wore on it proved that there were a bunch of the troops that were absolutely useless and they were going to do absolutely nothing. (Dallaire, 2009, p. 348)

The fact that states who had committed their troops to a peacekeeping mission prioritized the welfare of these troops when they were needed most may seem callous but it also is surely logical; domestic publics are invariably critical of any government that sends its soldiers abroad to be killed absent some obvious national interest. This disposition may well, as Dallaire's account graphically demonstrates, totally undermine a UN mission but it can hardly be surprising and there is no reason to suggest that this mindset will change.

The obstacles to reform

The need to substantially reform international law and the institutions that regulate it, in particular the Security Council, has long been acknowledged by many. Attempts to reform international law and the Security Council, so that decision making is more pluralist and based on clear guidelines as opposed to subjective discretion, have, however, been regularly blocked by the P5 including the three Western democracies (Archibugi, 2003, p. 8). At the 2005 World Summit, the US's stance on the sanctioning of force and the responsibility to protect reflected an explicit desire to both maintain the Security Council's monopoly on the authorization of the use of force and avoid any compulsion to take military action in the face of any particular mass atrocity (Hehir, 2008a, pp. 72–5). Attempts to convince the P5 to reform the decision making process have failed; in his 2005 report prior to the World Summit, the then Secretary General Kofi Annan called on the Security Council to 'add transparency to its deliberations and make its decisions more likely to be respected by both Governments and world public opinion'. He argued, 'genocide, ethnic cleansing and other such crimes against humanity' constitute issues, 'against which humanity should be able to look to the Security Council for protection'. He specifically recommended that the Security Council 'adopt a resolution setting out these principles and expressing its intention to be guided by them when deciding whether to authorize or mandate the use of force' (Annan, 2005, p. 33). This call was, however, 'politely ignored' by the P5 at the 2005 World Summit who simply asserted that existing Charter provisions and practice were adequate (Chesterman, 2011b, p. 19).

The Security Council has even demonstrated an unwillingness to hear reports on ongoing crises from the UN's own bodies. Indicatively, Francis Deng, current UN Special Adviser on the Prevention of Genocide, noted that his work is continually hampered by a persistent reluctance amongst the P5 to engage with his office in an official capacity. As noted in Chapter 4, the Security Council has often refused to even allow the Special Adviser to address the Council lest his address would focus too much attention on a particular case. The Security Council is, in effect, willing to countenance the existence of the Special Adviser so long as the powers afforded to Deng are minimal and the P5's engagement with the Special Adviser is discretionary. As Deng himself noted, 'those who would be called upon to intervene to stop [mass atrocities] tend to be resistant to discussing this issue' (Deng, 2009). Deng, indeed, suggested that formally addressing the Security Council was of limited utility anyway:

> every time an issue is brought to the Security Council, you can predict ... how Russia, China and the others, will vote. This is

> another consideration when it comes to my relationship with the Security Council; if you go there and say 'I am here concerned about what's happening in this or that country', not only are you raising the stakes but you're also generating controversy because you are going to get one member or another of the P5 to defend that country. (Deng, 2009)

This highlights the fact that even if the P5 have no direct vested interests, their respective allies may be embroiled and hence they will block any substantive response. As Alberto Coll notes, 'No matter how hideous its human rights violations, a state will almost always be able to find a patron in the Security Council willing to cast its veto on that state's behalf to protect it against humanitarian intervention' (2001, p. 136). The result of this, unsurprisingly, is that 'disreputable heads of government have good reason to believe that they can get away with using violence to acquire or maintain power or accumulate wealth' (Meyer, 2009, 51).

The question of the Security Council's lack of a 'duty' to intervene is, as Peters notes, 'very salient' because the problem historically has been that 'the Security Council has abstained from authorising robust military activities even in situations such as Rwanda or Darfur, which fulfil the narrow criteria of admissible humanitarian interventions' (2009, p. 538). The 'responsibility' of the international community to protect citizens suffering within states is clearly of limited utility if this is merely a discretionary responsibility. The discretionary nature of the Security Council's powers has profound implications for the legitimacy of this body. This is, Chesterman suggests, an aspect of the Charter which must be considered for reform as 'legitimacy requires more than reliance on discretion granted by the Charter' (2011b, p. 21).

It is, therefore, surely clear that the existing rules are fundamentally flawed and, as Karen Feste argues, 'will be ineffective and unacceptable in the foreseeable future' (2003, p. 5). While some supporters of R2P acknowledge this – such as Meyer who states, bluntly, 'implementation of R2P will not be possible within the current structure of the UN' (2009, 45) – it is surprising that substantive reform of the Security Council is so rarely discussed amongst R2P advocates. The Global Centre for the Responsibility to Protect published a document in June 2009 designed to address some of the 'Frequently Made Assertions' surrounding R2P. One assertion they addressed – related to the preceding discussion – was 'R2P puts too much emphasis on the Security Council, which historically has proved unwilling or unable to act effectively to prevent and halt mass atrocities. R2P is meaningless if the Security Council fails to act'. Their response is worth quoting in full:

> The [Secretary General's 2009] report is clear that the UN Security Council failed to respond to some of the worst atrocities of the twentieth century. The report also recognizes that the whole UN system and its member states remain 'underprepared to meet their most fundamental and protection responsibilities.' This is the challenge of putting words to deeds: to fill the gaps in capacity, will and imagination that will make mass atrocities a thing of the past. Fulfilling the responsibility to protect requires action by a wide range of actors. The onus is on them to make action by the Security Council unnecessary. Yet, in the case of a state's manifest failure to protect its populations, the World Summit outcome challenges the Security Council to take timely and decisive action. Upholding R2P requires the Security Council to work better. (Global Centre for R2P, 2009a, p. 3)

This statement begins with the surely irrefutable assertion that the Security Council has a dismal record. In terms of redressing this tendency, however, there is, essentially, very little beyond an idealistic call for 'will and imagination' and an appeal to the Council 'to work better'. It is unclear why anyone compelled to ask the question concerning the centrality of the Security Council could be placated by this reply. Later in the same document the Global Centre for R2P state:

> Notwithstanding concerns about the structure and functioning of the Security Council, making the implementation of R2P contingent on UN reform and amendment of the UN Charter would result in unconscionable delays to the UN's efforts to saving lives through the prevention of mass atrocities. (Global Centre for R2P, 2009a, p. 3)

This justification is inherently paradoxical; the shameful record of inertia in the face of mass atrocities, it is acknowledged, has been caused by both the Security Council's power and outlook; changing this record of inertia, however, does not require any alteration to the Security Council. In fact, addressing this key causal factor in the litany of inaction would cause 'unconscionable delays' and would itself constitute a barrier 'to saving lives through the prevention of mass atrocities'. In effect this position can be summarized as 'we know what has caused the problem but trying to remedy the cause of this problem would not solve the problem'.

Likewise the International Coalition for R2P (ICR2P) evidences a striking lack of any policies on UN reform. ICR2P has five aims, none of which even mention the UN let alone the Security Council; the Number 1 aim is to 'Strengthen normative consensus for R2P' (ICR2P, 2011a). The ICR2P presents its 'understanding of R2P' and with respect to enforcing the norm notes: 'The international community also has the responsibility to use appropriate diplomatic, humanitarian and other peaceful means under Chapter VI and VIII of the UN Charter to help protect populations threatened by these crimes' (ICR2P, 2011b). This clearly means that the sanctioning of action is to remain the preserve of the Security Council (and hence the P5) as Chapter VI and VII are each dependent on the Security Council's assent. Yet, it is precisely this systemic configuration which has inhibited the international legal system.

The problem, as noted in Chapters 3 and 5, is not the lack of laws but the politicization of their enforcement. An example is the fate of the 1966 *International Covenant on Civil and Political Rights*. This covenant came into force in 1976 and had 160 signatories by 2007; by any standard an impressive achievement. Yet, the efficacy of the Covenant continues to be undermined by the international legal system, regardless of how many states sign it. The Covenant binds all signatories 'to respect and to ensure to all individuals within its territory and subject to its jurisdiction the rights recognised in the present Convention, without distinction of any kind'. While this is an admirable aim, and the Covenant *is* binding under international law, as Martin Dixon notes, 'the system of enforcement is not really designed to provide a remedy for individuals in concrete cases'. This is because, again, enforcement is the problem; Dixon writes: 'A state may sign the Covenant and accept only the obligation to submit a report at five-yearly intervals and even then reports are routinely late, lacking in detail or not submitted at all' (2007, p. 349).

The *International Covenant on Civil and Political Rights* is illustrative of the fate of all human rights treaties within the present legal and political system; they are designed to preserve the pre-eminence of the state and to minimize any international oversight which might create a binding obligation upon the Security Council to enforce compliance (Armstrong, Farrell and Lambert, 2007, p. 158). The international system is thus compromised by the paucity of clear guidelines and rules on enforcement. This is not unique to international law, of course, but while there is an analogous ambiguity in many domestic systems, the structure of domestic judicial bodies and in particular the separation of politics from the judiciary, largely mitigates these grey areas. As Pierre Buhler explains:

> international law is still sufficiently vague to offer considerable freedom of interpretation – permitted by the contradictory rules, deliberate ambiguity in the wording, and so on. But unlike internal systems where vagueness, also inevitable, is constantly being removed by the courts, the lawmakers, or by the executive, in the interstate system no superior authority can reduce it either by 'setting the law' or, *a fortiori*, by ensuring its appeal. (2008, p. 14)

Again it is clear that the structure of the international legal system is the key problem and within that structure it is the power of the Security Council at the zenith, which corrupts the entire legal system. The ultimate end point of the approach advocated by the ICR2P and the Global Centre for R2P is, therefore, to change the disposition of the P5; to somehow convince them to, in the words of the Global Centre for R2P, 'work better'. This reliance on moral pressure naturally leads to what essentially amounts to pleading, as evident in the ICISS's appeal to the P5 to observe a 'code of conduct' (2001a, p. 51) and the Secretary General's plea to the P5 to 'refrain from employing or threatening to employ the veto in situations of manifest failure to meet obligations relating to the responsibility to protect' (Ki-Moon, 2009a, p. 27). Yet, there is little evidence that such moral pressure can be, or has been, effective with respect to the P5's outlook; 'self-abnegation' on the part of the P5, Buchanan and Keohane note, 'is highly unlikely' (2011, p. 51).

A new direction

To refute the claim that states have previously never accepted responsibilities to protect, Monika Hakimi compiled a list of circumstances under which states have accepted an obligation to protect individuals from harm inflicted by a third party (2010, pp. 343–4). As these obligations, such as the protection of aliens, protection from genocide and non-refoulement, predate the emergence of R2P there is, given the bloody pre-Charter history, clearly something flawed about the regulatory regime governing the protective obligations incumbent on third parties. Hakimi, indeed, describes this regime as 'disjointed' and asserts:

> No generalized framework exists for appraising when a state must protect against third-party harm or what that obligation requires. Decision makers answer those questions *ad hoc*, often overlooking relevant precedents or failing to consider all of the interests at state. Not surprisingly, their practice is at times misguided, inconsistent, or conceptually confused. (Ibid, p. 345)

As discussed in Chapter 3, international human rights legislation is too dependent on individual states to comply with, and enforce, these rights. The fact that within the UN, various bodies with the remit to regulate the enforcement of these rights, such as the Human Rights Council – and its infamous predecessor the Commission on Human Rights (Mertus, 2009, p. 41) – are themselves comprising states with dubious human rights records is obviously problematic. As the High Level Panel on Threats, Challenges and Change stated in 2004, 'Standard setting to reinforce human rights cannot be performed by States that lack a demonstrated commitment to their promotion and protection' (2004, p. 89).

As the previous section highlighted, however, the primary failing within the present system is the fact that the objective enforcement of the various proscriptions against human rights abuses, and obligations to protect third-party human rights, is overly reliant on the Security Council which, it must surely be accepted, has manifestly failed to consistently and impartially address intra-state humanitarian crises or articulate a set of criteria establishing the basis upon which a humanitarian intervention undertaken by others can be legitimized. This is due to a desire amongst the P5 to retain discretionary power. Rather than attempting to maintain the present framework and contrive new norms governing the use of force as R2P proposes, those keen to see an end to inertia in the face of intra-state mass atrocities, must explore innovative and far-reaching reforms of the existing enforcement structure with a view to facilitating the impartial, effective and consistent application of the many human rights laws which already exist, but in particular those related to the four crimes proscribed in paragraph 138 of the 2005 World Summit *Outcome Document*. Such a reform would clearly pose enormous challenges but as argued in Chapter 7 it is not necessarily the case that states in the developing world are opposed to external constraints on their internal behaviour, provided these constraints are designed by consensus, consistently and universally applied, and based on the principle of sovereign equality.

Unilateral intervention and mitigation

There have been many calls for UN reform from a wide variety of observers (Chesterman, 2011b; Glennon 2008b, p. 162; Simma, 1999, p. 2; Guicherd, 1999, p. 20). Any attempt to reform the UN, including the powers of the Security Council, however, confronts the obstacle posed by the Security Council's veto power. This is because Article 108 of the Charter stipulates that amendments to the Charter must be approved by the P5, hence, ironically, altering the power of the Security Council requires the assent of the Security Council (Bourantonis, 2007, pp. 10–11). Clearly this makes the task very difficult. Recognizing this fact, many have argued that the mitigation approach is the most viable solution (Brownlie, 1973, p. 146; Chesterman, 2002, p. 231). This involves a situation whereby technically illegal interventions – interventions without the Security Council's explicit consent – are tolerated rather than condemned and punished; an example regularly cited is that of Tanzania's intervention in Uganda in 1979. Though there were some dissenting voices in 1979, and the intervention was generally deemed illegal, the international community, 'responded with mute, but evident, satisfaction' (Franck, 2005, p. 219). In defence of this near-vigilante like approach Adam Roberts argues: 'in reality the UN, which simply cannot offer a full system of collective security, sometimes needs states to be willing to act in support of its stated goals even if there is no explicit authorization to them to do so' (2008, p. 33). In certain cases this may be appropriate; given the difficulty of securing Security Council unanimity, it would surely be excessively punctilious to condemn an intervention which saved thousands of lives because proper procedure was not observed. In any event, there is no guarantee that states will refrain from intervening absent Security Council consent; as the ICISS note:

> if the Security Council fails to discharge its responsibility in conscience-shocking situations crying out for action, then it is unreasonable to expect that concerned states will rule out other means and forms of action to meet the gravity and urgency of these situations. (2001a, p. 55)

The problem, however, is not when such unilateral intervention takes place for the right reasons and has positive humanitarian benefits but rather when it does not take place for the wrong reasons, such as with respect to Darfur, and when it does take place for the wrong reasons, such as the invasion of Iraq in 2003. In the first case, permitting unilateral intervention in the event of Security Council paralysis does not in any way solve the problem of non-intervention; that is, when there is an obvious need to intervene but no state has the will (or indeed the capacity) to act. We cannot surely be content with a situation, which is still totally dependent on political will, lest we are destined to witness yet more instances of non-intervention in response to mass atrocities. Additionally, as Meyer observers, 'unilateral and self-interested intervention can be uncoordinated and inefficient and can escalate the violence' (2009, 47). The invasion of Iraq was an instance of unilateral intervention justified – to a significant extent – on humanitarian grounds (Bellamy, 2004b). The invasion, as is relatively obvious, did not have positive humanitarian consequences for the Iraqi population and, more profoundly, challenged the very efficacy of international law and destabilized the international system (Thakur and Sidhu, 2006; Bowring, 2008). Such interventionism can only degrade the international system and encourage more states to intervene militarily more often (Byers and Chesterman, 2003). In this vein, Koskenniemi accepts that 'pragmatic instrumentalism' is a feature of the approach states take to international law and this is, he maintains, neither surprising nor in every case negative. He warns, however, that there is 'a dark side' to this; 'pragmatism inculcates a heroic mindset: we *can* do it! It is the mindset of well-placed, powerful actors confident in their possessing the "right" purpose ... It is the mindset of the civilising mission and of "regime change" if necessary' (Koskenniemi, 2006, p. 65). Such righteous selectivity 'creates a consistent bias in favour of dominant actors with many policy alternatives from which to choose and sufficient resources to carry out their objectives' (ibid).

Nonetheless, while I agree with Koskenniemi there is, in reality, very little, if indeed anything, that can be done to stop states unilaterally using military force; if states believe it is in their interests to do so, they will (Weiss, 2007a, p. 37). This is explored later in this chapter. The more persuasive argument against mitigation in the context of humanitarian intervention is not so much that states will illegitimately use force, but rather that this is not a viable solution to the problem of illegitimate non-intervention. There is, therefore, no reason to believe that a genuine humanitarian intervention could not occur without the Security Council's approval. The problem, however, is firstly the obvious scope for abuse, though I have already suggested this is not something that can be negated, but also, and more importantly, the extent to which such reliance on the whims of the powerful will necessarily lead to great selectivity. Certain humanitarian crises, therefore, will go unchecked.

The parameters of reform

A viable solution to the dilemma posed by intra-state humanitarian crises can only be found, I believe, through institutional reform conducted via an inclusive deliberation process which recognizes the need to maintain the basic idea of sovereign equality while contriving new methods of regulation and enforcement. Institutional reform in the area of enforcement would, I argue, transcend the circular debate on humanitarian intervention and offer the possibility of a viable means of responding to the periodic eruption of intra-state humanitarian crises. On the basis of the analysis and critique offered in the preceding chapters, and with a view to advancing the reform agenda, below are principles which I believe must inform any attempt to address the question of intra-state humanitarian crises:

- Sovereignty has normative content and is worth preserving.
- States do not naturally behave altruistically in international relations and evidence suggest they cannot be persuaded by force of argument to do so consistently.
- States generally agree that they have a responsibility to protect their own citizens.
- States accept that moral and legal norms change.
- The developing world do not trust the benevolence of the West.
- The developing world will only accept a change in the norms governing the use of force if such change is codified (or evolves through customary practice).
- The developing world has a preference for institutional design which guarantees non-political and consistent regulation and application.

Each principle is derived from an analysis of the debate to date and, I believe, collectively, these principles constitute the foundation upon which effective institutional design can be contrived. The necessary reforms require two major innovations; the establishment of an international judicial body and a standing UN army. Each is discussed in turn below.

Given the evident unwillingness of the P5 to respond to intra-state crises on the basis of need, due to the pervasive influence of their respective national interests, I suggest that an alternative body should be established with the power to judge how to respond to a particular intra-state humanitarian crisis. This judicial body would not be more powerful than the Security Council but rather would operate as an alternative when the P5 are paralysed. The new body would, therefore, challenge what Buchanan and Keohane describe as the Security Council's 'unconditional exclusive legitimacy' rather than its legitimacy *per se* (2011, p. 41). The judicial body would be mandated to deal only with intra-state humanitarian crises; there is still, arguably, some merit to the idea that the Security Council should have exclusive authority to determine how to respond to inter-state crises, though reform in voting procedures and the composition of the Security Council are surely required in this area too.

Thus, if a crisis erupts in a state and the Security Council is divided as to how to respond, or collectively decides not to act, this alternative judicial body would be mandated to make a judgement. With respect to a situation such as NATO's Security Council-mandated intervention in Libya in 2011 the judicial body would not have been involved as action was sanctioned by the P5. If, however, as is more often the case, a situation arises where there is evidence that one or more of the four crimes listed in the 2005 World Summit *Outcome Document* – genocide, war crimes, ethnic cleansing and crimes against humanity – are taking place in a state, the host state is unable or unwilling to halt these crimes, and the Security Council does not take action, then the judicial body would be mandated to make a judgement. The body would initially assess evidence from NGOs, national intelligence agencies, independent observers and, crucially, UN fact-finding missions. On the basis of this evidence, the body would be in a position to make two determinations; first, whether one or more of the four crimes were taking place, and second, the appropriate response. It may be the case that once a finding that, for example, ethnic cleansing was occurring, the appropriate response may *not* be military intervention; this should always be a last resort and may not be appropriate in certain circumstances. If, however, one or more of the four crimes were verifiably occurring, and the body determined that the only solution was military intervention, it could make such a recommendation.

The added value of this body with respect to the latter scenario is twofold; a ruling that intervention was necessary, made by this independent body, could possibly compel the Security Council to revise its response and to take more robust action. Unlike NGOs and UN fact-finding missions, the ruling of this new body could not be easily dismissed as subjective or illegitimate and could, potentially, serve as a catalyst for the P5 to act. Of course, it may not and there is no guarantee that such a ruling would not simply be ignored. In this situation, individual states could decide to intervene without the P5's explicit approval. This would clearly constitute a form of unilateral intervention but, crucially, it would have the backing of an independent international judicial body and thus have a defensible claim to legitimacy and legality.

In the hypothetical scenario discussed earlier advanced by Annan with respect to Rwanda in 1994, states determined to intervene to stop the genocide without Security Council approval would have faced the charge that they had acted illegally, which would have been technically true. There is surely something wrong with a legal system which criminalizes legitimate action. As Paul Christopher states, 'surely in those cases where we find our legal and moral rules at odds, we should endeavour to reconcile these differences' (2004, p. 248). Had there been a ruling by an independent judicial body that intervention was necessary, this charge of illegality would have been nullified. Again, however, there is no guarantee that states would decide to intervene if a ruling by this new judicial body called for such action and thus it is quite possible that the following scenario could occur; an intra-state crisis erupts; reports suggest one or more of the four crimes is occurring; the Security Council does not take action; the new judicial body rules that military intervention is required; the Security Council still takes no action; no states are willing to intervene unilaterally; the violence continues. Clearly, given the possibility that such a situation could occur, this would not constitute a solution to the problem of non-intervention; hence the need for a standing UN army.

Again, this force would not be the first port of call but rather the last resort failing Security Council or unilateral intervention following a recommendation to intervene by the judicial body. If states were willing to intervene then this force would not be required. As per the last scenario above, however, this is not guaranteed. It would be untenable, and highly embarrassing, for a judicial body to determine that intervention was necessary if no intervention subsequently occurred. Likewise, it would be ridiculous to create a standing UN army which could only be deployed by the Security Council as the spectacle of inertia would be even more pronounced then at present (Kinloch-Pichat, 2004, p. 211). Additionally, James Pattison warns that, without change in the international institutions, states would oppose the deployment of the force '*ad infinitum*' due to the existing suspicion as to the P5's motives and accountability (2008, p. 134). To avoid this, the UN should have a standing force capable of being deployed (by a body other than the Security Council) absent the deployment of troops by member states.

The composition of both the judicial body and the standing

army could broadly comprise the following. The judicial body could be organized along similar lines to the structure of the ICC insofar as the judges would be elected by member states of the UN. The ICC judges are elected by those states that have signed the Rome Statute but as the judicial body proposed here would be part of the UN – unlike the ICC – UN member states would constitute the electorate. On the basis of 'one state one vote' a panel of twelve judges would be elected, comprising at least one member from each continent, for a period of three years. Like the ICC, this body would comprise a presidency of three judges – a president and two-vice presidents – with responsibility for the administration of the body. The body would thus have no national affiliations and would be independent of existing UN organs and institutions, though the body would be accountable to the General Assembly. The body would be empowered to independently sanction a fact-finding mission to a particular conflict zone and to make public recommendations to the Security Council on the basis of the findings. In the event that the Security Council failed to implement its recommendation, the judicial body could initially issue a warning with a further recommendation for action within a set period of time. Failing subsequent action the judicial body could declare the Security Council to be paralysed and to appeal for states to unilaterally take the requisite action. Failing this, the body could deploy the UN standing army.

The standing army itself need not, I believe, constitute a traditional army with heavy machinery such as tanks and major offensive weapons. Rather, the force should be designed and equipped to engage in the type of robust peacekeeping missions currently deployed, such as the UN Operation in Côte d'Ivoire. The force would not be one used to defeat an opposing army but rather to halt atrocities and repel further attacks. It would, in effect, be a rapid reaction force which would not have to be huge; according to Sir Brian Urquhart:

> Experience ... shows that even a small, highly trained group with high morale and dedication, arriving at the scene of action immediately after a Security Council decision, would in most cases have a far greater effect than a larger and less well-prepared force arriving weeks or even months later. (Langille, 2002, pp. 70–1)

Additionally, an aspect of such a force's efficacy, not related to size, is the fact that, as the UN Commission on Global Governance noted, 'the very existence of an immediately available and effective UN Volunteer Force could be a deterrent in itself' (1995, p. 112). The influence of the force would not, therefore, only be exercised by its active use but rather also by its potentiality (Cooper and Kohler, 2009, p. 243). A smaller force would, of course, also be more feasible logistically and financially.

At present the UN requires states to volunteer troops to its peacekeeping missions; as previously discussed, this has meant, however, that there have been occasions when a peacekeeping mission has been sanctioned only to be compromised by insufficient troops and military equipment. As David Hamburg notes, missions have often been undermined by 'the unwillingness of key states to deploy troops in cases where they do not perceive their vital interests are involved or fear adverse effects on domestic affairs' (2008, p. 217). To overcome this, the military force suggested here would comprise soldiers under UN command; individuals would, therefore, join the UN army directly, as opposed to being seconded to UN missions, as is currently the case and would thus be loyal only to the UN army. The military force would have bases on each continent from which to potentially deploy troops and could utilize the existing infrastructure at the disposal of the UN Department of Peacekeeping Operations such as the UN Logistics Base in Brindisi, Italy. The force would, finally, be funded through UN member states fees; studies suggest that a force of 5–10,000 troops would cost $500 million to establish and $200 million per year (Pattison, 2008, p. 129). This force could also, of course, be used to supply troops to traditional peacekeeping missions.

The advantages of institutional reform

The proposal presented above clearly requires more detail; the underlying rationale and key features of the proposal, however, do, I contend, have merit. The idea of a standing UN military is neither new nor as fantastical as it may initially seem; indeed Weiss argued that the need for major institutional reform, including a standing UN army, is 'obvious' (2009b, p. 180). The Charter itself contains provisions for a UN military force; Article

43 of the Charter was intended to provide the UN with an organized military force at the Security Council's disposal. Article 43.1 commits all states to 'make available to the Security Council, on its call and in accordance with a special agreement or agreements, armed forces, assistance and facilities'. This never materialized and thus the Security Council has not been able to enact Article 42 which enables the Council to *authorize* and *require* the use of force (Dixon, 2007, pp. 330–1). The Security Council has at times, such as in response to Iraq's invasion of Kuwait in 1991, authorized the use of force but has not, as such, *required* such action. The Security Council's role in deploying troops during the 1990s was, in many respects, limited to legitimizing action taken by coalitions rather than actively authorizing action itself (Job, 2006, p. 63). Articles 45 and 47 of the Charter outline the scope and structure of the Military Staff Committee which was designed as a means by which the UN would have something akin to a standing army, but this entity was a victim of the Cold War and has never played a significant role (Chesterman, 2011b, p. 24).

Since the inception of the UN, calls have been made for the establishment of a UN military force. In 1948, the UN Secretary-General Trygve Lie proposed the creation of a 'small guard force ... recruited by the Secretary-General and placed at the disposal of the Security Council'. Additionally, a 'Peace Force' was proposed by Secretary-General U Thant in 1963 (Teichrib, 2000). Various statesmen and military officials have advocated the establishment of a multinational force, most recently at the 2010 EU summit, and the foreign offices of a number of states, including the Nordic states, the Netherlands, the UK and Canada, have explored the possibility of formally integrating elements of their national armies within a UN framework as was attempted in 1996 with the creation of the Multi-National Stand-By High Readiness Brigade for UN Operations (SHIRBRIG) which was established as a brigade available to the UN as a rapidly deployable peacekeeping force. Though SHIRBRIG eventually comprised 16 full members and 7 observer states it ceased operations in 2009 following a number of deployments in Africa.

Many academics, activists and practitioners have also advanced proposals for the creation of a UN military force (Urquhart, 1993; Hillen, 1994; Conetta and Knight, 1995;

Arbuckle, 2006; Pattison, 2010), while a number of high-profile international commissions – such as the 2000 Report of the Panel on UN Peace Operations and the 2004 High Level Panel on Threats, Challenges and Change – and various non-governmental organizations, have made similar proposals. The forces suggested, however, are generally advanced in the context of traditional peacekeeping operations which, unlike coercive humanitarian interventions, are undertaken with the consent of the host state. Thus, while a standing UN peacekeeping force would certainly constitute a major institutional innovation, it would not be mandated to undertake the type of interventions discussed here. This proposal is, therefore, more ambitious but much of both the rationale and logistical analysis offered for a standing peacekeeping force remains applicable.

There have been a number of studies detailing the logistical and financial requirements of such a force. Arguably the most comprehensive proposals to date were the reports, *Bridging the Commitment–Capacity Gap* (Langille, 2002) and *A United Nations Emergency Peace Service* (Johansen, 2006). Both reports emphasized the pressing need for a standing UN army and called for more research into, and proposals on, the logistics of establishing and maintaining this force. Peter Langille advocated the creation of a 'UN Emergency Service' and noted, 'It is time for an in-depth, transnational study to identify the general and specific requirements for starting, maintaining and operating a UN Emergency Service [which] should offer guidance into appropriate composition, structure and organization' (2002, p. 16). Likewise, Robert Johansen argued that such a force was 'desperately needed' and called for 'further research and more detailed analyses and blueprints to supplement the current proposal with additional materials', citing in particular outstanding questions regarding logistics, structure, legality and authorisation (2006, pp. 10 and 70). Such minutia and further details are, I feel, unnecessary here; while there are doubtless myriad areas where further clarification is required, the basic ethos and structure of these innovations do, I believe constitute a viable solution to the problem posed by intra-state crises. The following sections defend this proposal by first outlining the advantages offered by these reforms and then addressing the key critiques.

Legitimacy and objectivity

The question 'who decides?' has consistently been asked with respect to humanitarian intervention. Currently international law provides an answer – the Security Council – which, as I have argued, is untenable. The P5 has not demonstrated a willingness to engage in any type of action which does not directly correlate with their national interests (Berdal, 2003, p. 20). This is hardly a revelation; it is a fact which has been born out time and time again. It is, additionally, hardly a surprise; surely it would be illogical for any of the P5 to act in way which did not complement their interests and they are arguably not to blame for so doing, especially given their respective national responsibilities. If we cannot rely on the P5 to make objective decisions, and if, by virtue of their record, the legitimacy of their decisions is widely seen as lacking, then, under the present system we are left with unilateral intervention as the only alternative. Again, such action is both illegal and also tainted by the charge of illegitimacy; can states be trusted to act in defence of suffering strangers? While unilateral intervention cannot be rejected in every case as nefarious, as discussed in Chapter 7, such interventionism is widely deemed to be illegitimate and potentially destabilizing. Again, history suggests that a system, which enables individual states to intervene when they alone consider it necessary, is disorderly and more prone to violence (Bellamy, 2004b, p. 132). As discussed in Chapter 7, states appear to prefer the obviously imperfect authority of the Security Council to unilateralism. This should be seen, however, as reflecting a 'lesser of two evils' choice; a rejection of the latter rather than an endorsement of the former (Cronin and Hurd, 2008, p. 15).

Quite logically, if a legal system comprises a disreputable body with decision making powers at its zenith that system is fundamentally compromised. The function of law must be to do more than advance rules; clearly it must enforce these rules and, crucially, do so in a manner which is seen as legitimate. Kelsen, in defence of international judicial decision making, argued:

> The objective examination and unbiased decision of the question of whether or not the law has been violated is the most important, the essential stage in any legal procedure. As long as it is not possible to remove from the interested states the

> prerogative to answer the question of law and transfer it once and for all to an impartial authority, namely, an international court, any further progress on the way to the pacification of the world is absolutely excluded. (1972, p. 13)

In Kelsen's view, transferring power to international judicial bodies contributes to 'the pacification of the world'; the goal of the judicial body advanced here is more modest, though this progressive (in both senses of the word) evolution is not discounted.

An independent judicial body, unlike the Security Council, would be obviously free from national interests and also the suspicion that national interests were behind decisions made. The body's independent capacity to gather data and its freedom from any particular national bias would give it a credibility and legitimacy that the Security Council lacks. Obviously, a ruling may anger a particular state, and its allies, but charges of subjectivity and political interests would be manifestly baseless.

Kelsen, though supportive of an international coercive force argued that this could only be operable once a judicial body had been established with international legitimacy through which the force could be mobilized (1972, pp. 13–16). Danilo Zolo thus summarizes Kelsen's perspective as comprising, 'two essential theses, a cosmopolitan one and a judicial one'. The cosmopolitan thesis holds that international peace can only be guaranteed by a centralized system of international law. The judicial thesis comprises a belief in 'an international court of justice operating in relation to disputes between states as a higher, impartial third party, with an international police force under its command' (Zolo, 1998, p. 319). Zolo suggests that for a force capable of actually enforcing international law would require enormous military resources to rival the national armies of existing superpowers (ibid, p. 321). Indeed, Kelsen also argued, 'It is the essential characteristic of the law as a coercive order to establish a community monopoly on the use of force' (1972, p. 3). This implies not only the establishment of an international coercive force with preponderant capacity but additionally the disarming of existing national militaries; quite obviously a highly ambitious aim (Armstrong, Farrell and Lambert, 2007, p. 18). The force proposed here, however, would not need a monopoly on the use of force due to its very narrow remit, which, unlike the model discussed by Kelsen, would enforce only one aspect of international law. Of course, the proposal here, if operationalized, could no doubt serve as a key stage in the evolution towards a much more expansive model, which, in principle, I support.

Consistency

Linked to the above, the proposal advanced here would ensure the consistent application and enforcement of international law prohibiting the commission of the four crimes cited in paragraph 138 of the 2005 World Summit *Outcome Document*. So long as the response of the 'international community' is predicated on the whims of the P5, as will continue to be the case while R2P avoids the issue of reform, the response to intra-state crises will be inconsistent. Certain intra-state crises will prompt robust action, while other, more serious crises will not. This has been one of the themes of the preceding chapters and an obvious feature of the post-Cold War era where, for example, the non-intervention in Rwanda in 1994 contrasted sharply with the sanctioning of intervention in Haiti that same year. It surely cannot be acceptable to articulate a set of norms and codify a set of laws prohibiting certain acts only to selectively implement these laws on the basis of particular sectional interests. Such erratic enforcement domestically would be rightly cited as evidence that a state was 'failed'.

Given the powers of the P5, their respective national interests and the horse-trading that accompanies decision making – usually behind closed doors (Buchanen and Keohane, 2011, p. 47) – it is entirely predictable that future responses to intra-state crises will vary. The NATO intervention in Libya in 2011 may well have been the right thing to have done, given the scale of the atrocities under way and publicly promised by Gaddafi, but this cannot be cited as evidence of a new consistency. If anything, it is consistent with the record of inconsistency which has marked the Security Council's response to such crises in the post-Cold War era (Chesterman, 2011a).

The creation of a standing army would serve as a means by which the decisions of the judicial body would be enforced to remove the possibility that the sanctioning of intervention would not result in actual intervention. So long as military response is itself dependent on the political interests of states, who are often naturally reluctant to send their troops into conflict zones where they have no strategic interests, the record of intervention will continue to be erratic, as evidenced by the international response to the genocide in Rwanda in 1994 and the poorly resourced UN peacekeeping mission deployed in Darfur in 2007 (Barnett, 1997, p. 559; Wheeler, 2002, p. 227; Schulz, 2009, p. 153). As Kofi Annan observed in his 1999 report on the Rwandan Genocide to the General Assembly, 'the failure to intervene was driven more by the reluctance of Member States to pay the human and other costs of intervention, and by doubts that the use of force would be successful, than by concerns about sovereignty' (Wheeler, 2001, p. 126). In the contemporary era, the willingness of governments to contribute to peace support operations has declined, though the need for a UN response capability has become more acute (Canadian Peacebuilding Coordinating Committee, 2001, p. 4). Indicatively, Ed Luck, the UN Special Adviser on the Responsibility to Protect, warned that while it is relatively unproblematic to determine that grave violations of human rights proscribed by R2P have occurred, responding effectively is compromised by the current system as, 'finding the material, human, financial and ... military resources to implement is rarely assured' (2008, p. 8). Currently, to launch a military operation US cooperation is 'a *sine qua non*' (Macfarlane, Thielking, and Weiss, 2004, p. 985). This has obviously negative implications for the consistency of response, and a standing UN army would remove this dependence on US assent.

A guard against spurious humanitarian interventionism

One of the main arguments advanced against legalizing humanitarian intervention is that it would lead to a proliferation of intervention's spuriously legitimized as 'humanitarian' (Schachter, 1991, p. 126; Stromseth, 2005, p. 257). Indicatively, Gareth Evans warned, 'any formalisation of the principle would, in the long tradition of *missions civilisatrices*, only encourage those who were all too inclined to misuse it' (2004, p. 71). This argument is not convincing, particularly in the context of the proposal advanced here, which would, I believe, actually limit the scope for illegitimate interventionism.

This proposal, if ever realized, will not be able to prevent unilateral intervention spuriously justified as humanitarian but no legal system is so perfect that its laws are never violated or illegitimately invoked. If a state or group of states is determined to subvert both the Security Council and the new organ then they will doubtless do so. International law has never been able to absolutely guard against violations of the law, and thus the occurrence of such illegal action will not constitute a break with historical tradition (Byers, 2005a). It must be noted, however, that doing so in the context of the establishment of the new organ forecloses the argument, routinely proffered during both the intervention in Kosovo and the invasion of Iraq, that paralysis at the Security Council forced states to 'do the right thing' in defiance of an anachronistic system. Action taken without either Security Council or the new judicial body's approval would be so difficult to legitimize that it is difficult to conceive how it would not be a blatant violation of international law and perceived as such whatever the protestations of its instigators. Without approval from both the Security Council and the new judicial body, any intervention would be manifestly unjustified.

Additionally, because humanitarian intervention without Security Council approval would be permissible under certain circumstances via this proposal does not mean it would be permissible in all cases. James Connelly and Don Carrick argue that it is 'deeply flawed' to assume 'that if something is legally required, permitted or forbidden then it is also, automatically, morally required, permitted or forbidden' (2011, p. 46). There has been, they argue, an 'unquestioned equivocation between law and morality' which pervades thinking on these issues (ibid, p. 46). While this has obvious implications for acts which are illegal but legitimate it also has implications for acts which may be legal but not necessarily legitimate, or morally defensible. Hence, legalizing humanitarian intervention does not, and certainly should not, constitute the opening of the floodgates whereby such action is undertaken whenever there is sufficient evidential basis to support its legality. It may still be better, on moral or prudential grounds, not to intervene. Indicatively, as Nicholas Rengger has argued, even if we accept that there was a legal basis for the invasion of Iraq, or imagine that the Security Council had sanctioned the invasion, the invasion was still not defensible on both moral and prudential grounds (2005, p. 145). The proposal advanced here, therefore, does not remove the need for the exercise of judgement beyond narrow legal analysis. Domestically, judges routinely use discretion in applying the law and do not behave as automatons when handing out sentences; the broader context, including the history and likely impact, is, or at least should be, a factor.

An assault on sovereignty?

One of the more prominent fears related to R2P, and humanitarian intervention more generally, is that such action constitutes an unacceptable assault on sovereignty. These arguments were dealt with at length in Chapter 7; suffice to say here they are less than convincing and are invariably advanced in the context of unilateral humanitarian intervention. While I, in principle, support humanitarian intervention, I have argued throughout this book that sovereignty must be preserved in some form. Thus, a system based on a hierarchy of states whereby certain ostensibly 'more advanced' states have special rights, such as where democratic coalitions are empowered to intervene in the affairs of others, would constitute an unacceptable reversion to the pre-Charter era and surely usher in a new era of subjugation. The key point made in Chapter 7, however, was that the supposed choice between sovereignty and intervention, independence and subjugation, is false; it is quite possible for the accepted understanding of sovereignty to alter in such a way that it preserves the key tenets of the concept so that states retain a meaningful independence, but which also increases international regulation of intra-state affairs.

The proposal above would ensure that states retained control by virtue of the fact that the new body would be independent of any ideology, national interest or normative allegiance and remain accountable to the General Assembly; the same cannot be said of the Security Council, or individual/groups of states engaging in unilateral intervention. The great, and perfectly reasonable, fear expressed routinely in many speeches and declarations from the developing world regarding humanitarian intervention – namely, that it constitutes either the subjective imposition of particular norms, or the wilful exercise of power – would necessarily be assuaged by the judicial body by virtue of the inclusive process by which it would be established, its composition and narrow remit. No state can today claim a cultural right to commit the four crimes prescribed at the World Summit in 2005 and nor could an independent, accountable judicial body be deemed biased.

Sovereignty, as discussed in Chapter 7, has been defended as a necessary ordering principle in international relations and thus many have expressed concerns about diverting power to international bodies. Yet even Hedley Bull, inherently wary and sceptical of intervention, acknowledged that provided there was agreement amongst states as to their own duties and rights, 'The spread of the doctrine that states are not the only subjects of international law would be likely to represent a strengthening of the contribution of international law to international order' (2002, p. 146). Likewise Jean Cohen makes the point that the contemporary debate on intervention and sovereignty has demonstrated not that both are inherently problematic but rather that a new relationship between the two must emerge, which preserves the basic foundation of sovereignty and actually strengthens it by virtue of regulating external intervention. There is, she maintains, a choice:

> we can either opt for strengthening international law by updating it, making explicit the particular conception of sovereignty on which it is now based and showing that this is compatible with cosmopolitan principles inherent in human rights norms; or we can abandon the principle of sovereign equality and the present rules of international law for the sake of human rights, thus relinquishing an important barrier to the proliferation of imperial projects. (Cohen, 2004, p. 3)

Thus, far from diminishing sovereignty, new laws on humanitarian intervention would actually strengthen the sovereignty of states by virtue of clarifying, and regulating, the scope for legitimate external intervention. A law governing intervention, which ensures consistency and automaticity, would require the creation of an obligation. This, contrary to the claims of some, would actually be of benefit to sovereignty; as Peters notes, 'such an obligation is recommendable precisely to obliterate the need for unilateral action and to forestall the pretexts' (2009, p. 540)

The idea that states would endorse a body which necessarily impacts on their sovereignty has, however, been discounted by some. According to Richard Cooper and Juliette Voinov Kohler, 'many states resist the adoption of a precise regulatory framework that will govern the collective use of force [and] resist empowering the UN with the capacity to deliver on its promise to protect populations from atrocity crimes' (2009, pp. 247–8). It is certainly true that some states, by virtue of their own oppressive policies, will resist such a body and no doubt articulate the shibboleth that it would constitute an 'unacceptable assault on sovereignty'. These arguments can invariably be discounted as devoid of merit; it was obviously no surprise that Sudan, for example, was critical of external intervention at the 2009 General Assembly debate but the government's actions in Darfur surely discredit, and explain, their position.

Nonetheless, it may seem difficult to conceive of even non-oppressive states voluntarily aggregating power and aspects of their sovereign inviolability to a coercive international force. As discussed in Chapters 6 and 7, however, states seek predictability and security and, by virtue of their desire to achieve both, they are likely to determine that ceding certain powers to a higher authority can cohere with their national interests, provided this is done collectively and the higher authority is demonstrably legitimate and accountable. As the DIIA noted, 'States are attracted to international law by the expectation that it will further their interests' (1999, p. 20). Law would never work domestically or internationally if individuals or states implacably refused to countenance a trade-off between the abrogation of certain personal freedoms and the acceptance of constraints, and the benefits that accrue from this in the form of security and predictability. Under the present system, states are at the mercy of the Security Council, and indeed powerful states more generally, and thus have little guard against illegitimate intervention. The new judicial body, however, would constitute a surely more attractive locus of authority given its objectivity. This is a view shared by Sir Arthur Watts who argued that that the alternative to the rule of law is 'anarchy and disorder, even chaos' and, therefore, 'The occasional constraints and disadvantages of the international legal system are overwhelmingly outweighed by the advantages which it confers on States.' Watts also argued that debates and events in the contemporary era had exposed the profound weaknesses with the existing system, specifically with respect to the enforcement of international law and the response to intra-state humanitarian crises. Given these deficiencies, he asserted, 'There is a choice: the international community must either establish an international force to maintain order, or let states perform that function themselves.' The latter option, has been tried but, he notes, this in effect creates 'self-appointed guardians of the peace ... that cannot be a satisfactory basis on which to organize a legal order (Watts, 2001, p. 7).

During the 2009 General Assembly debate on R2P, a number of states *did* support more tangible reform akin to the above proposal; South Korea and New Zealand, for example, called for the creation of a rapid-reaction force; Gambia suggested the creation of a neutral arbiter in the form of a representative committee that would advise on reactions to intra-state crises; Italy called for a Rule of Law Standing Capacity on the model of the Standing Police Capacity; and Singapore called for the Security Council to be made more formally accountable to the General Assembly (Hehir, 2011).

These, and other tentative signs of an emerging consensus in favour of transnational decision making dealt with in Chapter 7 should not, however, be exaggerated; 'The ethics of human rights', Jackson warns:

> have to be fitted into the pluralist framework of international society and cannot sidestep that framework. That is the only operational context within which human beings can be defended in contemporary world politics. Human rights and humanitarianism have no actuality outside that pluralist framework. Solidarism is clearly subordinate to pluralism. (2000, p. 289)

The world is, therefore, likely to remain divided into a plurality of states for some time and attempts to protect human rights must work with, rather than against, states. This proposal does this by virtue of the fact that the new bodies are accountable to states but not controlled by any state(s) and charged with a very specific mandate related only to the four crimes universally endorsed as illegal.

What about the P5?

While, as discussed above and in Chapter 7, we can point to some evidence to support the claim that the developing world – often I believe mistakenly cited as purveyors of sovereign inviolability –

are not necessarily implacably opposed to the spirit of this proposal, the willingness of the P5 to countenance such change is a different matter. As Mats Berdal notes, 'The UN was consciously designed, through the provisions of the Charter, to account for the realities of power and hierarchy in international relations, not to supersede the state system' (2008, p. 182). While this is undoubtedly true, it does not suggest that altering the system is necessarily contrary to its historical genesis or more specifically that the changes advocated earlier disregard the influence of power and, if realized, *would* supersede the state system; this is not a blueprint for a world government but rather a reform designed to work in narrowly prescribed circumstances. That the P5 have managed to withstand the clamour of calls made in recent years to increase the representativeness of the veto-wielding powers on the Security Council, suggests that a reform of the scale proposed here has little chance of success. This is a widely held view; according to Weiss, major states 'show no desire to let an independent UN official ... make the key decisions about use of force or other important responses' (2009b, p. 139). With specific reference to the current world superpower, Vittorio Parsi claims, 'to consider a reform of the United Nations that could reduce the power of the United States is pure fantasy' (2006, p. 118), while Koskenniemi cautioned that 'an empire is never an advocate of an international law that can seem only an obstacle to its ambitions' (2001, p. 34).

With respect to the most obvious question of what would happen if the judicial body sanctioned a military intervention against one of the P5, the answer is simple; this would not happen. Any such military action would, quite obviously, be suicidal and the judicial body would, as stated earlier, take the likely consequences of intervention into consideration before sanctioning action. This would also be additionally true of the P5's closest allies who would also be potentially immune from intervention if they had an agreement with one of the P5 that guaranteed military support in the event of external intervention; there are, however, very few such cases and it is additionally questionable whether any of the P5 would actually attack a UN force to defend another state found guilty of committing one of the four crimes.

In a different context, that of establishing an International Marshals Service (IMS) for the ICC to enable the court to apprehend indicted suspects, Cooper and Kohler acknowledge that restraining the exclusive authority of the Security Council to sanction coercive action would pose significant problems: 'The P5 may resist allowing the IMS to enforce action on their territory or on the territory of their allies. They may equally resist a triggering mechanism that limits their discretionary power' (2009, p. 257). As discussed throughout this book, the P5 have indeed resisted any attempt to limit their discretionary power, most notably at the 2005 World Summit, and, as discussed in Chapter 4, curtailed the modest powers of the Special Adviser on the Prevention of Genocide to ensure they retained the capacity to block even the Special Adviser's submissions.

On this evidential basis, it is certainly highly likely that any proposal seeking to compel the Security Council to act would utterly fail. This proposal, however, does not suggest this but rather creates an alternative body that can be mobilized when the P5 fail to act. This means that if a crisis erupts in a state of little strategic interest to the P5 pushing the matter to the new judicial body may actually not be such an unattractive proposition for the P5. The P5 may, in fact, view this as a means by which the pressure on them, and the US in particular, to 'do something' would be somewhat relieved by virtue of the existence of the alternative body. This body would also, importantly, not have any role in inter-state affairs or regulating the use of force beyond humanitarian intervention. Divisive and sensitive issues, such as self-defence in particular, would not, therefore, be under the new organ's purview.

Additionally, the establishment of the ICC is evidence that the P5 do not have the ability to block the establishment of new international bodies; thus the barrier posed by Article 108 with respect to amending the Charter mentioned earlier would not be a problem in this case. As discussed in Chapter 7, the ICC has extensive competencies and 'restricts state power and sovereignty prerogatives' (Scheipers, 2009, p. 2). The ICC thus obviously compromises traditional notions of sovereignty, and yet it was primarily driven by states from the developing world. The lesson of the establishment of the ICC is, therefore, that even if the P5 did oppose the creation of a new judicial body and military force specifically tasked with addressing humanitarian crises it is not the case that this opposition would necessarily foreclose the possibility that this reform could occur. Scheipers, in fact, argues that the 'anarchical' nature of the international system potentially facilitates the development of radical challenges to hegemonic power:

> the meaning of the normative foundations of the international society – sovereignty and human rights – is fluid and subject to continuous contestation and conflict. Hegemonic interpretations may emerge, but they are likely to be challenged by counter-discourse, so that the anarchical condition of the international society will prevail. (Scheipers, 2009, p. 139)

Thus the fatalistic lament 'the Security Council will never support it' may be true – though I contend the reforms are less objectionable than they may first seem – but this is not necessarily the death knell of these reforms.

Conclusion: 'progress rather than perfection'

It is my contention that the debate on humanitarian intervention which erupted in the 1990s highlighted a profound structural flaw at the heart of the UN system, a system which according to Cassese, 'has substantially failed' (2005, p. 339). This flaw is the mechanisms for the enforcement of international law and specifically the powers of the Security Council. The 'problem' with the Security Council, and the UN system of international law more generally, was once ascribed to the Cold War; in the absence of that (somewhat plausible) excuse it is increasingly clear that the ideological division was not exclusively to blame. Predicating the enforcement of international law on the whims of the world's five most powerful states is an aspect of the current system which is untenable and the debate on humanitarian intervention is profoundly important precisely because, to my mind, it has illustrated the P5's stranglehold more starkly than any other issue. It is this issue, therefore, which more than any other has the potential to catalyse a new era in international politics. Indeed, Jennifer Welsh speculated that the implications of debate which erupted in the wake of NATO's intervention in Kosovo may mean that this case could constitute 'the first step on the road to a post Security Council era' (2006, p. 182).

Reforms of the nature outlined above are obviously extensive;

so extensive that they may, not unreasonably, be deemed idealistic. There is, however, a difference between utopianism and the articulation of an ambitious proposal which demands extensive reform; between something that cannot ever be realized and something that may not be. R2P is predicated on an assumption that the disposition of states can be altered through the application of moral pressure. As I have argued, this is neither empirically nor theoretically sound and so long as the structure of the international political and legal system remains unchanged the litany of inhumanitarian non-intervention will surely continue. The 'solution' proposed by R2P has been tried before, and it has consistently failed; to assume that a new set of actors can persuade states to behave better because they have rebranded their appeals as 'R2P' rather than 'Never Again!' is unconvincing and possibly born from either naivety or hubris. Thus there is no choice but extensive reform; if a solution is sought to the problem of inhumanitarian non-intervention, we cannot be surprised that this requires fundamental change. Indeed, it would be truly remarkable if a problem of this magnitude could be solved through a solution as simple as that suggested by R2P.

Those concerned with regulating humanitarian intervention so as to avoid the spectacle of inertia cannot ignore the glaring problem posed by the Security Council's monopoly on the authorization of the use of force. If we wish to put an end to the record of lamentable responses to intra-state humanitarian crises we must, therefore, be prepared to grasp the nettle of major reform and think imaginatively about the contours of a new system. As Weiss argues:

> We require more creative thinking about the absolute necessity for more robust intergovernmental institutions, as well as more passionate (or less embarrassed) advocacy of steps leading toward world government – rather than hoping that the decentralized system of states and a pooling of corporate and civil society efforts will somehow be sufficient to ensure human survival and dignity. (2009b, pp. 227–8)

What Chesterman describes as 'inhumanitarian non-intervention' (2003, p. 54) has been the norm for centuries and the major reforms precipitated by the UN Charter did little to alter this depressing trend. The hope that the end of the Cold War would precipitate a new era for the UN and a greater respect for human rights has not been realized; it must be accepted, therefore, that the system, rather than just its members' disposition, is flawed.

Critics of the notion that the Security Council has failed to respond adequately to intra-state crises can rightly argue that the Security Council's function is, as Dominic Zaum noted, not one of 'maintaining the international rule of law [but rather] an institutionalized process for managing international crises' (2009, p. 402). It is indeed true that the Security Council was not established to function as a traditional custodian of the law and that it had as its primary *raison d'être* the avoidance of major conflict; but this can surely no longer be a viable mandate over twenty years after the end of the Cold War. Additionally, the idea that there exists a choice between international peace and stability or law enforcement and humanitarian intervention is exaggerated. Finally, the notion that genocide, for example, does not constitute an 'international crisis' is curious indeed; the Security Council has consistently failed to respond adequately to many such crises which, despite their intra-state nature, obviously have consequences for international peace and stability as the devastating repercussions of the Rwandan genocide on peace and stability in the surrounding region illustrated (H. Weiss, 2009).

While changes to the UN Charter are rare – three since 1945 (Chesterman, 2011b) – major changes in the international system do periodically occur; elements of the contemporary system such as the EU and the ICC would doubtless seem incredible to early twentieth-century statesmen. These changes are generally a product of a particular sequence of events; the emergence of a new disposition/norm, a change in the calculus of states as to their interests, the codification of these new norms as laws and the creation of new institutions to regulate these laws. Without the latter legal and institutional reforms, changes in moral norms are largely irrelevant and, crucially, the calculus of states remains the same. National interests are, of course, influenced by external as well as internal change but states are naturally more likely to ignore a nebulous moral discourse than a legal proscription; the emergence of a critical mass opposed to slavery had to be accompanied by legal expression – including punitive sanctions – for states to decide it was in their interests to cease this practice. Indeed, all the talk of normative power and moral persuasion emanating from R2P advocacy groups begs the question, 'why do we have laws?' If states can be persuaded to 'do the right thing' why did we ever need legal codes? The world presented by proponents of R2P in which 'good people' persuade receptive world leaders to behave responsibly suggests legal codes are unnecessary; we can simply discuss disputes, exchange alternative views and ultimately sense will prevail. In such a scenario why do we need positive law? Why bother crafting an elaborate set of guidelines and detailed instructions when we can work out logically and in a spirit of compassion, the best course of action. Of course, bitter experience amply demonstrates that effective regulation – both internal and external – cannot be achieved on the basis of morality alone hence the proliferation of positive law. This form of naivety, which observes good practice and concludes that those involved must therefore be inherently good, was critiqued at length by Reinhold Niebuhr and it is a theme I draw on in the concluding chapter (1986, p. 160).

Idealists fail to appreciate the extent to which effective systems must be based on rules and constraints; in short, they must be based on laws. Systems work not because they are run by 'good' people, but because they have sufficient checks and balances against the inevitable influence of self-interest. The proposal advanced here clearly privileges law over politics and morality but does not assume that the exercise of law is not political or based on moral principles. As Koskenniemi observes, 'A court's decision or a lawyer's opinion is always a genuinely political act' (2006, p. 72). It is, therefore, a question of limiting, rather than eradicating, the influence of politics. The goal is progress rather than perfection.

Thus, it is international law and more robust international legal institutions which hold the only hope for solving this problem. Law, almost by definition, implies constraint but, read another way, it constitutes freedom. As Koskenniemi writes, international law, 'exists as a promise of justice and thus as encouragement for political transformation' (2006, p. 57). Law, therefore, enables the achievement of positive political transformation, based on new moral codes and norms. To have freedom as humans and for this freedom to mean something, we require law. Niebuhr advanced this view at length; freedom, he argued, is the necessary condition for the individual but this is achievable only through societal organization, what he described as 'a contrived order in his community' (1986, p. 163). Likewise,

Koskenniemi argues that, without law, 'the acting persons or entities exist as subjects of interests and preferences, both liberated and weighed down by their irreducible particularity'. While this superficially appears to constitute freedom, each actor becomes what Koskenniemi describes as a '*homo economicus*, poised to perpetuate the realization of its idiosyncratic preference'. Such actors, driven by an instrumental worldview and pure interest-fulfilment, create literal and metaphysical chaos. The paradox, therefore, is that 'a single-minded instrumentalism is bound to be frustrated in the end: at the mercy of a dangerous and incomprehensible world where every action creates unforeseen consequences, and always falls short of satisfying the ever intensifying interests' (Koskenniemi, 2006, p. 69). A viable long-term solution to the cessation of egregious human rights abuses perpetrated by states against their own people is objective and consistent law enforcement rather than a reliance on the benevolence of powerful strangers.

Chapter 9

Conclusion: The Future of Humanitarian Intervention?

This book is about the responsibility to protect but it is also about humanitarian intervention. The idea that R2P can, or should, distance itself from the issue of humanitarian intervention is, I contend, illogical. The very first sentence of the 2001 report *The Responsibility to Protect* reads:

> This report is about the so-called 'right of humanitarian intervention': the question of when, if ever, it is appropriate for states to take coercive – and in particular military – action against another state for the purpose of protecting people at risk in that other state. (ICISS, 2001a, p. VII)

The focus is very clear. How R2P has evolved to the point where today many of its most vocal proponents are at pains to stress that it is about much more than military intervention is curious, if not disingenuous (Evans, 2008, p. 56; Bellamy, 2009, p. 198). Indicatively the International Coalition for the Responsibility to Protect (ICR2P) published an 'educational tool' in September 2011 specifically focused on distancing the concept from humanitarian intervention. The coalition wrote, 'The third pillar of R2P [timely and decisive response] must not be equated with humanitarian intervention' (ICR2P, 2011c, p. 1). It is hard not to conclude that this widely evident attempt to move away from humanitarian intervention is, as Weiss claims, simply 'evasiveness' born from an unwillingness to tackle the difficult issues related to intervention (2011, p. 2). There is no doubt that tackling these highly contentious issues – specifically the powers vested in the Security Council – is likely to generate controversy and cause division, but a disposition desirous of maintaining cordiality and avoiding disagreement creates false consensus which preserves the status quo, as personified by the insipidity of the current UN Secretary-General Ban Ki-Moon. R2P was, it is important to reiterate, in the words of the ICISS a 'response' to the question asked by Kofi Annan in 1999 namely, 'how should we respond ... to gross and systematic violations of human rights that affect every precept of our common humanity?' (ICISS, 2001a, p. VII). At present, R2P has answered this question by reaffirming the discredited system it was established to reform. Naturally an issue like humanitarian intervention encompasses more than simply a discussion about military intervention but military intervention – humanitarian intervention – is ultimately the key issue here (Pattison, 2010, p. 250). What has really been achieved if today the decision to intervene is, as Alex Bellamy admits, 'made in an *ad hoc* fashion by political leaders balancing national interests, legal considerations, world opinion, perceived costs and humanitarian impulses – much as they were prior to the advent of R2P' (2009, p. 3).

In a 2004 article, David Brooks excoriated the international reaction to the slaughter in Darfur. He contrasted the various political commitments made since 1945 and especially since the 1994 Rwandan genocide with the shameful response and concluded: 'The "never again" always comes' (Brooks, 2004). The Security Council mandated intervention in Libya in 2011 certainly constitutes an instance of, in my view, welcome and timely action to halt and prevent slaughter, but it does not mean the problems which caused the non-intervention in Darfur have been removed. We must be cautious, therefore, about inferring too much from this one event and the justificatory rhetoric that accompanied it. As Chesterman notes, formulations of the phrase 'responsibility to protect' have been used previously, prior even to the 2005 World Summit; he notes that in the context of the situation in Georgia, the Abkhazi were said by the Council in a resolution in 2002 to have 'a particular responsibility to protect' returnees (2011a, p. 2)

If the record of humanitarian intervention has been inconsistent then this means by definition that there have been interventions as well as non-interventions. If non-intervention had always been the response then the record would be consistent, albeit even more lamentable. The *inconsistency* is a function of those cases where the Security Council has mandated action or groups of states have determined to act unilaterally, such as Iraq in 1992, Haiti in 1994 and Kosovo in 1999, but failed to do so in response to other crises such as Rwanda, Darfur, the DRC and Sri Lanka. If we wish to improve this record then we must, logically, remove that factor most obviously responsible for this record, namely the power of the permanent five members of the Security Council (P5) and the more general reliance on states to take action. Without reforming international law so that a particular entity is charged with a legal duty, rather than a discretionary entitlement, to intervene, the promises now routinely made by states will count for little and the optimism which greeted the intervention in Libya will be replaced by a new despair regarding inaction elsewhere.

Rhetoric and reality

I have endeavoured to demonstrate that R2P adds little to the key issues in the debate on humanitarian intervention nor has it proposed, or envisaged, reforming the existing system for responding to intra-state humanitarian crises. For this reason I have sought to offer both a critique and a proposal in the hope that this might go some way towards demonstrating the viability of an alternative strategy to that espoused by R2P. The proposal derives from a number of underlying beliefs which adherents to R2P no doubt share and may, I hope, appeal to many currently championing the moral advocacy approach.

In February 2002 UN Secretary-General Kofi Annan expressed his admiration for the linguistic appeal of the term 'The Responsibility to Protect', remarking, 'I admire your diplomatic skill in redirecting the debate, and – believe me – I wish I had thought of this myself' (Chesterman, 2006, p. 172). There is no doubt that the International Commission on Intervention and State Sovereignty's (ICISS) terminology is worthy of merit, creating as it did a simple slogan that encapsulated the essence of the debate and the spirit of the pro-intervention movement. Creative wordplay can only take you so far, however, and beyond this linguistic flourish the concept's efficacy is questionable. There is no doubt that R2P has become 'a commonly accepted frame of reference for preventing and responding to mass atrocities' (Bellamy, 2011, p. 1) but whether this is a particularly significant achievement is questionable. 'Sustainable development' is a commonly accepted frame of reference for tackling poverty but its actual influence is a different matter. R2P has, therefore, become a semantic incantation. Quite logically, R2P advocates William Pace, Nicole Deller and Sapna Chhatpar warn, 'The promise of R2P will have failed if governments begrudgingly admit that such a commitment exists, only to resist its application to specific conflicts' (2009, p. 225).

For millennia, people have argued that states *should* protect their own people and also that states *should* intervene to help those suffering overseas in oppressive states. The idea that R2P has radically altered our understanding of the responsibilities of the state is untrue. As Theresa Reinold argues:

> We do not need the notion of the responsibility to protect to understand that it is morally objectionable to remain passive while scores of innocent civilians are being slaughtered. We also do not need R2P to understand that the host state has a duty to prevent genocide ... this duty was accepted sixty years ago. (2010, p. 67)

What *is* required, she notes, is international consensus that the international community's duty to intervene is a legally binding obligation; R2P has not achieved consensus in this area. In terms of new competencies and mechanisms by which to intervene, R2P has not added anything new. As noted by the ICISS, under the UN Charter, the Security Council has 'considerable latitude to define the scope of what constitutes a threat to international peace and security' (2001a, p. 50). This means that since 1945, if the P5 collectively wanted to intervene to stop an intra-state crises, they could have done so in accordance with the provisions of the Charter. The barrier to consistent humanitarian intervention, therefore, has been the superpower rivalry during the Cold War and since 1991 the absence of political will and disunity amongst the P5 rather than barriers posed by, or gaps within, international law (Chesterman 2002, p. 54). Despite this, as discussed in Chapter 5, the enforcement of R2P in situations where forcible action is required to prevent or halt mass atrocities is wholly predicated on the political will of the Security Council; as the ICISS admitted, 'unless the political will can be mustered to act when action is called for, the debate about human protection purposes will largely be academic' (2001a, p. 70). More recently, Ed Luck, the UN Special Adviser on the

Responsibility to Protect, similarly stated: 'Ultimately, of course, it is all about political will' (2010). Mobilizing political will and changing the behaviour of states through moral advocacy alone on such fundamental issues as human rights and sovereignty is, if history is a guide, extremely onerous, if not impossible.

The various statements and declarations of support made by states regarding R2P invariably promise support for the concept but the record of actual state practice since 2001 contrasts sharply with these hortatory speeches. Indeed, while the 2005 World Summit *Outcome Document* is regularly cited as a key moment in the international acceptance of R2P others have argued that many state signatories actually did not read the document (Reinold, 2010, p. 64). Following the drafting of the *Outcome Document*, the then US Ambassador to the UN John Bolton declared, with typical subtlety, 'I plan to never read it again. I doubt many others will either' (Bellamy, 2009, p. 92). The fact that states overwhelmingly spoke in favour of R2P at the 2009 General Assembly debate is also hardly surprising given that there is nothing inherently threatening in the contemporary variant of R2P; there are no obligations on any states to intervene, no punishments for not intervening and the ambiguity surrounding how violations of a state's internal responsibility to protect should be dealt with provides significant scope to commit crimes without censure. R2P's key documents, as Carsten Stahn observed, 'are silent on the fundamental question of how to deal with violations of the responsibility to protect' (2007, p. 117).

All this means that, even with the emergence of R2P, the Security Council continues to enjoy a discretionary right to intervene which is totally dependent on the interests of the P5. Each member of the P5, Mats Berdal observes, is committed 'to using the Security Council as a means of promoting its interests in the world' (2003, p. 20). National interests, therefore, rather than the protection and promotion of international human rights, are the guiding determinant for each of the P5. As Cherif Bassiouni noted, 'If the responsibility to protect existed, the Security Council would have had a duty to send forces to the DRC long ago' (2009, p. 35). In practice this also means that allies of the P5 need not fear external intervention given the capacity of P5 states to use the veto. During the 2009 General Assembly debate the Sudanese ambassador was perhaps the most critical of the Security Council's powers and record, stating:

> In a nutshell, what is needed are not romantic words to dress up the failures of the United Nations, but serious reform within the Security Council ... To give the Security Council the privilege of being executor of the concept of the responsibility to protect would be tantamount to giving a wolf the responsibility to adopt a lamb. (Sudan, 2009)

Given the extreme and sustained violence orchestrated by the government of Khartoum in Darfur since 2003, Sudan has very limited, if any, moral authority, though the sentiment underlining the above statement is not easily dismissed.

The key fact is that the manner in which large-scale intra-state humanitarian crises are dealt with today, and will be dealt with for the foreseeable future, is to all intents and purposes exactly the same as would have been the case twenty-five years ago. Twenty-five years ago, such a crisis would have *potentially* generated international media attention and gradually moved on to the agenda of the General Assembly and the Security Council. The state deemed to be the aggressor would have invariably denied the charges, other states would have discussed this defence and ultimately the Security Council would have decided whether or not to take action. Exactly the same scenario would take place today should such a crisis erupt. Security Council unanimity would arguably have been more difficult to achieve twenty-five years ago than it is today but this was a function of the Cold War rather than contemporary consensus on R2P. The same controversy surrounding the politicization of the P5 would arise, the dispute about the legality of unilateral action would re-emerge and onlookers would decry the unedifying obfuscation. At times, the interests of the P5 and humanitarian need do align – as per Libya in 2011. The problem is these are coincidences; rare and predicated on a very rare alignment of factors – including personalities, regional politics and geopolitics. This is not a propitious way of consistently addressing intra-state crises.

'The children of light'

In H.G. Wells' novella *The Time Machine* an eccentric 'time traveller' journeys into the future where he encounters a group of humanoid creatures he calls the Eloi. These beings are described as 'pretty little people' possessed of 'a graceful gentleness, a certain child-like ease' (Wells, 1961, p. 25). The time traveller initially believes he has discovered paradise as these creatures are devoid of aggressive impulses and live a care-free existence without social problems of any kind. The time traveller soon discovers, however, that this external utopia in fact conceals a horror in the form of a subterranean species, the Morlocks. These nocturnal creatures, though seldom seen, are the architects of the Eloi's world and, in a grim twist, it transpires that they are actually harvesting the Eloi. The world of the 'pretty little people' is a façade and the Eloi's initially appealing naivety and gentleness is exposed as the means by which the mendacious and cruel Morlocks thrive.

The R2P industry, and its relationship with the real world of international relations, I believe, shares many characteristics with this fable. At its core, the novella describes a corrupt, asymmetrical relationship between a one group of self-interested, aggressive entities and another group whose benevolence and optimism, though endearing, is their fatal flaw. As I have argued throughout this book, R2P is predicated on a belief in the capacity of 'good' people to convince states to change their ways and behave responsibly and altruistically. In the absence of sustained calls for fundamental reform of the existing international system, R2P's advocates necessarily imagine a world where the enlightened convince the recalcitrant to change their ways. The fact that in recent years states have increasingly expressed their support for R2P has been routinely cited as evidence of the efficacy of the enlightened. In fact, when states nod their heads in solemn endorsement of R2P, they are arguably engaging in a form of theatrics designed for public consumption. This is because R2P has been denuded by powerful states of its more controversial aspects leaving it today to constitute a linguistic conceit which reaffirms the status quo (Chesterman, 2011, p. 2). Indeed, one must ask, 'why would states, particularly the Great Powers, *not* support such a nebulous concept? What possible disadvantages could result?' Neither the principle of discretion nor the power vested in the P5 have been affected by R2P and the structure of the system remains the same in all significant respects. So long as the R2P industry champions moral advocacy rather than legal reform they will sponsor a debate which obscures the real structural problems to the advantage of the purveyors and beneficiaries of the current system.

While the websites of many R2P advocacy groups contain myriad articles, opinion pieces and transcripts of conference proceedings, it is not at all clear that this has much resonance outside the veritable 'R2P bubble' that exists, particularly in New York. Indicatively, the violence which ravaged the Democratic Republic of Congo (DRC) and the Great Lakes region generally for so long in the 1990s and early 2000s went largely unreported in the mainstream media despite the fact that it constituted arguably the largest humanitarian crisis in the world at the time and was the subject of much discussion amongst NGOs (H. Weiss, 2009). Recalling the lack of public and political interest in the crisis in Darfur Steve Crawshaw of Human Rights Watch remarked:

> I looked at how odd it had been that the 10th anniversary of Rwanda was April 2004, so in real time people were going 'oh my God we failed so badly 10 years ago'. At the same time as utterly refusing – utterly and completely refusing – to look at what was happening in Darfur in real time. (2009)

Previously, Crawshaw had lamented the limited impact of humanitarian NGO advocacy on policymakers, suggesting that the 'reports thudding on to their desks from human-rights and humanitarian NGOs' may appeal for action but in terms of actually acting as a catalyst for action, 'that doesn't quite count' (2004). Even if NGO advocacy does spark the interest of the media and create public pressure for states to take action it seems clear that the P5 *can* resist such calls. As Allen Buchanan and Robert Keohane note, 'The permanent members most likely to use the veto against humanitarian intervention are extremely powerful and not likely to suffer severe political or economic consequences for using it to thwart such interventions' (2011, p. 47). The idea that the P5 are today less likely to veto interventions because of the existence of vocal proponents of R2P does not equate with reality. Even Chesterman, who argues that R2P has made it harder for the P5 to say 'no' to a request for intervention, cautions that this may not be as significant a development as some believe: 'The hand-wringing response to ongoing massacres in Darfur ... suggested that this negative aspect of the responsibility to protect may be working, but also that anxiety about doing nothing is a far cry from effective intervention to protect the population at risk' (2011b, p. 23).

The R2P industry in addition to exhibiting similarities to the unfortunate Eloi, coheres with the Reinhold Niebuhr's 'children of light'. Niebuhr defined the children of light as, 'those who seek to bring self-interest ... in harmony with a more universal good' (1986, p. 166). Niebuhr criticized 'the social and historical optimism' prevalent among this group as 'the typical illusion of an advancing class which mistook its own progress for the progress of the world' (ibid, p. 162). The children of light seek to advance humanity without recognizing the existence of the 'children of darkness' who take advantage of the normative idealism of the children of light. While the children of light construct democratic systems, nationally and internationally, and accept promises at face value, the children of darkness exploit the regulatory weakness of these systems to pursue their own self-interest. The children of light, Niebuhr argues,

> are virtuous because they have some conception of a higher law than their own will. They are usually foolish because they do not know the power of self-will. They underestimate the peril of anarchy in both the national and the international community. Modern democratic civilisation ... has an easy solution for the problem of anarchy and chaos on both the national and international level of community, because of its fatuous and superficial view of man. It does not know that the same man who is ostensibly devoted to the 'common good' may have desires and ambitions, hopes and fears, which set him at variance with his neighbour. (Ibid, p. 166)

Democracy exists, Niebuhr argues, not because man is inherently virtuous but precisely because man is not (ibid, p. 160).

The key point raised by Niebuhr, of great relevance to the debate on R2P, is the danger inherent in assuming that 'good' is universally understood and that self-interest can be harnessed by moral advocacy and demonstrating the virtues of collective action without concomitant need for legal regulation and the establishment of punitive capacity. Indicative of the view Niebuhr critiques, is Stanley Hoffman's exhortation: 'The concept of "national interest" ... should be widened to incorporate ethical concerns' (1995,

p. 29). Of course, an understanding of the national interest which incorporates an ethical universalism would be a positive development but simply willing this to happen – in the form of the ubiquitous 'should' – provides us with very little instruction as to how to achieve, and crucially to regulate, this.

The power of self-interest among states remains the guiding force in international relations and this is arguably most evident with respect to the P5. To ignore this and assume we can convince these states to change their ways through moral advocacy alone is unlikely to achieve positive results. 'The children of light', Niebuhr argued, 'have not been as wise as the children of darkness.' The fatal mistake they have made, he warned, is that they 'underestimated the power of self-interest' (Niebuhr, 1986, p. 166). Self-interest, therefore, exists, and will likely always exist, but this need not induce fatalism. The influence of self-interest is tempered myriad times on a daily basis by domestic, and in certain cases international, law. Increased legal regulation, therefore, offers a viable, and I suggest the only viable, means of mitigating the pervasive influence of self-interest.

The future of humanitarian intervention?

I have argued that the only means to avoid the perennial cycle of inhumanitarian non-intervention is wholesale reform of the international system. Key to this is establishing obligations rather than rights. International law does *not* impose an obligation upon any state, organization or institution to intervene and this is a profoundly significant deficiency. It is, therefore, the absence of obligations and the prevalence of mere discretionary rights which has, since 1945, inhibited the effective enforcement of international human rights law. As Anne Peters argues:

> The relevant question is, therefore, not the right to intervene, but that of an eventual, though exceptional, obligation of third states or (organized) groups of states to intervene in certain extreme situations, notably in the face of impending mass atrocities. (2009, p. 535)

The proposals I advanced in Chapter 8 seek to preserve the basic ethos of sovereignty while enabling intervention in limited circumstances according to objective criteria and independent judgement. The principle informing these proposals is the achievement of consistency and automaticity, which by definition demands the delegation of obligations. My analysis of sovereignty and the objections raised in the developing world to humanitarian intervention in Chapter 7 suggest that many states are sceptical of humanitarian intervention and any diminution in the principle of sovereign inviolability, but also that there is much evidence to suggest that these objections stem from a fear of subjective interpretations of humanitarian necessity and the abuse of humanitarian intervention. The proposals I advance seek to allay these fears while allowing for intervention when the need is clear. This approach differs significantly from many of the more vocal critics of humanitarian intervention but, as I argued, the notion of absolute sovereign inviolability is legally and morally untenable. This nuanced position – for humanitarian intervention in certain circumstances but against the exclusive authority of the Security Council – has been articulated by others (Pattison, 2010). Even Mohammed Ayoob, a self-confessed intervention sceptic, accepted that need for intervention in certain circumstances. To this end he proposed a 'Humanitarian Council' comprising fifty states from across the world, which would have the power to sanction intervention. Removing the Security Council's monopoly over the decision to intervene, he argued, is 'essential' (Ayoob, 2002, pp. 95–6). I believe the state-based composition and sheer size of Ayoob's council would undermine its impartiality and effectiveness but the basic ethos behind the proposal is one I endorse. The need for a standing military force is also an idea that has long been debated and I believe it is humanitarian intervention which most starkly highlights the need for such a force. This force would overcome the need to periodically plead with states to supply troops for military interventions, eliminate state interference in UN military operations and lend interventions an obvious legitimacy derived from the force's independence that is currently lacking with respect to UN-mandated coalitions of the willing.

The obstacles to the reforms I outlined in Chapter 8 are significant but not as insurmountable as they may initially seem. Hans Kelsen argued that reforming international law so that greater authority is delegated to trans-state institutions is 'not a logical impossibility', though he did caution: 'what is logically possible may be politically undesirable' (1972, p. 40). The political undesirability of these proposals doubtless stems from the unwillingness of the P5 to renounce their monopoly on the authorization of the use of force. The obstacle to effect reform is, therefore, evident: the political interests of the P5. Greater acceptance of this barrier would go a long way towards enabling those keen to regulate and facilitate humanitarian intervention to focus on developing the means by which the self-interest of the P5 can be circumvented rather than tempered by eloquent appeals.

What is arguably suggested by the record of humanitarian intervention is that states undertaking such action, either alone or in coalitions, rarely achieve positive results. This suggests, however, that, rather than abandoning all hope, for humanitarian intervention to ever be effective, we should contrive innovative means by which they can be executed and, specifically, empower a new actor to organize and undertake the intervention. This is not to suggest that consequences should not be factored into decision making; there are many scenarios, hypothetical and real, where to intervene would worsen a situation. A blind faith in 'doing good' is not always a prudent, logical or even moral course of action. As Fiona Terry notes, 'To say "let humanitarianism prevail though the heavens fall" ... is absurd' (2002, p. 244).

The contemporary UN system is, as I have argued, fundamentally flawed and this has been a key causal factor on the record of humanitarian intervention. But, this should not induce fatalism; rather it should compel us to think innovatively about how this system may be changed. In this vein, Mats Berdal describes the UN as 'structurally ill equipped ... to plan, mount and sustain enforcement operations'. He cautions, however, that this current predicament should not be seen as immutable: 'It does not follow from this ... that it is inherently incapable of adapting functionally to changing circumstances and new challenges' (2003, p. 24). The UN Charter was drafted over sixty-five years ago and was largely the brainchild of Stalin, Churchill and Roosevelt; elder statesmen from a world long gone. It is hardly surprising, therefore, that the UN is 'structurally ill equipped' to deal with the myriad new challenges facing the world today. What is surprising, however, is that the UN's structural failings and outdated rules of procedure have been overlooked so often by those eager to improve the record of humanitarian intervention. Part II of this book has sought to demonstrate that this is a vital area of research and one which holds great potential. These reforms go beyond the typical call for an expanded, ostensibly more representative, Security Council. The drive to expand the membership of the Security Council appears to conflate representativeness with effectiveness. In fact, increasing the size of the permanent members would most likely come at a significant cost to the effectiveness of the Security Council and it is difficult to see why this reform would have a positive effect on the record of humanitarian intervention (Chesterman, 2011b, p. 4).

This book has sought, therefore, to contribute to that element of the debate on humanitarian intervention which seeks to improve the record of intervention through regulation and the strengthening of international law. The fact that the constituency engaged in promoting humanitarian intervention is dominated by advocates of R2P has necessitated the critique advanced in Part I of this book. While Chapters 2, 3, 4 and 5 are largely critical in intent I hope that the more constructive analysis advanced in Chapters 6, 7 and 8 will be this book's abiding influence.

Conclusion: the reform imperative

The history of humanitarian intervention makes for grim reading. The litany of inaction in the face of mass atrocity is an unedifying trend which has persisted despite the tumultuous changes in international relations in the past 150 years. Additionally, when humanitarian rhetoric has been used most vociferously to defend intervention, it has generally been inversely legitimate (Weiss, 2007a, p. 37). Faced with this evidence, many have concluded that humanitarian intervention constitutes an invariably illegitimate, and usually counter-productive, action that should not be considered let alone undertaken. Indicative of this view, David Gibbs argued with regard to international responses to humanitarian crises, 'sometimes the best course of action is to take no action' (2009, p. 222). This, to my mind at least, is an unhelpful over-reaction. The fact that previous purportedly humanitarian interventions have failed certainly provides us with many examples of how not to intervene, but they do not necessarily mean we should not intervene. If continual failure in the face of a pressing problem led us to discontinue trying to solve that particular problem then human evolution would have stagnated millennia ago.

Weiss describes his work as being infused with 'an unquenchable optimism' (2009b, p. 231). The proposals I advance are obviously ambitious but, I believe, they are achievable and thus I share this optimism, though, like Niebuhr, I do not ignore the realities of power and self-interest. Kelsen's vision of a new legal order has arguably been realized to some degree with respect to certain developments in the post-Cold War era. The changes which have occurred in this period surely constitute evidence that international law is becoming less of an irrelevant abstraction. In discussing the general theme of proposing changes in the international legal order Kelsen advised:

> A conscientious writer must direct his suggestions to what, after careful examination of political reality, may be considered as being possible tomorrow, although it, perhaps, seems not yet possible today. Otherwise there would be no hope for progress. His scheme should involve no revolution of international relations but reform of their order by an improvement of the social technique prevailing in this field. (1972, pp. viii–ix)

All proposals, therefore, by definition involve the articulation of hypothetical structures and practices that are currently lacking and only 'possible tomorrow'. It would be unhelpful, however, albeit possibly engaging, to advocate a totally unrealistic 'revolution of international relations'; while we may dream up systems and norms of behaviour that states *should* abide by, they must surely be tempered by some relationship with the real world. I hope the tentative proposals outlined in this book constitute an ambitious template for tomorrow rather than a proposal for an impossible revolution.

Bibliography

Akhavan, P. (1995) 'Enforcement of the Genocide Convention: A Challenge to Civilization', *Harvard Human Rights Journal*, 8/2, pp. 229–58.

Akhavan, P. (2005) 'Report on the Work of the Office of the Special Adviser of the United Nations Secretary-General on the Prevention of Genocide', McGill University, Faculty of Law, Montréal, Canada, 7 November. Available online, http://www.un.org/en/preventgenocide/adviser/publications.shtml [accessed July 2011].

Ali, T. (ed.) (2000) *Masters of the Universe? NATO's Balkan Crusade* (London: Verso).

Amin, S. (2008) *The World We Wish To See* (New York, NY: Monthly Review Press).

Anghie, A. (2006) 'The Evolution of International Law: Colonial and Postcolonial Realities', *Third World Quarterly*, 27/5, pp. 739–53.

Annan, K. (1999) 'Two Concepts of Sovereignty', *The Economist*, 18 September, pp. 49–50.

Annan, K. (2000) 'Annex 1: Opening Remarks' in Sherman, J. (Rapporteur) 'Humanitarian Action: A Symposium Summary', *International Peace Academy*, International Policy Conference, 20 November, http://www.ciaonet.org/wps/shj04/ [accessed May 2009].

Annan, K. (2001a) 'Report of the SG on the Prevention of Armed Conflict', A/55/985–S/2001/574, 7 June.

Annan, K. (2001b) 'Message Honouring Raphael Lemkin', Press Release SG/SM/7842, 13 June. Available online, http://www.un.org/News/Press/docs/2001/sgsm7842.doc.htm [accessed November 2010].

Annan, K. (2004) 'Letter from the Secretary-General to the President of the Security Council', S/2004/567, 12 July. Available online, http://daccessdds.un.org/doc/UNDOC/GEN/N04/424/63/PDF/N0442463.pdf?OpenElement [accessed June 2010].

Annan, K. (2005) 'In Larger Freedom', A/59/2005, 21 March. Available online, http://daccess-dds-ny.un.org/doc/UNDOC/GEN/N05/270/78/PDF/N0527078.pdf?OpenElement [accessed September 2011].

Anscombe, G. (1981) 'The Justice of the Present War Examined', *Ethics Religion and Politics* (Oxford: Blackwell).

Arbuckle, J. (2006) *Military Forces in the 21st Century* (London: Routledge).

Archibugi, D. (2003) 'Cosmopolitical Democracy' in D. Archibugi (ed.) *Debating Cosmopolitics* (London: Verso).
Arend, A. and Beck, R. (1993) *International Law and the Use of Force* (London: Routledge).
Armstrong, D. and Farrell, T. (2005) 'Introduction' in D. Armstrong, T. Farrell and B. Maiguashca (eds) *Force and Legitimacy in World Politics* (Cambridge: Cambridge University Press).
Armstrong, D., Farrell, T. and Lambert, H. (2007) *International Law and International Relations* (Cambridge: Cambridge University Press).
Ayoob, M. (2002) 'Humanitarian Intervention and State Sovereignty', *International Journal of Human Rights*, 6/1, pp. 81–102.
Bain, W. (2003) 'The Political Theory of Trusteeship and the Twilight of International Equality', *International Relations*, 17/1, pp. 59–77.
Bain, W. (ed.) (2006) *The Empire of Security and the Safety of the Peoples* (London: Routledge).
Bain, W. (2010) 'Responsibility and Obligation in the "Responsibility to Protect"', *Review of International Studies*, 36, pp. 25–46.
Bandow, D. (2000) 'NATO's Hypocritical Humanitarianism' in T. G. Carpenter (ed.) *NATO's Empty Victory* (Washington, DC: Cato Institute).
Barnard, A. (2011) 'China Sought to Sell Arms to Qaddafi, Documents Suggest', *The New York Times*, 4 September. Available online, http://www.nytimes.com/2011/09/05/world/africa/05libya.html?_r=2&pagewanted=1&hp [accessed September 2011].
Barnett, M. (1997) 'The UN Security Council, Indifference, and Genocide in Rwanda', *Cultural Anthropology*, 12/4, pp. 551–78.
Barnett, M. (2002) *Eyewitness to a Genocide* (New York, NY: Cornell University Press).
Barnett, M. (2010) *The International Humanitarian Order* (London: Routledge).
Bass, G. (2008) *Freedom's Battle: The Origins of Humanitarian Intervention* (New York, NY: Vintage Books).
Bassiouni, C. (2009) 'Advancing the Responsibility to Protect through International Criminal Justice', in R.H. Cooper and J.V. Kohler (eds) *Responsibility to Protect: The Global Moral Compact for the 21st Century* (Basingstoke and New York: Palgrave Macmillan).
Bellamy, A. (2002) *Kosovo and International Society* (Basingstoke: Palgrave Macmillan).
Bellamy, A. (2003) 'Humanitarian Intervention and the Three Traditions', *Global Society*, 17/1, pp. 3–20.
Bellamy, A. (2004a) 'Motives, Outcomes, Intent and the Legitimacy of Humanitarian Intervention', *Journal of Military Ethics*, 3/3, pp. 216–32.

Bellamy, A. (2004b) 'Ethics and Intervention; The "Humanitarian Exception" and the problem of Abuse in the Case of Iraq', *Journal of Peace Research*, 41/2, pp. 131–47.

Bellamy, A. (2005) 'Responsibility to Protect or Trojan Horse? The Crisis in Darfur and Humanitarian Intervention after Iraq', *Ethics and International Affairs*, 19/2, pp. 31–54.

Bellamy, A. (2006a) 'Whither the Responsibility to Protect? Humanitarian Intervention and the 2005 World Summit', *Ethics and International Affairs*, 20/2, p. 143–69.

Bellamy, A. (2006b) *Just Wars: From Cicero to Iraq* (London: Polity).

Bellamy, A. (2009) *Responsibility to Protect: The Global Effort to End Mass Atrocities* (London: Polity).

Bellamy, A. (2010) 'Kosovo and the Advent of Sovereignty as Responsibility', in A. Hehir (ed.) *Kosovo, Intervention and Statebuilding* (London: Routledge).

Bellamy, A. (2011) 'Libya and the Responsibility to Protect: The Exception and the Norm', *Ethics and International Affairs*, 25/3, pp. 1–7. Available online, http://www.carnegiecouncil.org/resources/journal/index.html [accessed September 2011].

Benin (2009) 'Statement by the Permanent Mission of Benin to the UN', 28 July. Available online, http://www.responsibilitytoprotect.org/Benin_FR.pdf [accessed October 2011].

Berdal, M. (2003) 'The UN Security Council: Ineffective but Indispensable', *Survival*, 45/2, pp. 7–30.

Berdal, M. (2008) 'The UN, Multilateralism, and International Order', in G. Andreani and P. Hassner (eds) *Justifying War?: From Humanitarianism to Counterterrorism* (Basingstoke: Palgrave Macmillan).

Berman, F. (2007) 'Moral Versus Legal Legitimacy' in C. Reed and D. Ryall (eds) *The Price of Peace* (Cambridge: Cambridge University Press).

Blair, T. (1999) 'Doctrine of the International Community', Speech at the Economic Club, Chicago, 24 April. Available online, http://www.pbs.org/newshour/bb/international/jan-june99/blair_doctrine4-23.html [accessed November 2010].

Bolton, J. (2005) 'Letter to President Ping', 30 August. Available online, http://www.responsibilitytoprotect.org/files/US_Boltonletter_R2P_30Aug05%5B1%5D.pdf [accessed July 2011].

Booth, K. (2001) 'Three Tyrannies' in T. Dunne and N. Wheeler (eds) *Human Rights in Global Politics* (Cambridge: Cambridge University Press).

Bosco, D. (2009) *Five to Rule Them All* (Oxford: Oxford University Press).

Boucher, D. (1998) *Political Theories of International Relations* (Oxford: Oxford University Press).
Bourantonis, D. (2007) *The History and Politics of Security Council Reform* (London: Routledge).
Bowring, B. (2008) *The Degradation of the International Legal Order?: The Rehabilitation of Law and the Possibility of Politics* (Oxford: Routledge-Cavendish).
Branigan, T. (2011) 'Chinese Arms Companies "offered to sell weapons to Gaddafi regime"', *The Guardian*, 5 September. Available online, http://www.guardian.co.uk/world/2011/sep/05/chinese-arms-companies-weapons-gaddafi-regime [accessed September 2010].
Brauman, R. and Saligon, P. (2004) 'Iraq: In Search of a "Humanitarian Crisis"' in F. Weissman (ed.) *In the Shadow of 'Just Wars': Violence, Politics and Humanitarian Action* (London: Hurst)
Brazil (2009) 'Statement by the Permanent Representative of Brazil to the UN', 23 July. Available online, http://www.responsibilitytoprotect.org/Brazil_ENG.pdf [accessed June 2010].
Briggs, H. (1945) 'Power Politics and International Organization', *American Journal of International Law*, 39/4, pp. 664–79.
Brooks, D. (2004) 'Another Triumph for the UN', *The New York Times*, 25 September. Available online, http://www.nytimes.com/2004/09/25/opinion/25brooks.html [accessed June 2011].
Brown, A. (2008) 'Reinventing Humanitarian Intervention?: Two Cheers for the Responsibility to Protect', House of Commons Library Research Paper 08/55, International Affairs and Defence Section, 17 June.
Brown, A. (2009) *Human Rights and the Borders of Suffering* (Manchester: Manchester University Press).
Brown, C. (2001) 'Ethics Interests, and Foreign Policy' in K. E. Smith and M. Light (eds) *Ethics and Foreign Policy* (Cambridge: Cambridge University Press).
Brown, C. (2003) 'In Defence of Inconsistency' in D. Chatterjee and D. Scheid (eds) *Ethics and Foreign Intervention* (Cambridge: Cambridge University Press).
Brown, C. (2006a) *Sovereignty, Rights and Justice: International Political Theory Today* (London: Polity).
Brown, C. (2006b) 'Foreword', in C. Bickerton, P. Cunliffe and A. Gourevitch (eds) *Politics Without Sovereignty* (London: Routledge).
Brownlie, I. (1973) 'Thoughts on Kind-Hearted Gunmen', in R. B. Lillich (ed.) *Humanitarian Intervention and the United Nations* (Charlottesville, VA: University Press of Virginia).
Buchanan, A. and Keohane, R. (2011) 'Precommitment Regimes for Intervention: Supplementing the Security Council', *Ethics and International Affairs*, 25/1, pp. 41–63.

Buhler, P. (2008) 'Military Intervention and Sources of Legitimacy' in G. Andreani and P. Hassner (eds) *Justifying War?: From Humanitarianism to Counterterrorism* (Basingstoke: Palgrave Macmillan)

Bull, H. (1979) 'Human Rights and World Politics', in R. Pettman (ed.) *Moral Claims in World Affairs* (Canberra: Australian National University Press).

Bull, H. (1984) *Justice in International Relations: Hagey Lectures* (Ontario: University Publications Distribution Service).

Bull, H. (2002) *The Anarchical Society: A Study of Order in World Politics* (Basingstoke: Palgrave Macmillan).

Burton, M. (1996) 'Legalising the Sublegal', *Georgetown Law Journal*, 85, 417–54.

Byers, M. (2005a) 'Not Yet Havoc: Geopolitical Change and the International Rules on Military Force' in D. Armstrong, T. Farrell and B. Maiguashca (eds) *Force and Legitimacy in World Politics* (Cambridge: Cambridge University Press).

Byers, M. (2005b) 'High Ground Lost on UN's Responsibility to Protect', *Winnipeg Free Press*, 18 September.

Byers, M. and Chesterman, S. (2003) 'Changing the Rules About Rules?' in J. Holzgrefe and R. Keohane (eds) *Humanitarian Intervention: Ethical, Legal and Political Dilemmas* (Cambridge: Cambridge University Press).

Campbell, D. (1998) 'Why Fight: Humanitarianism, Principles, and Post-structuralism', *Millennium*, 27/ 3, pp. 497–521.

Canada (2009) 'Canadian Statement at the UN General Assembly', 23 July. Available online, http://www.canadainternational.gc.ca/ prmny-mponu/canada_un-canada_onu/statements-declarations/general_assembly-assemblee-generale/240709_r2p.aspx?lang=eng [accessed November 2010].

Canadian Peacebuilding Coordinating Committee, United Nations Association Committee, World Federalists of Canada (2001) 'Report from the NGO-Government Dialogue: Towards a Rapid Reaction Capability for the UN', November. Available online, http://www.globalpolicy.org/un-reform/un-reform-topics/un-standing-force.html [accessed November 2010].

Caplan, R. (2000) 'Humanitarian Intervention: Which Way Forward?', *Ethics and International Affairs*, 14, pp. 23–38.

Carnegie Commission on Preventing Deadly Conflict (1997) 'Preventing Deadly Conflict Final Report With Executive Summary', December. Available online, http://www.wilsoncenter.org/subsites/ccpdc/pubs/rept97/finfr.htm [accessed August 2010].

Carr, E.H. (2001) *The Twenty Years Crisis* (Basingstoke: Palgrave Macmillan).

Carroll, R. (2004) 'US Chose to Ignore Rwandan Genocide', *Guardian*, 31 March.

Cassese, A. (2005) *International Law* (Oxford: Oxford University Press).

Chandler, D. (2000) 'International Justice', *New Left Review*, 6, Nov/Dec, 55–66.

Chandler, D. (2002) *From Kosovo to Kabul* (London: Pluto).

Chandler, D. (2004) 'The Responsibility to Protect? Imposing the "Liberal Peace"', *International Peacekeeping*, 11/1, pp. 59–81.

Chandler, D. (2009) 'Unravelling the Paradox of "The Responsibility to Protect"', *Irish Studies in International Affairs*, 20, pp. 27–39.

Charlesworth, H. and Kennedy, D. (2009) 'Afterword', in A. Orford (ed.) *International Law and its Others* (Cambridge: Cambridge University Press).

Chatterjee, D. and Scheid, D. (2003) 'Introduction' in D. Chatterjee and D. Scheid (eds) *Ethics and Foreign Intervention* (Cambridge: Cambridge University Press).

Chesterman, S. (2002) *Just War or Just Peace?* (Oxford: Oxford University Press).

Chesterman, S. (2003) 'Hard Cases Make Bad Law' in A. Lang (ed.) *Just Intervention* (Washington, DC: Georgetown University Press).

Chesterman, S. (2011a) '"Leading from Behind": The Responsibility to Protect, the Obama Doctrine, and Humanitarian Intervention after Libya', *Ethics and International Affairs*, 25/3, pp. 1–7. Available online, http://www.carnegiecouncil.org/resources/journal/index.html [accessed September 2011].

Chesterman, S. (2011b) 'The Outlook for UN Reform', New York University School of Law, Public Law & Legal Theory Research Paper Series, Working Paper No. 11–55, August. Available online, http://ssrn.com/abstract=1885229 [accessed September 2011].

Chile (2009) 'Statement by the Permanent Representative of Chile to the UN', 23 July. Available online, http://www.responsibilitytoprotect.org/Chile_ENG_SP.pdf [accessed June 2010].

China (2009) 'Statement by the Permanent Representative of China to the UN', 23 July. Available online, http:// responsibilitytoprotectorg/Statement%20by%20Ambassador%20Liu%20Zhenmin.pdf [accessed June 2010].

Chomsky, N. (1999) *The New Military Humanism: Lessons from Kosovo* (London: Pluto).

Chopra, J. and Weiss, T. (1992) 'Sovereignty is no Longer Sacrosanct', *Ethics and International Affairs*, 6, pp. 95–117.

Christopher, P. (2004) *The Ethics of War and Peace* (Upper Saddle River, NJ: Prentice Hall).

Clapham, C. (1998) 'Rwanda: The Perils of Peacemaking' *Journal of Peace Research*, 35/ 2, pp. 193–210.

Clapham, C. (1999) 'Sovereignty and the Third World State', *Political Studies*, 47:3, 522–37.

Coalition of NGOs on Darfur (2008) 'Rhetoric vs. Reality: The Situation in Darfur'. Available online, http://www.hrw.org/sites/default/files/related_material/darfur1208.pdf [accessed June 2011].

Cohen, J. (2004) 'Whose Sovereignty? Empire Versus International Law', *Ethics and International Affairs*, 18/3, pp. 1–24.

Coicaud, J.M. and Wheeler, N. (2008) 'Introduction: The Changing Ethics of Power Beyond Borders' in J.M. Coicaud and N. Wheeler (eds) *National Interests and International Solidarity* (New York, NY: United Nations University Press).

Colclough, E. (2004) *'A Colorful Character': Wearing the Blue Helmet* (Limerick: Warleigh Press).

Coll, A. (2001) 'Kosovo and the Moral Burdens of Power', in A. Bacevich and E. Cohen (eds) *War Over Kosovo* (New York, NY: Columbia).

Collins, B. (2002) 'New Wars and Old Wars? The Lessons of Rwanda' in D. Chandler (ed.) *Rethinking Human Rights* (Basingstoke and New York: Palgrave Macmillan).

Cooper, R.H. and Kohler, J.V. (2009) 'Introduction: The Responsibility to Protect', in R H. Cooper and J. V.Kohler (eds) *Responsibility to Protect: The Global Moral Compact for the 21st Century* (Basingstoke and New York: Palgrave Macmillan)

Conetta, C. and Knight, C. (1995) *Vital Force: A Proposal for the Overhaul of the UN Peace Operations System and the Creation of a UN Legion* (Cambridge, MA: Commonwealth Institute).

Connelly, J. and Carrick, D. (2011) 'Ethical and Legal Reasoning about War in a Time of Terror' in A. Hehir, N. Kuhrt and A. Mumford (eds) *International Law, Security and Ethics* (London: Routledge).

Considine, S. C. and Sonner, H. (2009) 'Interview between author and Sapna Chhatpar Considine, Project Manager, International Coalition for the Responsibility to Protect and Heather Sonner, International Secretariat of the Institute for Global Policy', Tuesday, 18 August, New York.

Crawshaw, S. (2004) 'Genocide? What Genocide', *Financial Times*, 21 August.

Crawshaw, S. (2009) 'Interview between author and Steve Crawshaw, Human Rights Watch', 17 August, New York.

Cronin, B. (2008) 'International Consensus and the Changing Legal Authority of the UN Security Council', in B. Cronin and I. Hurd (eds) *The UN Security Council and the Politics of International Authority* (London: Routledge).

Cronin, B. and Hurd, I. (2008) 'Introduction' in B. Cronin and I. Hurd (eds) *The UN Security Council and the Politics of International Authority* (London: Routledge).

Dallaire, R. (2003) *Shake Hands With the Devil* (London: Arrow Books).
Dallaire, R. (2004) 'Looking at Darfur, Seeing Rwanda', *New York Times*, 4 October.
Dallaire, R. (2009) 'Interview with Romeo Dallaire' in S. Totten and P. R. Bartop (eds) *The Genocide Studies Reader* (London: Routledge).
Danielsen, D. (2009) 'Corporate Power and Global Order' in A. Orford (ed.) *International Law and its Others* (Cambridge: Cambridge University Press).
Danish Institute of International Affairs (DIAA) (1999) *Humanitarian Intervention: Legal and Political Aspects* (Copenhagen: Danish Institute of International Affairs).
de Brichambaut, M.P. (2000) 'The Role of the UN Security Council in the International Legal System' in M. Byers (ed.) *The Role of Law in International Politics* (Oxford: Oxford University Press).
de Cuellar, J.P. (1991) 'Report of the Secretary-General on the Work of the Organization', UN Document A/46/1, 13 September.
Democratic People's Republic of Korea (2009) 'Statement by Democratic People's Republic of Korea to the UN', United Nations General Assembly, 100th Plenary Meeting, 28 July, A/63/PV.100.
Deng, F. (2009) 'Interview between author and Francis Deng, Special Adviser on the Prevention of Genocide', New York, 20 August.
Deng, F. (2010) 'JISB Interview: The Responsibility to Protect', *Journal of Intervention and Statebuilding*, 4/1, pp. 83–9.
Deng, F., Kimaro, S., Lyons, T., Rothchild, D. and Zartman, W. (1996) *Sovereignty as Responsibility: Conflict Management in Africa* (Washington, DC: The Brookings Institution).
Derrida, J. (2005) *Rogues: Two Essays on Reason* (Stanford, CA: Stanford University Press).
Dinstein, Y. (2005) *War, Aggression and Self-Defence* (Cambridge: Cambridge University Press).
Dixon, M. (2007) *Textbook on International Law* (Oxford: Oxford University Press).
Docking, T. (2008) 'US Foreign Policy Towards Africa' in J.M. Coicaud and N. Wheeler (eds) *National Interests and International Solidarity* (New York, NY: United Nations University Press).
Doehring, K. (2002) 'Self Determination' in Simma, Bruno (ed.) *The Charter of the United Nations: A Commentary* (Oxford: Oxford University Press).
Donaldson, T. (2002) 'Kant's Global Rationalism' in T. Nardin and D. R. Mapel (eds) *Traditions of International Ethics* (Cambridge: Cambridge University Press).
Donnelly, J. (2002) 'Twentieth Century Realism' in T. Nardin and D. Mapel (eds) *Traditions of International Ethics* (Cambridge: Cambridge University Press).

Douzinas, C. (2009) 'Speaking Law: On Bare Theological and Cosmopolitan Sovereignty' in Anne Orford (ed.) *International Law and its Others* (Cambridge: Cambridge University Press).

Drinan, R. (2001) *The Mobilization of Shame* (New Haven, CT: Yale University Press).

Egypt (2009) 'Statement on Behalf of the Non-aligned Movement', 23 July. Available online, http://www.responsibilitytoprotect.org/NAM_Egypt_ENG.pdf [accessed August 2010].

Evans, G. (2004) 'When Is It Right To Fight', *Survival*, 46/3, 59–82.

Evans, G. (2006) 'The Responsibility to Protect: Unfinished Business', *Issues and Instruments*, 17 July. Available online, http://www.gevans.org/opeds/oped73.html [accessed March 2011].

Evans, G. (2008) *The Responsibility to Protect: Ending Mass Atrocity Crimes Once and For All* (Washington, DC: Brookings Institution Press).

Evans, G. (2009) 'From an Idea to an International Norm' in R. H. Cooper and J. V. Kohler (eds) *Responsibility to Protect: The Global Moral Compact for the 21st Century* (Basingstoke and New York: Palgrave Macmillan).

Evans, M. (2005) 'Moral Theory and the Idea of a Just War' in M. Evans (ed.) *Just War Theory: A Reappraisal* (Edinburgh: Edinburgh University Press).

Fake, S. and Funk, K. (2009) 'R2P: Disciplining the Mice, Freeing the Lions', *Foreign Policy in Focus*, 23 March. Available online, http://www.fpif.org/fpiftxt/5984 [accessed March 2011].

Farer, T. (2003) 'The Ethics of Intervention in Self Determination Struggles' in D. Chatterjee and D. Scheid (eds) *Ethics and Foreign Intervention* (Cambridge: Cambridge University Press).

Fein, H. (2009) 'The Threes P's of Genocide Prevention', in S. Totten and P. R. Bartop (eds) *The Genocide Studies Reader* (London: Routledge).

Feinstein, L. (2006) *Darfur and Beyond: what is needed to prevent mass atrocities,* Council on Foreign Relations, Council Special Report No. 22. Available online, www.cfr.org/content/publications/attachments/DarfurCSR22.pdf [accessed June 2011].

Feinstein, L. (2007) 'Beyond Words: Building Will and Capacity to Prevent More Darfurs', *Washington Post*, 26 January.

Feinstein, L. and De Bruin, E. (2009) 'Beyond Words: US Policy and the Responsibility to Protect' in R. H. Cooper and J.V. Kohler (eds) *Responsibility to Protect: The Global Moral Compact for the 21st Century* (Basingstoke and New York: Palgrave Macmillan).

Feste, K. (2003) *Intervention: Shaping the Global Order* (Westport, CT: Praeger).

Fisher, D. (2007) 'Humanitarian Intervention' in C. Reed and D. Ryall (eds) *The Price of Peace* (Cambridge: Cambridge University Press).

Fitzmaurice, M. (2006) 'The Practical Working of the Law of Treaties' in M. Evans (ed.) *International Law* (Oxford: Oxford University Press).

France (2009) 'Statement by the Permanent Representative of France to the UN', 23 July, 2009. Available online, http://www.responsibilitytoprotect.org/France_FR.pdf [accessed June 2010].

Franck, T. (2005) 'Interpretation and Change in the Law of Humanitarian Intervention' in J.L. Holzgrefe and Robert O. Keohane (eds) *Humanitarian Intervention: Ethical, Legal and Political Dilemmas* (Cambridge: Cambridge University Press).

Franck, T. and Rodley, N. (1973) 'After Bangladesh: The Law of Humanitarian Intervention by Military Force', *American Journal of International Law*, 67, 275–305.

General Assembly (2000) 'United Nations Millennium Declaration', 55/2, 8 September. Available online, http://www.un.org/millennium/declaration/ares552e.htm [accessed June 2010].

General Assembly (2005) '2005 World Summit Outcome', A/60/L.1, 15 September. Available online, http://www.who.int/hiv/universalaccess2010/worldsummit.pdf [accessed October 2011].

Gibbs, D.N. (2009) *First Do No Harm: Humanitarian Intervention and the Destruction of Yugoslavia* (Nashville, TN: Vanderbilt University Press).

Glennon, M. (1999) 'The New Interventionism', *Foreign Affairs*, 78:3, 2–7.

Glennon, M. (2008a) 'War and Counterterrorism', in G. Andreani and P. Hassner (eds) *Justifying War?: From Humanitarianism to Counterterrorism* (Basingstoke: Palgrave Macmillan).

Glennon, M. (2008b) 'Law, Legitimacy, and Military Intervention' in G. Andreani and P. Hassner (eds) *Justifying War?: From Humanitarianism to Counterterrorism* (Basingstoke: Palgrave Macmillan).

Glenny, M. (1999) *The Balkans, 1804–1999* (London: Granta Books).

Global Centre for R2P (2009a) 'Frequently Made Assertions', 16 June. Available online, http://globalr2p.org/media/pdf/Frequently_made_assertions_16_June_Final.pdf [accessed June 2011]

Global Centre for R2P (2009b) 'Implementing the Responsibility to Protect. The 2009 General Assembly Debate: An Assessment', GCR2P Report, August. Available online, http://globalr2p.org/media/pdf/GCR2P_General_Assembly_Debate_Assessment.pdf [accessed August 2010].

Gompert, D.C., Richardson, C., Kugler, R.L. and Bernath, C.H. (2005) 'Learning from Darfur: Building a Net-Capable African Force to Stop Mass Killing', Centre for Technology and National Security Policy, The National Defense University. Available online,

http://www.ndu.edu/CTNSP/Def_Tech/DTP%2015%20Darfur.pdf [accessed June 2011].
Gow, J. (1997) *Triumph of the Lack of Will: International Diplomacy and the Yugoslav War* (New York, NY: Columbia University Press).
Gow, J. (2005) *Defending the West* (Cambridge: Polity).
Gow, J. (2011) 'Principles of Pre-emption' in A. Hehir, N. Kuhrt and A. Mumford (eds) *International Law, Security and Ethics* (London: Routledge).
Gowlland-Debbas, V. (2000) 'Functions of the United Nations Security Council in the International Legal System' in M. Byers (ed.) *The Role of International Law in International Politics* (Oxford: Oxford University Press).
Gray, C. (2000) *International Law and the Use of Force* (Oxford: Oxford University Press).
Gray, C. (2001) 'No Good Deed Shall Go Unpunished' in K. Booth (ed.) *The Kosovo Tragedy* (London: Frank Cass).
Guicherd, C. (1999) 'International Law and the War in Kosovo', *Survival*, 41/2, pp. 19–34.
Hakimi, M. (2010) 'State Bystander Responsibility', *The European Journal of International Law*, 21/2, pp. 341–85.
Hamburg, D. (2008) *Preventing Genocide* (Boulder, CO: Paradigm).
Hamburg, D. (2009) 'Interview between author and David Hamburg, Chairman of the Office of the Special Adviser for the Prevention of Genocide Advisory Committee', New York, 18 August.
Hayden, P. (2005) *Cosmopolitan Global Politics* (Aldershot: Ashgate).
Hehir, A. (2008a) *Humanitarian Intervention after Kosovo: Iraq, Darfur and the Record of Global Civil Society* (Basingstoke: Palgrave Macmillan).
Hehir, A. (2008b) 'The Changing Conception of Self-defence' in I. Wilson III and J. Forest (eds) *Defence Politics*, (London: Routledge).
Hehir, A. (2010a) *Humanitarian Intervention: An Introduction* (Basingstoke: Palgrave Macmillan).
Hehir, A. (2010b) 'Responsibility to Protect: Sound and Fury Signifying Nothing?', *International Relations*, 24/2, pp. 218–39.
Hehir, A. (2011) 'The Responsibility to Protect in International Political Discourse: Encouraging Statement of Intent or Illusory Platitudes?', *International Journal of Human Rights*, 15/8, pp. 1329–46.
Held, D. (1995) *Democracy and the Global Order* (London: Polity).
Heneghan, T. (2011) 'Gaddafi Tells Rebel City, Benghazi, "We Will Show No Mercy"', *Huffington Post*, 17 March. Available online, http://www.huffingtonpost.com/2011/03/17/gaddafi-benghazi-libya-news_n_837245.html [accessed August 2011].
Henkin, L. (1990) 'Compliance with International Law in an Inter-State System', *Académie de droit international, Recueil des cours 1989* (Dordrecht: Martinus Nijhoff).

Henkin, L. (1999) 'Kosovo and the Law of "Humanitarian Intervention"', *American Journal of International Law*, 93/4, pp. 824–54.

Hertz, J. (1957) 'Rise and Demise of the Territorial State', *World Politics*, 9/4, pp. 473–93.

High Level Panel on Threats, Challenges and Change (2004) *A More Secure World: Our Shared Responsibility*, 2 December. Available online, http://www.un.org/secureworld/report.pdf [accessed August 2011].

Hillen, J. (1994) 'Policing the New World Order: The Operational Utility of a Permanent UN Army', *Strategic Review*, 22/2, pp. 54–62.

Hilpold, P. (2001) 'Humanitarian Intervention: Is There a Need for a Legal Reappraisal?', *European Journal of International Law*, 12/3, pp. 437–67.

Hintjens, H.M. (1999) 'Explaining the 1994 Genocide in Rwanda' *The Journal of Modern African Studies*, 37/2, pp. 241–86.

Hoffmann, S. (1995) 'The Politics and Ethics of Military Intervention', *Survival*, 37/4, pp. 29–51.

Hoffmann, S. (2003) 'Intervention: Should it go on? Can it go on?' in D. Chatterjee and D. Scheid, (eds) *Ethics and Foreign Intervention* (Cambridge: Cambridge University Press).

Hoffmann, S. (2008) 'Foreword: Intervention, Sovereignty, and Human Rights' in G. Andreani and P. Hassner (eds) *Justifying War?: From Humanitarianism to Counterterrorism* (Basingstoke: Palgrave Macmillan).

Holbrook, J. (2002) 'Humanitarian Intervention and the Recasting of International Law', in D. Chandler (ed.) *Rethinking Human Rights* (Basingstoke: Palgrave Macmillan).

Howard, M. (1984) *The Causes of War and Other Essays* (Cambridge, MA: Harvard University Press).

Human Rights Council (2007) 'Report of the High-Level Mission on the situation of human rights in Darfur pursuant to Human Rights Council decision S-4/101' A/HRC/4/80, 9 March.

Human Rights Council (2009) 'Annual Report of the United Nations High Commissioner For Human Rights and Reports of the Office of the High Commissioner and the Secretary-General: Efforts of the United Nations system to prevent genocide and the activities of the Special Adviser to the Secretary-General on the Prevention of Genocide. Report of the Secretary-General', A/HRC/10/30, 18 February.

Hurd, I. (2007) *After Anarchy* (Princeton, NJ: Princeton University Press).

Hurrell, A. (2005) 'Legitimacy and the Use of Force: Can the Circle be Squared?' in D. Armstrong, T. Farrell and B. Maiguashca (eds) *Force and Legitimacy in World Politics* (Cambridge: Cambridge University Press).

Hutchful, E. (2000) 'Understanding the African Security Crisis' in A.F. Musah and J. K. Feyemi (eds) *Mercenaries: An African Security Dilemma* (London: Pluto).

Huttenbach, H.R. (2005) 'From the Editor: can genocide be prevented? No! Yes? Perhaps', *Journal of Genocide Research*, 7/3, pp. 307–8.

Huttenbach, H.R. (2008) 'From the Editors: genocide prevention: sound policy or pursuit of a mirage?', *Journal of Genocide Research*, 10/4, pp. 471–3.

Institute for Global Policy (2009) 'Global Consultative Roundtables on the Responsibility to Protect'. Available online, http://www.responsibilitytoprotect.org/index.php/africa [accessed December 2008].

(ICISS) International Commission on Intervention and State Sovereignty (2001a) *The Responsibility to Protect* (Ottawa: International Development Research Centre).

(ICISS) International Commission on Intervention and State Sovereignty (2001b) *The Responsibility to Protect: Research, Bibliography, Background* (Ottawa: International Development Research Centre).

(IICK) Independent International Commission on Kosovo (2000) *Kosovo Report* (Oxford: Oxford University Press).

International Coalition for R2P (2009) 'Report on the General Assembly Plenary Debate on the Responsibility to Protect', 15 September. Available online, http://www.responsibilitytoprotect.org/ICRtoP%20Report-General_Assembly_Debate_on_the_Responsibility_to_Protect%20FINAL%209_22_09.pdf [accessed June 2010].

International Coalition for R2P (2011a) 'Founding Purposes of the Coalition'. Available online, http://www.responsibilitytoprotect.org/index.php/about-coalition/founding-purposes [accessed June 2011].

International Coalition for R2P (2011b) 'The Coalition's Common Understanding of RtoP'. Available online, http://www.responsibilitytoprotect.org/index.php/about-coalition/our-understanding-of-rtop [accessed June 2011].

International Coalition for R2P (2011c) 'Clarifying the Third Pillar of the Responsibility to Protect'. Available online, http://responsibilitytoprotect.org/Clarifying%20the%20Third%20Pillar%20of%20the%20Responsibility%20to%20Protect_Timely%20and%20Decisive%20Response.pdf [accessed September 2011].

International Commission of Inquiry on Darfur (2005) 'Report of the

International Commission of Inquiry on Darfur to the United Nations Secretary-General', 25 January. Available online, http://www.un.org/news/dh/sudan/com_inq_darfur.pdf [accessed December 2010].

Iran (2009) 'Statement by the Permanent Representative of Iran to the UN', 23 July. Available online, http://www.responsibilitytoprotect.org/Iran_ENG.pdf [accessed June 2010].

Jackson, R. (1996) *Quasi-states: Sovereignty, International Relations and the Third World* (Cambridge: Cambridge University Press).

Jackson, R. (2000) *The Global Covenant: Human Conduct in a World of States* (Oxford: Oxford University Press).

Jackson, R. (2006) 'The Safety of the People is the Supreme Law: Beyond Hobbes but not as far as Kant' in W. Bain (ed.) *The Empire of Security and the Safety of the People* (London: Routledge).

Janssen, D. (2008) 'Humanitarian intervention and the prevention of genocide', *Journal of Genocide Research*, 10/2, pp. 289–306.

Janzekovic, J. (2006) *The Use of Force in Humanitarian Intervention: Morality and Practicalities* (Aldershot: Ashgate).

Jentleson, B.W. (2009) 'The Dilemma of Political Will' in S. Totten and P.R. Bartop (eds) *The Genocide Studies Reader* (London: Routledge).

Job, B. (2006) 'International Peace and Security and State Sovereignty: Contesting Norms and Norm Entrepreneurs' in R. Thakur and W.P.S. Sidhu (eds) *The Iraq Crisis and World Order: Structural, Institutional and Normative Challenges* (New York, NY: United Nations University Press).

Johansen, R. (ed.) (2006) *A United Nations Emergency Peace Service*, (New York: World Federalist Movement).

Jones, B.D. (1995) '"Intervention without Borders": Humanitarian Intervention in Rwanda 1990–94', *Millennium*, 24/2, pp. 225–49.

Johnstone, D. (2000) 'NATO and the New World Order', in P. Hammond and E. Herman (eds) *Degraded Capability: The Media and the Kosovo Crisis* (London: Pluto).

Kegley Jr., C.W. and Wittkopf, E.R. (2006) *World Politics: Trend and Transformation* (London: Thomson Wadsworth).

Kelsen, H. (1945) *General Theory of Law and State* (Cambridge, MA: Harvard University Press).

Kelsen, H. (1972) *Peace Through Law* (Cambridge, MA: Harvard University Press).

Kennedy, D. (2009) 'Reassessing International Humanitarianism: The Dark Sides' in A. Orford (ed.) *International Law and its Others* (Cambridge: Cambridge University Press).

Kennedy, P. (2006) *The Parliament of Man: The Past, Present and Future of the United Nations* (New York, NY: Random House).

Ki-Moon, B. (2009a) 'Implementing the Responsibility to Protect: Report of the Secretary-General', A/63/677, 12 January. Available online, http://globalr2p.org/pdf/SGR2PEng.pdf [accessed June 2010].

Ki-Moon, B. (2009b) 'Secretary-General, moved by statements of Member States, is eager to move forward', UN Department of Public Information, 14 September. Available online, http://www.un.org/News/Press/docs/2009/sgsm12452.doc.htm [accessed June 2010].

Ki-Moon, B. (2011) 'Statement by the Secretary-General on Libya', 17 March. Available online, http://www.responsibilitytoprotect.org/index.php/crises/190-crisis-in-libya/3269-ban-says-historic-resolution-was-clearly-the-international-community-fulfilling-of-its-responsibility-to-protect [accessed June 2011].

Kinloch-Pichat, S. (2004) *A UN Legion: Between Utopia and Reality* (London: Routledge).

Kissinger, H. (1992) 'Humanitarian Intervention has its Hazards', In*ternational Herald Tribune*, 14 December.

Kober, S. (2000) 'Setting Dangerous International Precedents' in T.G. Carpenter (ed.) *NATO's Empty Victory* (Washington, DC: Cato Institute).

Koskenniemi, M. (2001) *The Gentle Civilizer of Nations* (Cambridge: Cambridge University Press).

Koskenniemi, M. (2006) 'What is International Law For?' in M. Evans (ed.) *International Law* (Oxford: Oxford University Press).

Krasno, J. and Das, M. (2008) 'The Uniting for Peace Resolution and Other Ways of Circumventing the Authority of the Security Council', in B. Cronin and I. Hurd (eds) *The UN Security Council and the Politics of International Authority* (London: Routledge).

Krieger, H. (2001) *The Kosovo Conflict and International Law* (Cambridge: Cambridge University Press).

Kuhrt, N. (2011) 'The Human Security Agenda after 9/11' in A. Hehir, N. Kuhrt and A. Mumford (eds) *International Law, Security and Ethics* (London: Routledge).

Kuperman, A. (2001) *The Limits of Humanitarian Intervention: Genocide in Rwanda* (Washington, DC: Brookings Institution Press).

Landman, T. (2005) *Studying Human Rights* (London: Routledge).

Lang, A. (2002) *Agency and Ethics: The Politics of Military Intervention* (New York, NY: University of New York Press).

Lang, A. (2003) 'Humanitarian Intervention: Definition and Debates' in A. Lang, (ed.) *Just Intervention* (Washington, DC: Georgetown University Press).

Langille, P. (2002) *Bridging the Commitment-Capacity Gap* (New York, NY: The Centre for UN Reform Education).

Layne, C. (1994) 'Kant or Cant: The Myth of the Democratic Peace', *International Security*, 19/2, pp. 5–49.
Levy, B.-H. (2011) '(2011) 'After Qaddafi, Assad', *The New Republic*, 19 May. Available online, http://www.tnr.com/article/world/88662/bashar-al-assad-syria-qaddafi-arab-spring?page=0,0 [accessed September 2011].
Lillich, R. (1967) 'Forcible Self-Help by States to Protect Human Rights', *Iowa Law Review*, 53, 290–314.
Linklater, A. (2000) 'The Good International Citizen and the Crisis in Kosovo' in A. Schnabel and R. Thakur (eds) *Kosovo and the Challenge of Humanitarian Intervention* (New York, NY: United Nations University Press).
Lu, C. (2006) *Just and Unjust Interventions in World Politics: Public and Private* (Basingstoke: Palgrave Macmillan).
Luck, E. (2008) 'The UN and the Responsibility to Protect', *Policy Analysis Brief*, The Stanley Foundation, August. Available online, http://www.humansecuritygateway.com/documents/TSF_theUNandR2P.pdf [accessed November 2010].
Luck, E. (2010) 'The Responsibility to Protect: Growing Pains or Early Promise?', *Ethics and International Affairs*, 24/4, September. Available online, http://www.carnegiecouncil.org/resources/journal/24_4/response/001.html [accessed June 2011].
Lund, M. (2004) 'Operationalizing the Lessons from Recent Experience in Field-Level Conflict Prevention Strategies' in A. Wimmer, R. Goldstone, D. Horowitz, U. Joras and C. Schetter (eds) *Facing Ethnic Conflicts: Towards a New Realism* (Oxford: Rowman & Littlefield).
Lyons, G. and Mastanduno, M. (1995) 'Introduction' in G. Lyons and M. Mastanduno (eds) *Beyond Westphalia: State Sovereignty and International Intervention* (Baltimore, MD: Johns Hopkins University Press).
Macfarlane, N., Thielking, C. and Weiss, T. (2004) 'The Responsibility to Protect: Is anyone interested in humanitarian intervention?' *Third World Quarterly*, 25/5, pp. 977–92
Malanczuk, P. (2006) *Akehurst's Modern Introduction to International Law* (London: Routledge).
Malinowski, T. (2011) 'The Timeliness Paradox', *The New Republic*, March 27. Available online, http://www.tnr.com/article/politics/85856/the-speed-paradox [accessed September 2011].
Malone, D. (2006) *The International Struggle Over Iraq: Politics in the UN Security Council 1980–2005* (Oxford: Oxford University Press).
Mamdani, M. (2009) *Saviours and Survivors: Darfur, Politics, and the War on Terror* (New York, NY: Pantheon Books).
Mandelbaum, M. (1999) 'A Perfect Failure; NATO's War Against Yugoslavia', *Foreign Affairs*, 78/5, pp. 2–8.

Mayall, J. (2006) 'Humanitarian Intervention and International Society: Lessons From Africa' in J. Welsh (ed.) *Humanitarian Intervention and International Relations* (Oxford: Oxford University Press).

Mayroz, E. (2008) 'Ever Again? The United States, Genocide Suppression, and the Crisis in Darfur', *Journal of Genocide Research*, 10/3, pp. 359–88.

Mearsheimer, J. (1994) 'The False Promise of International Institutions', *International Security*, 19/3, pp. 5–49.

Mertus, J. (2009) *The United Nations and Human Rights* (London: Routledge).

Meyer, S. (2009) 'In Our Interest: The Responsibility to Protect', in R.H. Cooper and J.V. Kohler (eds) *Responsibility to Protect: The Global Moral Compact for the 21st Century* (Basingstoke and New York: Palgrave Macmillan).

Mgbeoji, I. (2006) 'The Civilised Self and the Barbaric Other: Imperial Delusions of Order and the Challenges of Human Security', *Third World Quarterly*, 27/5, pp. 855–69.

Miall, H. (2004) 'Transforming Ethnic Conflict: Theories and Practices', in A. Wimmer, R. Goldstone, D. Horowitz, U. Joras and C. Schetter (eds) *Facing Ethnic Conflicts: Towards a New Realism* (Oxford: Rowman & Littlefield).

Michalek, S.J. (1971) 'The League of Nations and the UN in World Politics', *International Studies Quarterly*, 15/4, pp. 387–441.

Milanović, M. (2006) 'State Responsibility for Genocide', *The European Journal of International Law*, 17/3, pp. 553–604.

Molloy, S. (2006) *The Hidden History of Realism* (Basingstoke and New York: Palgrave Macmillan).

Morgenthau, H. J. (1954) *Politics Among Nations: The Struggle for Power and Peace* (New York, NY: Alfred Knopf).

Mueller, J. (2005) 'Force, Legitimacy, Success, and Iraq' in D. Armstrong, T. Farrell and B. Maiguashca (eds) *Force and Legitimacy in World Politics* (Cambridge: Cambridge University Press).

Murphy, S. (1996) *Humanitarian Intervention* (Philadelphia, PA: University of Pennsylvania Press).

Nardin, T. (2003) 'The Moral Basis of Humanitarian Intervention' in A. Lang (ed.) *Just Intervention* (Washington, DC: Georgetown University Press).

Neff, S.C. (2006) 'A Short History of International Law' in M. Evans (ed.) *International Law* (Oxford: Oxford University Press).

New York Times (1998) 'Clinton in Africa; Clinton's Painful Words of Sorrow and Chagrin', 26 March.

Newman, M. (2009) *Humanitarian Intervention: Confronting the Contradictions* (London: Hurst).

Nicaragua (2009) 'Statement by the Permanent Representative of Nicaragua to the UN', 23 July. Available online, http://www.responsibilitytoprotect.org/index.php/component/content/article/35-r2pcs-topics/2493-general-assembly-debate-on-the-responsibility-to-protect-and-informal-interactive-dialogue- [accessed June 2010].

Niebuhr, R. (1986) 'The Children of Light and the Children of Darkness', in R. McAfee Brown *The Essential Reinhold Niebuhr* (New Haven, CT: Yale University Press).

Nolan, C. J. (2006) 'Great Powers and International Society' in W. Bain (ed.) *The Empire of Security and the Safety of the People* (London: Routledge).

Obama, B., Cameron, D. and Sarkozy, N. (2011) 'Libya's Pathway to Peace', *New York Times*, 14 April. Available online, http://www.nytimes.com/2011/04/15/opinion/15iht-edlibya15.html [accessed September 2011].

O'Connell, M.E. (2000) 'The UN, NATO and International Law after Kosovo', *Human Rights Quarterly*, 22/1, pp. 57–89.

O'Connell, M.E. (2008) 'Opposing the New Militarism', *Foreign Voices*, 1, pp. 5–8.

Onuf, N. (2003) 'Normative Frameworks for Humanitarian Intervention' in A. Lang (ed.), *Just Intervention* (Washington, DC: Georgetown University Press).

Oppenheim, L. (2006) *International Law: A Treatise* (London: Lawbook Exchange).

Organisation of African Unity (2000) 'International Panel of Eminent Personalities to Investigate the 1994 Genocide in Rwanda and Surrounding Events', *Special Report*, 7 July. Available online, http://www.issafrica.org/Af/profiles/Rwanda/IPEPRwanda.pdf [accessed June 2011].

Orford, A. (2003) *Reading Humanitarian Intervention* (Cambridge: Cambridge University Press).

Orford, A. (2009) 'A Jurisprudence of the Limit' in A. Orford (ed.) *International Law and its Others* (Cambridge: Cambridge University Press).

Pace, W., Deller, N. and Chhatpar, S. (2009) 'Realizing the Responsibility to Protect in Emerging and Acute Crises' in R.H. Cooper and J. V. Kohler (eds) *Responsibility to Protect: The Global Moral Compact for the 21st Century* (Basingstoke and New York: Palgrave Macmillan).

Parsi, V. E. (2006) *The Inevitable Alliance: Europe and the United States Beyond Iraq* (Basingstoke and New York: Palgrave Macmillan).

Pattison, J. (2008) 'Humanitarian Intervention and a Cosmopolitan UN Force', *Journal of Political Theory*, 4/1, pp. 126–45.

Pattison, J. (2010) *Humanitarian Intervention and the Responsibility to Protect* (Oxford: Oxford University Press).
Pattison, J. (2011) 'The Ethics of Humanitarian Intervention in Libya', *Ethics and International Affairs*, 25/3, pp. 1–7. Available online, http://www.carnegiecouncil.org/resources/journal/index.html [accessed September 2011].
Peters, A. (2009) 'Humanity as the A and Ω of Sovereignty', *The European Journal of International Law*, 20/3, pp. 513–44.
Philippines (2009) 'Statement by the Philippines' July 23. Available online, http://www.responsibilitytoprotect.org/Philippines_ ENG.pdf [accessed August 2010].
Power, S. (2001) 'By-standers to Genocide' *The Atlantic*, September. Available online, http://www.theatlantic.com/doc/200109/power-genocide [accessed August 2010].
Power, S. (2009) 'Foreword' in R.H. Cooper and J.V. Kohler (eds) *Responsibility to Protect: The Global Moral Compact for the 21st Century* (Basingstoke and New York: Palgrave Macmillan).
Prosecutor v. Tadic (1996) Judgment, ICTY Case No. IT-94-1-AR72 (Jurisdiction), Appeals Chamber, 1995, 35 ILM 35.
Prunier, G. (1997) *The Rwanda Crisis: History of a Genocide* (New York, NY: Columbia University Press).
Ramcharan, B.G. (2008) *Preventive Diplomacy at the UN* (Indiana, IN: Indiana University Press).
Reindorp, N. (2009) 'Interview between author and Nicola Reindorp, Global Centre for RtoP', *New York*, 19 August.
Reinold, T. (2010) 'The Responsibility to Protect: Much Ado About Nothing?', *Review of International Studies*, 36, pp. 55–78.
Reisman, M. (2000) 'Unilateral Action and the Transformations of the World Constitutive Process: The Special Problem of Humanitarian Intervention', *European Journal of International Law*, 11/1, pp. 3–18.
Rengger, N. (2005) 'The Judgment of War: On the Idea of Legitimate Force in World Politics' in D. Armstrong, T. Farrell and B. Maiguashca (eds) *Force and Legitimacy in World Politics* (Cambridge: Cambridge University Press).
Reus-Smit, C. (2001) 'Human Rights and the Social Construction of Sovereignty', *Review of International Studies* 27/4, pp. 519–38.
Reus-Smit, C. (2005) 'Liberal Hierarchy and the Licence to Use Force' in, D. Armstrong, T. Farrell, and B. Maiguashca (eds) *Force and Legitimacy in World Politics* (Cambridge: Cambridge University Press).
Reuters (2008) 'Interview – Myanmar must act now to clear red tape', 7 May. Available online, http://www.reuters.com/article/idUSBKK328448 [accessed June 2010].

Roberts, A. (2006) 'The United Nations and Humanitarian Intervention' in J. Welsh (ed.) *Humanitarian Intervention and International Relations* (Oxford: Oxford University Press).

Roberts, A. (2008) 'Why and How Intervene?' in G. Andreani and P. Hassner (eds) *Justifying War?: From Humanitarianism to Counterterrorism* (Basingstoke: Palgrave Macmillan).

Robertson, G. (2002) *Crimes Against Humanity* (London: Penguin).

Rodley, N. and Cali, B. (2007) 'Kosovo Revisited: Humanitarian Intervention on the Fault Lines of International Law', *Human Rights* Law Review, 7/2, pp. 275–97.

Schabas, W. (2000) *Genocide in International Law: The Crime of Crimes* (Cambridge: Cambridge University Press).

Schachter, O. (1991) *International Law in Theory and Practice* (Dordrecht: Martinus Nijhoff).

Scheffer, D. (2009) 'Atrocity Crimes: Framing the Responsibility to Protect' in R.H. Cooper and J.V. Kohler (eds) *Responsibility to Protect: The Global Moral Compact for the 21st Century* (Basingstoke and New York: Palgrave Macmillan).

Scheipers, S. (2009) *Negotiating Sovereignty and Human Rights* (Manchester: Manchester University Press).

Schulz, W. (2009) 'Spread wide the Word', in R.H. Cooper and J.V. Kohler (eds) *Responsibility to Protect: The Global Moral Compact for the 21st Century* (Basingstoke and New York: Palgrave Macmillan).

Security Council (1999) 'Report of the Independent Inquiry into the actions of the United Nations during the 1994 genocide in Rwanda', S/1999/1257, 15 December.

Shawcross, W. (2000) *Deliver Us From Evil* (London: Bloomsbury).

Simma, B. (1999) 'NATO, the UN and the Use of Force', *European Journal of International Law*, 10/1, pp. 1–22.

Simmons, A. and Donnellan, A. (2009) 'Reaching Across Borders', in R.H. Cooper and J.V. Kohler (eds) *Responsibility to Protect: The Global Moral Compact for the 21st Century* (Basingstoke and New York: Palgrave Macmillan).

Simpson, G. (2004) *Great Powers and Outlaw States* (Cambridge: Cambridge University Press).

Singapore (2009) 'Statement by the Permanent Representative of Singapore to the UN', 23 July. Available online, http://www.responsibilitytoprotect.org/Singapore_ENG.pdf [accessed June 2010].

Slaughter, Anne-Marie (2011) 'A Day to Celebrate, but Hard Work Ahead', *Foreign Policy*, 18 March. Available online, http://www.foreignpolicy.com/articles/2011/03/18/does_the_world_belong_in_libyas_war?page=0,7 [accessed June 2011].

Slim, H. (2004) 'Dithering over Darfur?', *International Affairs*, 80/5, pp. 811–28.

Smith, M. (1998) 'Humanitarian Intervention: An Overview of Ethical Issues', *Ethics and International Affairs*, 12/1, pp. 63–79.

Spiked (2011) 'About *Spiked*: Frequently Asked Questions'. Available online, http://www.spiked-online.com/index.php/about/article/193/ [accessed October 2011].

Spykman, N. (1942) *America's Strategy in World Politics* (New York, NY: Harcourt, Brace).

Sri Lanka (2009) 'Statement by the Permanent Representative of Sri Lanka to the UN', 23 July. Available online, http://www.responsibilitytoprotect.org/index.php/component/content/article/35-r2pcs-topics/2493-general-assembly-debate-on-the-responsibility-to-protect-and-informal-interactive-dialogue- [accessed June 2010].

Stahn, C. (2007) 'Responsibility to Protect: Political Rhetoric or Emerging Legal Norm?', *American Journal of International Law*, 101/1, pp. 99–120.

Stanton, G.H. (2009) 'Early Warning' in S. Totten and P.R. Bartop (eds) *The Genocide Studies Reader* (London: Routledge).

Stavropoulou, M. (2009) 'Interview between author and Maria Stavropoulou, Political Affairs Officer, OSAPG', New York, 21 August.

Steiner, H. (2006) 'International Protection of Human Rights' in M. Evans (ed.) *International Law* (Oxford: Oxford University Press).

Strauss, E. (2010) *The Emperor's New Clothes?: The United Nations and the Implementation of the Responsibility to Protect* (Baden-Baden: Nomos).

Stromseth, J. (2005) 'Rethinking Humanitarian Intervention' in J.L. Holzgrefe and R. Keohane (eds) *Humanitarian Intervention* (Cambridge: Cambridge University Press).

Sudan (2009) 'Statement by the Mission of Sudan to the UN', 23 July. Available online, http://www.responsibilitytoprotect.org/Sudan_ENG.pdf [accessed June 2011].

Switzerland (2009) 'Statement by the Permanent Representative of Switzerland to the UN', 23 July. Available online, http://www.responsibilitytoprotect.org/Switzerland_ENG_FR.pdf, p. 6 [accessed November 2010].

Teichrib, C. (2000) 'World Peace Through World Force: Creating the UN Army', *Discerning the Times Digest*. Available online, http://www.unwatch.com/shirbrig.shtml [accessed November 2010].

Terry, F. (2002) *Condemned to Repeat? The Paradox of Humanitarian Action* (Ithaca, NY: Cornell University Press).

Tesón, F. (1996) 'Collective Humanitarian Intervention' *Michigan Journal of International Law*, 17, pp. 323–71.

Tesón, F. (1998) *Humanitarian Intervention: An Enquiry into Law and Morality* (New York, NY: Transnational Publishers).

Thakur, R. (2001) 'Global Norms and International Humanitarian Law', *International Review of the Red Cross*, 83/841, pp. 19–44.

Thakur, R. (2004) 'Developing Countries and the Intervention-Sovereignty Debate' in R.M. Price, and M.W. Zacher (eds) *The United Nations and Global Security* (New York, NY: Palgrave Macmillan).

Thakur, R. (2011) 'The World's Responsibility to Protect Libyans', *The Epoch Times*, 19 March. Available online, http://www.theepochtimes.com/n2/content/view/53257/99999999/1/1/ [accessed July 2011].

Thakur, R. and Sidhu, W.P.S. (2006) 'Iraq's Challenge to World Order', in R. Thakur and W.P.S. Sidhu (eds) *The Iraq Crisis and World Order: Structural, Institutional and Normative Challenges* (New York, NY: United Nations University Press).

Thakur, R. and Weiss, T. (2009) 'R2P: From Idea to Norm – and Action?', *Global Responsibility to Protect*, 1/1, pp. 1–32

Thomas, N. and Tow, W. (2002) 'The Utility of Human Security: Sovereignty and Humanitarian Intervention', *Security Dialogue*, 33/2, pp. 127–40.

Thomas, R. (ed.) (2003) *Yugoslavia Unraveled: Sovereignty, Self Determination, Intervention* (Oxford: Lexington Books).

Totten, S. and Bartop, P.R. (2009) 'The Prevention of Genocide' in S. Totten and P.R. Bartop (eds) *The Genocide Studies Reader* (London: Routledge).

UK (2009) 'Statement by the Permanent Representative of the United Kingdom to the UN', 23 July. Available online, http://www.responsibilitytoprotect.org/UK_ENG(1).pdf [accessed June 2010].

UK House of Commons Foreign Affairs Select Committee (2000) Foreign Affairs – Fourth Report, No. HC 28–1 of 7 June. Available online, http:www.publications.parliament.uk/pa/cm199900/cmselect/cmfaff/28/2802.htm [accessed August 2010].

United Nations (1999) 'Report of the Independent Inquiry into the Actions of the United Nations During the 1994 Genocide in Rwanda', S/1999/1257, 15 December. Available online, http://www.un.org/News/dh/latest/rwanda.htm [accessed June 2010].

United Nations (2000) 'Report of the Panel on UN Peace Operations', A/55/305-S/2000/809, 21 August.

United Nations Association of the United States of America (2006) 'Strengthening the United Nations' Capacity to Prevent Genocide',

Project Report of the United Nations Association of the United States of America on supporting the Special Adviser to the Secretary-General on the Prevention of Genocide, New York, April.

United Nations Commission on Global Governance (1995) *Our Global Neighbourhood* (Oxford: Oxford University Press).

United Nations Economic and Social Council (2004) 'Report of the United Nations High Commissioner for Human Rights and Follow-Up to the World Conference on Human Rights: Situation of Human Rights in the Darfur region of Sudan', E/CN.4/2005/3, 7 May. Available online, http://www.unhchr.ch/ huridocda/ huridoca.nsf/ AllSymbols/863D14602AA82CAEC1256EA80038E268/$File/ G0414221.doc?OpenElement [accessed February 2011].

United Nations General Assembly (2008) 'Human rights situations that requires the Council's attention: Report of the Special Rapporteur on the situation of human rights in the Sudan, Sima Samar', UN Index: A/HRC/9/13, September 2, 2008. Available online, http://www.reliefweb.int/rw/RWFiles2008.nsf/FilesByRWDoc UnidFilename/EGUA-7JJNR2-full_report.pdf/$File/full_report.pdf [accessed September 24, 2008].

United Nations High Commissioner for Human Rights (2004) 'Report of the United Nations High Commissioner for Human Rights and Follow-Up to the World Conference on Human Rights: Situation of Human Rights in the Darfur region of Sudan', E/CN.4/2005/3, 7 May. Available online, http://www.unhchr.ch/huridocda/huridoca. nsf/(Symbol)/E.CN.4.2005.3.En [accessed October 2011].

United States of America (2009) 'Statement by the Permanent Representative of the United States to the UN', 23 July. Available online, http://responsibilitytoprotect.org/USA_ENG-1.pdf [accessed November 2010].

Urqhart, B. (1993) 'For a UN Volunteer Military Force', *New York Review of Books*, 10 June.

US Department of State (2004) 'The Crisis in Darfur: Secretary Colin Powell, Testimony before the Senate Foreign Relations Committee, September 9'. Available online, www.ithaca.edu/faculty/cduncan/ 375/powell.doc [accessed August 2010].

US Department of State (2009) 'Report to Congress on Incidents During the Recent Conflict in Sri Lanka'. Available online, http:// www.state.gov/documents/organization/131025.pdf [accessed June 2011].

Uvin, P. (2001) 'Reading the Rwandan Genocide' *International Studies Review*, 3/3, pp. 75–99.

van der Stoel, M. (2004) 'Looking Back, Looking Forward: Reflections on Preventing Inter-Ethnic Conflict' in A. Wimmer, R. Goldstone, D. Horowitz, U. Joras and C. Schetter (eds) *Facing Ethnic Conflicts: Towards a New Realism* (Oxford: Rowman & Littlefield).

Voeten, E. (2008) 'Delegation and the Nature of Security Council Authority' in B. Cronin and I. Hurd (eds) *The UN Security Council and the Politics of International Authority* (London: Routledge).

Walker, R.B.J. (1993) *Inside/Outside: International Relations as Political Theory* (Cambridge: Cambridge University Press).

Waltz, K. (1979) *Theory of International Politics* (Oxford: Oxford University Press).

Waltz, K. (1991) 'Realist Thought and Neo-realist Theory' in R.L. Rothstein (ed.) *The Evolution of Theory in International Relations* (Columbia, SC: University of South Carolina Press).

Walzer, M. (2006) *Just and Unjust Wars* (New York, NY: Basic Books).

Walzer, M. (2011) 'The Case Against Our Attack on Libya', *The New Republic*, 20 March. Available online, http://www.tnr.com/article/world/85509/the-case-against-our-attack-libya [accessed August 2010].

Watts, Sir A. (2001) 'The Importance of International Law' in M. Byers (ed.) *The Role of International Law in International Politics* (Oxford: Oxford University Press).

Weiss, H. (2009) 'The Democratic Republic of the Congo' in R.H. Cooper and J.V. Kohler (eds) *Responsibility to Protect: The Global Moral Compact for the 21st Century* (Basingstoke and New York: Palgrave Macmillan).

Weiss, T. (2000) 'The Politics of Humanitarian Ideas', *Security Dialogue*, 31/1, pp. 11–23.

Weiss, T. (2007a) *Humanitarian Intervention* (London: Polity).

Weiss, T. (2007b) 'Halting Genocide: Rhetoric versus Reality', Genocide Studies and Prevention, 2/1, pp. 7–30.

Weiss, T. (2009a) 'Interview between author and Professor Thomas Weiss, Director of the Ralph Bunche Institute for International Science', New York, 19 August.

Weiss, T. (2009b) *What's Wrong With the United Nations and How to Fix It* (Cambridge: Polity).

Weiss, T. (2011) 'R2P Alive and Well After Libya', *Ethics and International Affairs*, 25/3, pp. 1–6. Available online, http://www.carnegiecouncil.org/resources/journal/index.html [accessed September 2011].

Weller, M. (2002) 'Undoing the Global Constitution: UN Security Council Action on the International Criminal Court', *International Affairs*, 87/4, pp. 693–712.

Wells, H.G. (1961) *The Time Machine*, in *Selected Short Stories: H.G. Wells* (Harmondsworth: Penguin).

Welsh, J. (2006) 'Conclusion: The Evolution of Humanitarian Intervention in International Society' in J. Welsh (ed.) *Humanitarian Intervention and International Relations* (Oxford: Oxford University Press).

Welsh, J. (2010) 'Implementing the Responsibility to Protect: Where Expectations Meet Reality', *Ethics and International Affairs*, 24/4, pp. 415–30.

Welsh, J. (2011) 'Civilian Protection in Libya: Putting Coercion and Controversy Back into RtoP', *Ethics and International Affairs*, 25/3, pp. 1–8. Available online, http://www.carnegiecouncil.org/resources/journal/index.html [accessed September 2011].

Weltman, J. (1995) *World Politics and the Evolution of War* (London: Johns Hopkins).

Wesamba, C. (2009) 'Interview between author and Castro Wesamba, Political Affairs Officer OSAPG', New York, 21 August.

Wheeler, N. (1997) 'Agency, Humanitarianism and Intervention', *International Political Science Review*, 18/1, pp. 9–25.

Wheeler, N. (2001) 'Humanitarian Intervention after Kosovo: Emergent Norm, Moral Duty or the Coming Anarchy?', *International Affairs*, 77/1, pp. 113–28.

Wheeler, N. (2002) *Saving Strangers* (Oxford: Oxford University Press).

Wheeler, N. (2005) 'A Victory for Common Humanity? The Responsibility to Protect after the 2005 World Summit', *Journal of International Law and International Relations*, 2/1, pp. 95–106.

Wheeler, N. (2006) 'The Humanitarian Responsibilities of Sovereignty' in J. Welsh (ed.) *Humanitarian Intervention and International Relations* (Oxford: Oxford University Press).

White, N. (2000) 'The Legality of Bombing in the Name of Humanity', *Journal of Conflict and Security Law*, 5/1, pp. 27–43.

White, N. (2004) 'The Will and Authority of the Security Council After Iraq', *Leiden Journal of International Law*, 17/4, pp. 645–72.

White House (2011) 'Remarks by the President in Address to the Nation on Libya', 28 March. Available online, http://www.whitehouse.gov/the-press-office/2011/03/28/remarks-president-address-nation-libya [accessed September 2011].

Whitman, J. (2005) 'Humanitarian Intervention in an Era of Pre-emptive Self-defence', *Security Dialogue*, 36/3, pp. 259–74.

Wight, M. (1966) 'Why is there no International Theory?' in H. Butterfield and M. Wight (eds) *Diplomatic Investigations: Essays in the Theory of International Politics* (Cambridge, MA: Harvard University Press).

Wight, M. (1979) *Power Politics* (Harmondsworth: Penguin Books).

Williams, M. (2007) *Realism Reconsidered* (Oxford: Oxford University Press).

Williams, P. (2005) 'Peace Operations and the International Financial Institutions: Insights from Rwanda and Sierra Leone' in P. Williams and A. Bellamy (eds) *Peace Operations and the Global Order* (Oxford: Routledge).

Wood, E. M. (2000) 'Kosovo and the New Imperialism', in T. Ali (ed.) *Masters of the Universe? NATO's Balkan Crusade* (London: Verso).
Wright, R. (2006) *A Short History of Progress* (Edinburgh: Canongate).
Zaum, D. (2009) 'Book Review: Humanitarian Intervention After Kosovo', *International Affairs*, 85/2, pp. 402–3.
Zolo, D. (1997) *Cosmopolis* (Cambridge: Polity Press).
Zolo, D. (1998) 'Hans Kelsen: International Peace Through International Law', *European Journal of International Law*, 9, pp. 306–24.

Index